W9-CDD-956

Innovations in Secondary Education

SECOND EDITION

Glenys G. Unruh
University City, Missouri, Schools

William M. Alexander
University of Florida, Gainesville

HOLT, RINEHART AND WINSTON, INC.
New York   Chicago   San Francisco   Atlanta
Dallas   Montreal   Toronto   London   Sydney

Library of Congress Cataloging in Publication Data

Unruh, Glenys G.
  Innovations in secondary education.

  Includes bibliographical references.
  1. Education, Secondary—United States.
I. Alexander, William Marvin   joint
author. II. Title.
LA222.U57   1974   373.73   73-14622

ISBN 0-03-003971-1

5 6 7 8 9   090   9 8 7 6 5 4 3 2

Preface

Important changes have taken place in secondary education since 1970, when the first edition of *Innovations in Secondary Education* was published. This book picks up on new directions in innovation following the period of student riots in 1969 and 1970. The errors of the sixties are pointed out, and innovations that are promising but little used are identified. The book takes a positive and constructive approach and emphasizes "what works" in high school today. In fact, there is an air of excitement about newer innovations, which responds meaningfully to the writers who are emphasizing negativism, defeatism, and "frauds" in education, and whose books and articles have tended to depress the public regarding the potentialities of education. This textbook is intended as a comprehensive and basic source on innovative practices for high school personnel who are in training or on the job.

Chapter 1 is a discussion of the forces that necessitate innovation. The next six chapters classify and describe innovation in general categories: the student, the curriculum, the organization, the staff, media, and places for learning. The final chapter deals with the processes of innovation and change.

More emphasis is given in this edition to concerns within the school as well as to societal concerns. Student problems are identified by the students themselves in addition to those expressed by practitioners and theorists. A subtle but meaningful difference in approach is evident in curriculum innovations. The curriculum programs developed nationally during the sixties were assumed to be "teacher proof." Teachers subsequently were found to be "curriculum proof." This book makes very clear the effects of the ingenuity of teachers and administrators in leading schools who have drawn the best from the curriculum movement of the sixties and created new dimensions in response to the changing needs of students and society. In the earlier edition, flexible organizations were mostly confined within the standard school day and year; here, new concepts of time and attendance permeate the chapter on organization.

This new edition advances into more sophisticated interpretations of the role of the teacher and adds new concepts of staff development including teacher centers, competency-based teacher education programs, and the increasing scope of the concept of accountability. New types of technology are illustrated. In the chapter on space for learning, contemporary architectural designs for schools are presented as well as descriptions of learning areas in nonschool facilities.

When the first edition was written, schools and universities were enjoying the heyday of foundation and federal funding. In the concluding chapter of this book, the discussion of innovation and change reflects the lessons learned from reforms inspired by the advent of federal and private fundings. Emphasis here is on processes of innovation and change that will endure when transitory sources of funds are not available.

Innovation is defined as the introduction of a novel factor, perceived as new by a given school and community, supported by a driving force, and implemented as a practical advance that deviates from established or traditional forms. Innovations in this sense are based on broad and purposeful concepts drawn from the ideals of a democratic society: respect for individual differences, development of the self-concept, self-responsibility, humanistic ideals, a social conscience, a world view, and intercultural understandings.

No one innovation is advocated as a panacea. Different innovations and combinations of innovations are meeting the needs of the wide diversity of individuals and communities served by the high schools of the country. Most innovations are still confined to too few schools and affect too few students. But interest is high and change is occurring more rapidly in the mid-seventies after the setbacks of the late sixties and opening year of the seventies following the period of student activism. Now, students, educators, and in many instances citizens of the community are joining together to initiate deep and lasting secondary school reforms.

Illustrations from specific high schools and communities are interwoven with the text. Through visits and correspondence with approximately 150 high schools that were named by educators as examples of schools having innovations worth knowing about, we have been able to describe real situations. When possible we have referred the reader to other sources for more complete information. We are grateful to the many school systems and individual schools that have provided information about their innovative practices. We have also drawn heavily upon our own experience in schools in which we have visited and worked and upon published sources that describe particular innovations. The footnotes and other references identify not only our sources, but also significant sources for readers who want more information.

This text can be of immediate value to those who are seriously concerned about problems facing high schools. The spirit of *Innovations in Secondary Education* is positive and constructive.

As all who work in high schools become more knowledgeable about innovations and their wise use and become more experienced in processes of change and innovation, fundamental improvements will be made and will continue. It is our hope that this book, by drawing from research and development and from actual practices in advancing high schools, will be useful in stimulating progress.

University City, Missouri   G.G.U.
Gainesville, Florida   W.M.A.
January 1974

Contents

Tables and Figures

1

Why Innovate?

THE MILIEU OF INNOVATIONS

Innovations in the high schools of the mid-1970s arise from many sources. Educators are seeking to cope creatively with contemporary problems of American society and its youth by introducing new ideas and practices. Many citizens feel that the high school may be society's best chance to stem the tide of lawlessness, immorality, and frustration which threatens to engulf us. Past achievements of the high school and its graduates encourage and challenge us to make the high schools of today more effective for the 1970s and 1980s than their predecessor institutions were for earlier decades. And above all other factors, there is the enthusiasm, the excitement, and the contagion of the new and novel to raise morale and enhance motivation for living and learning. Thus even the negative forces which stimulate some schools to innovation may create positive poles to attract youth to continued and improved schooling.

In this chapter we describe the various issues, concerns, and problems which currently stimulate innovation. These are the sparks to ignite ever-improving programs of secondary education.

1

The high schools—and schools in general—are being vigorously questioned. Concerns of youth, concerns of the public, pressures of social change, challenges of diversity, questions of finance, and demands for accountability—all are sources of current questioning. What are the schools doing to help solve these problems? Why do the schools continue to call for increased funds? These are the questions being asked.

Schools have not generally provided very satisfactory answers to these questions, yet the public investment in schools is massive and the schools' fundamental responsibility is considerable. Some persons even believe that unless schools assume their responsibility to respond to basic issues, new educational forms may replace them. Superficial efforts are not enough; comprehensive rethinking is needed of purposes, programs, and relationships with students and the community. Past experience, used wisely, can help to prevent constant recycling of old errors and shortcomings.

The decade of the sixties, thought at the time to be a decade of change and reform, made too little progress toward solutions of fundamental problems. Frequently, surface changes, small and isolated innovations, lack of comprehensive approaches to change, and research based on weak assumptions seemed to say that the need for innovation was not taken seriously enough. Even the small innovations were not widespread. A survey conducted by the NEA Research Division in the spring of 1971 gave a nationwide sample of public school teachers a list of eleven instructional innovations and asked them to indicate those in which they were currently involved. Seventy percent of the teachers surveyed responded to the questionnaire and indicated participation in one or more minor innovations. However, the top-ranking innovation identified as "team teaching" was claimed by only 29 percent of secondary teachers. Involvement in other innovations ranged down to "use of dial access," which was claimed by 1 percent (see Table 1). Although the educational literature of the sixties advocated innovations, most of them do not seem to have become universally popular.

In addition to innovations in technique, new curriculum developments in the subject-matter fields also attracted attention. These innovations seemed to appeal largely to the more affluent suburban schools whose leaders hoped to improve student achievement of the conventional goals of the school: improvement of instruction in the subject-matter disciplines and preparation of students for college. An underlying assumption seemed to be that the school as an institution was headed in the right direction except that it needed to exert more effort toward its previous goals and make content and instruction more palatable to students. It was taken for granted that there was nothing wrong with the school; the student needed to be changed—the same assumption that dominated educational improvement efforts after the student-centered movement of the 1930s failed to catch on.

table I

How Secondary Teachers Defined Their Current
Involvement in Innovative Instructional Practices, 1971

PRACTICE	PERCENT INVOLVED
Team teaching	29.4
Programmed instruction	28.5
Videotape use	28.3
Cassette tape use	24.7
Differentiated staff	20.5
Modular scheduling	14.8
Nongraded classrooms	11.2
Classrooms without walls	6.2
Computer-assigned instruction	4.9
Computer use in science or mathematics	4.6
Dial access or remote access	1.3

Source: Research Division, National Education Association, "Use of New Techniques in Instruction," NEA Research Bulletin, 49:83 (October 1971).

Too frequently, the innovative programs of the sixties were not based on comprehensive new concepts about the role of secondary education, nor about the changing nature of the student, nor about the larger social forces that were operating outside of the school. Despite the emphasis of the sixties on new curriculum developments and new techniques of instruction, the instructional program of the schools improved too little in its quality and effectiveness; this was the opinion of eleventh graders of 1970 compared with eleventh graders of 1960 in a study conducted by the American Institutes for Research. Some 440,000 students representing a random sample of 1353 secondary schools throughout the country took the Project Talent battery in 1960. In 1970 a stratified random sample of schools was selected from the population of 1960 schools and 12,722 eleventh graders were tested in 134 schools around the country. Students cited similar dissatisfactions in both surveys: lack of interesting school work, problems in reading, and need for better teaching methods.[1]

As the sixties closed, the new instructional methodologies of process approaches and modes of inquiry had not yet achieved their promise. Brandwein, who recorded observations in 1100 classrooms, arrived at this conclusion:

I found the words inquiry and process . . . being espoused all over the land. But, let me give you my data: 90 percent of the teachers in the eleventh and twelfth grade lectured 90 percent of the time, 80 percent of

[1] John C. Flanagan and Steven M. Jung, *Progress in Education: A Sample Survey 1960–1970* (Palo Alto, Calif.: American Institutes for Research, December 1971), p. 26.

the teachers in the tenth and eleventh grade lectured 80 percent of the time. They were all teaching through "inquiry." We defraud ourselves . . . by using new words.[2]

The riots and demonstrations of the late sixties provided a shock effect and stimulated mutual concern of students, educators, and lay citizens for the goals, structure, control, and operation of the secondary schools. In the seventies it has become clear that the function of the high school is more than finding sophisticated methods of transmitting information to students. Answers to the question "Why innovate?" stem from basic issues facing the schools. These issues leave secondary schools little choice but to involve themselves in deep, complex, and interrelated innovations.

CONCERNS OF YOUTH

For some 20 to 30 percent of American youth aged fifteen through twenty, school and college is an unsatisfactory experience that does little to help them find direction for a full and useful life. Opportunities for many young people growing up today are too limited. The existing combination of secondary schools, community colleges, job opportunities, military service, and early marriage has failed to meet the needs of several million young people. Jobs are not available, schooling seems pointless, military service is unpopular, and early marriage is no solution to youths' concerns. These are among the conclusions of the study, *American Youth in the Mid-Seventies, an Extensive Review and Analysis of the Current Status of Youth*, conducted by the National Association of Secondary School Principals. While the number of teen-agers increased by 30 percent, unemployment rates in the fifteen- through twenty-year age group increased by 50 percent. Nationwide, this unemployed, largely apathetic or alienated group of young people presents a major problem for youth and for society generally.[3]

What are some of the concerns of youth that are among the responsibilities of the secondary schools? The failure of schools to involve them in decision-making processes, poor management of information, and neglect of their need to develop self-esteem are among the dissatisfactions of high-school students.

[2] Paul F. Brandwein, "The Role of the Teacher," *Proceedings: The Abington Conference* (Abington, Penn., 1968), p. 59.

[3] Robert J. Havighurst, Richard A. Graham, and Donald Eberly, "American Youth in the Mid-Seventies," *NASSP Bulletin*, 56:1–13 (November 1972).

Decision Making

Students want a part in decision making. They want to communicate with the school administration, to have opportunities to communicate their feelings and express concern to the adults who are in control of the school power structure.

Using a group interview form and staff of forty dedicated interviewers, DeCecco asked approximately 7000 students in the greater New York and Philadelphia areas how democracy worked in their schools, especially when they tried to do something new or make some old idea work in a new way:

> What over two-thirds of the students told us was very clear: they felt they were the victims of arbitrary rules, arbitrarily enforced, and that their situation would improve only with their involvement in rule making. The students felt powerless, trapped between conformity to school routines (which made increasingly little sense to them, to many of their teachers, and to their parents) or resistance and protest, which seemed to get them into more and more trouble.[4]

Students were not trying to say that high school administrators should give in to outrageous demands; they were saying that they want to discuss their concerns with adults as a regular process of democratic decision making in the school and not be insulated from their principals and other adult leaders by bureaucratic regulations and officious secretaries. It is common knowledge that in a large high school it is almost impossible for most students to speak with their principal or assistant principal, and it is even difficult to see the counselor without a definite appointment. Unless the student is in some difficulty, or has achieved a rare honor, or for some other reason it is to the adults' advantage to see him, the student seldom has the opportunity to communicate even indirectly with administrators, let alone be a recognized part of the decision-making process of the high school.

Participation in decision making at the governance level of the high school is important to youths today, but even more important is their need for more opportunities for interaction with the teacher in the classroom. When teachers continue to do 80 percent or more of the talking in a class period, students feel little involvement and personal commitment to the goals and objectives of the course. Changes in curriculum content, organizational arrangements, and methodologies of instruction cannot achieve their full potential until the process of teacher and student discussion achieves greater quality and meaning.

[4] John P. DeCecco, "Tired Feelings, New Life-Styles, and the Daily Liberation of the Schools," *Phi Delta Kappan*, 53:168–169 (November 1971).

Relevance

Mismanagement of subject matter in secondary school programs, otherwise known as lack of relevancy, persists despite exhortations in the educational literature. Students are frequently critical of entire courses and brush them aside as "not relevant." Relevance, however, is a term needing a reference to be meaningful. To say that a given subject, course, package, or unit is not relevant must refer to goals the students have in mind which the particular subject matter or teaching methods do not serve. Teacher–student involvement in goal setting and planning may bring new understandings to both parties. Inventiveness can provide new programs and courses of study to reach the goals and ideals of students without abdicating the school's responsibility for developing competence and excellence.

Today it is essential for schools to examine the contributions of the larger society to students' learning, and to understand how young people of the present era are profoundly different from previous generations of adolescents. The job of the school of the past was to transmit information; the job of the school of today is to develop skills for the management of information. Strategies are needed for making use of the information richness and information processing capabilities of students' out-of-school environment.

That the students have outgrown the schools is a problem that schools are slow to acknowledge, says Coleman. Not many years ago, the schools were the young person's chief source of information. Schools provided books, and books were the principal door to the world beyond a child's own direct experience. He lived in a society with a poverty of information. His vicarious experiences, gained through reading, were low in proportion to the direct experiences gained from work and play on the farm and in the city. In the earlier society, the family and school shaped the child's cognitive world by selecting the information that he was to receive. Thus the school and the home, by processes of selection and exclusion of information, had a very powerful effect on the student's values. Coleman emphasizes that schools as they now exist have perpetuated their previous mode and continue to design their programs for an information-poor society. He states:

> The emergence of electronic methods of communication such as television has shifted the balance between direct and vicarious experience toward vicarious experience for all of us, and it has done so most strongly for the young. Instead of information poverty they now confront information richness . . . As the environment has become rich in information, the child's cognitive world has begun to be shaped by neither family nor school, but by comic books, television, paperbacks, and the broad spectrum of newspapers and magazines that abound . . . A less-open society, a

society that exercises totalitarian control over the mass media, can and does reduce this pluralism of information sources, but probably only delays the impact of technology . . . Thus, two aspects of the communications structure of information-rich open societies are destroying two classical functions of the school. Information richness removes the function of the school in extending the child's horizons through vicarious experiences, and information pluralism removes from schools the function of shaping the child's values through selectivity.[5]

Knowledge transmitted by the electronic media spreads immediately and efficiently. Students now have almost instant access to information that would have required years to reach them in previous times. Also, when print and talk were the chief means of communication, students assimilated most knowledge in a linear fashion. Modern youths, on the other hand, learn from multisensory stimuli. Schools that neither recognize these conditions nor change their orientation well deserve the accusations of irrelevancy.

Self-esteem

A third area of concern to youth is development of self-esteem, a much broader exploratory function of the school. Here, whole new areas of study are opened to students, giving them much greater opportunities to explore their interests and/or competencies without penalty of failure. Opportunities for youth to be involved in serious social issues, in immediate community problems, in helping other students solve their problems, in studying the school itself are areas that could lead to enhancement of self-concept of students. Self-esteem, self-respect, and self-direction can grow and develop in a humane school. Trump names the following characteristics of a humane school:

1. Focuses on options rather than on uniformity in developing and administering policies and practices. In other words, it does not subject every individual to group standards even though it informs him about model behaviors and procedures.
2. Devises a program for each pupil in which he can move forward with success in terms of his own talents and interests no matter how diverse they may be.
3. Makes sure that every pupil is known as a total human being— educationally by a teacher-adviser who helps him personally to diagnose his needs, plan his program, make and change his schedule, evaluate his results and plan accordingly for the future. (This procedure goes far beyond the typical homeroom or the programing by school counselors or assistant principals.)

[5] James S. Coleman, "The Children Have Outgrown the Schools," *Psychology Today*, 5:73–76 (February 1972).

4. Creates an environment in which each teacher may make maximum utilization of his professional talents and interests, one that recognizes individual differences among teachers and provides differentiated staffing to identify better the role of the professional teacher.

5. Separates curriculum content so that each learner knows what is essential for everyone as distinct from the cognitive, skill, and affective behaviors that are important for those learners with special goals in the areas of hobbies and careers. The goal here is to reduce greatly the required learnings so that each pupil at all ages has more time to develop and follow his special interests.

6. Systematically tries to interest each pupil and teacher to learn more than he thinks he wants to learn. The technique is through motivational presentations and discussions.

7. Practices accountability for pupils and teachers, realizing that such procedures show that the school cares as opposed to permissiveness or vagueness that indicates that it does not worry about what happens to individuals.

8. Provides a variety of places in the school and in the community where pupils may study and work with supervision so that each pupil may find learning strategies that suit him best instead of being required to learn in one classroom from one teacher.

9. Has continuous progress arrangements so that each pupil may proceed at his own pace under competent supervision with a variety of self-directing, self-motivating, and self-evaluating materials and locations.

10. Evaluates pupil progress and teacher performance on the basis of the individual's own past record rather than on a comparison with others in the same group, while at the same time provides data that will help each person know what others are accomplishing.

11. Substitutes constructive reports of achievements for the threat of failure as the prime motivational device of the school. The school records the special projects that each pupil completes, no matter how small, that go beyond what the school requires of everyone.

12. Recognizes that the principal more than any one other person creates a humane environment in the school; and, therefore, frees him from routine managerial tasks to permit him to get out of the office to work with pupils and teachers to develop more humane programs and procedures for everyone.[6]

These characteristics of a humane school are exemplified in practice in programs described in the chapters of this book. Many schools are making unusually serious efforts to meet the needs and concerns of students for self-esteem and individual attention.

[6] J. Lloyd Trump, "On Humanizing Schools," NASSP Bulletin, 56:9–10 (February 1972).

CONCERNS OF THE PUBLIC

A rising tide of concern about the cost effectiveness of the public schools has been demonstrated by a negatively voting public time and again. A flow of exciting and disquieting publications about "crisis in the classroom" seems to have captured an audience not accustomed to reading about education. The concerns of Kozol, Holt, Postman, Silberman, and other writers have increased the anxieties of the public about its schools. "Gallup's Fourth Annual Poll of Public Attitudes toward Education" suggests that schools are not offering the programs that the public wants. The public gave the highest priority to the goal of getting better jobs, yet unemployment of young people is rising. The public also believed that a lack of discipline is the number one problem facing schools. However, all groups surveyed by Gallup (parents, educators, and adults without children in schools) agreed that the blame for lack of discipline should be placed chiefly on home life.

A study by Blum at Stanford's Institute for Public Policy Analysis substantiated the identification of parents as a source of greatest responsibility for problem students. In his study of the relationship between drug usage by teen-agers and home life, Blum found that the highest incidence of drug usage among teen-agers was found in families that tended to be permissive, to indulge in alcohol and pills, to have a notably high number of speeding violations. These encouraged their children to accept pleasure as a good thing whether in the form of staying out late, engaging in sex, or using chemicals. Low drug usage was found among youths from those families that emphasized a sense of community responsibility of obligation to others; temperance in use of alcohol and pills; discipline, affection, and respect for each other; and a generally positive attitude toward the police.[7]

Thus, concerns of the public are not only related to what goes on in the schools, but are related also to the irresponsibility of many homes. Some high schools are facing this problem by offering adult evening courses in parent education as well as courses on responsible parenthood to youths in school who will be tomorrow's parents.

The majority of parents are highly responsible, however, and are becoming more and more involved with the schools. In the mid-sixties, black parents in the ghettos and white parents in the suburbs began to question and in some cases even to revolt against the educational system. Quite a different situation developed from that in the era when more than one-third of the students were screened out or dropped out before

[7] Published in Richard Blum, *Horatio Alger's Children* and *The Dream Sellers* (San Francisco: Jossey-Bass, 1972).

completing high school. Until recently, parents accepted this situation without questioning the school's role.

Then a change took place. Questions of accountability arose. Parents began to ask: Is all that can be done for a student actually being done? Not satisfied with the school's responses, parents demanded more participation in decision making. Difficult questions were asked of the teacher, the principal, and the superintendent. Some schools anticipated the new involvements and responded by working with groups in the community, by assisting in organizing groups, by planning with them, and by providing them with the kinds of information that answered complaints and criticisms. By forming productive school and community partnerships, they are working to bring about the educational opportunities that are needed for the youth of our country today and tomorrow. Where this has not happened, community groups have worked apart from the school and tensions have developed.

PRESSURES FROM SOCIAL CHANGE

Involvement of the community is important, but so is involvement of high school students. Development of students' skills in decision making and value clarification are among the characteristics of modern programs in high schools that are approaching social change and value conflicts in constructive ways. Illustrations in later chapters describe representative programs designed to help young people constantly meet changing problems.

But some other high schools seem to be ignoring their responsibilities to equip students to live and work in a dynamic and changing society. Too many high schools, now as in the past, place emphasis on a one-dimensional or single-principle basis which produces unfortunate patterns of either/or thinking. These patterns should be combined into a comprehensive theory that substitutes for categorical positions on these time-worn issues: personal interest versus subject matter, life-centeredness versus subject-centeredness, content versus method, emotional development versus intellectual growth, basic skills versus the growth of the whole child, and so on.

Numerous examples could be given of single-principle thinking in secondary schools. Too many vestiges of the thinking of the Committee of Ten in 1893 still remain: that high school is designed for the intellectually elite as a college preparatory institution, and all others should be sent somewhere else. Thus, when the masses flood into the high schools, instructors and administrators are frequently unsure of what to do with those who are not highly motivated achievers. A pattern, then, develops of mediocrity as a matter of course.

Value Conflicts

Secondary teachers and the professors of their university courses are usually products of the same culture as the citizens who give economic goals of education the highest priority. The views that schooling is the road to achieving higher income and that "the way I did it" is the way that should be perpetuated have resulted in strong adherence to maintaining traditional course content, habits of grading, and definitions of the type of schooling needed for the well-educated person. This book highlights innovations in the growing number of schools that are moving away from these traditions.

Oddly, some traditionalists do not always apply the same thinking to moral values or attempt to teach value clarification. While in some secondary schools knowledge seems to be regarded as an unchanging entity centered only in the past, in the area of morals and values almost anything goes. Youth are seldom taught how to make value decisions. In fact, some seem to have no moral values, as exemplified by stealing in the shopping centers, violence in the halls, promiscuity in sex, drug abuse, and so on.

A recap of history may clarify these observations. In the nineteenth century, knowledge was conceived as more or less a fixed body. One could figuratively draw a circle around it and consider it as a body of absolutes which must be transmitted to the young. Likewise, concepts of right, truth, and morals were absolutes; the opposite of right was wrong, of truth was falsehood, and of morality was immorality. There were few "gray areas" of uncertainty.

In the early twentieth century, with the spread of printed knowledge and subsequently with the rapid diffusion of information through electronic media, youths and adults were exposed to floods of information, a variety of viewpoints, and many value systems. These changing societal conditions seemed to lead to "anything goes" in values, says Schaeffer:

> Until a few years ago it was still possible to discuss what was right and wrong, what was true and false. One could say "be a good girl," and while she might not have followed your advice, at least she would have understood what you were talking about. To say the same thing to a truly modern girl today would be to make a "nonsense" statement. The blank look you might receive would not mean that your standards had been rejected but that your message was meaningless. The shift has been tremendous. Thirty or more years ago you could have said such things as "This is true" or "This is right," and you would have been on everybody's wave length.[8]

8 Francis A. Schaeffer, *The God Who Is There* (Downers Grove, Ill.: Inter-Varsity Press, 1968), p. 14.

Shaeffer's final statement is no longer true. Ambivalence about values pervades secondary schools and society at large, with too few efforts being made to teach young people how to consider their objectives, analyze data, causes, and consequences, and work toward value decisions. Excellent examples, however, are given later in this book of positive programs for student involvement in value decision making which can provide ideas for expansion in secondary education.

Examples of value conflict other than issues of morality can be readily observed in educational literature and in practice in the high schools. The hassle over the concept of grades versus no grades continues, while educators should rather be providing students with analytic assessments which help them understand their strengths, current weak points, with suggestions and support for growth and improvement. Individualized instruction is another area of misunderstanding. Some view it as a method of grooming a few students who will become the elite. The concept of elitism is in itself misunderstood. To many educators it is a bad word connoting political elitism, that is, special power and privilege in which others are made to do one man's bidding (e.g., Hitler), and worthy egalitarian ideals are subverted into mediocrity. True elitism is a concept of individuality which should lead to the development of talent and leadership as positive expressions of competence (e.g., Einstein).

Pearl has criticized programs of individualized instruction which foster a spirit of anarchism or develop students who operate solely for themselves. He says:

> Students should certainly be encouraged to develop to the utmost their individual potential, but the core of the school must be interdependent group activities in which the student fulfills his social responsibility . . . there is only one way to build student responsibility and that is to allow them to be responsible for something. Allowing students to be responsible for each other's academic progress also builds feelings of belongingness.[9]

Standards

The matter of standards is another area of misunderstanding. In some instances teachers have interpreted criticism of traditional educational practices to be a message that students should be allowed to "do their own thing." Engaging in trivia or nothingness in order to pass an hour or a day without strain on one's mind is hardly "relevant" to the goals of the secondary school. To do your own thing does not mean to do away with standards; the question is, how to "do your thing" with competence. No thoughtful educator is promoting a "no standards" school which could lead to an entire society of bunglers and quacks. No one cares to see the

[9] Arthur Pearl, *The Atrocity of Education* (St. Louis: New Critics Press, 1972), p. 247.

medical profession become unreliable, lawyers become inept, automobile builders follow an "anything goes" concept, or a teaching profession that has nothing to profess.

Many parents, especially minorities or others dissatisfied with school offerings, have demanded high standards, basics in learning, program evaluation, and other procedures that lead to competence. Kenneth B. Clark, Director of the Metropolitan Research Center of New York City, has observed in reference to the struggle for community control in the schools of that city, that black parents are pointing out that permissiveness is a bypass leading nowhere and are demanding standards in education that will lead to upward mobility for their children.[10] In California, the San Francisco Youth Law Center sponsored a suit again the San Francisco Unified School District on behalf of a student who was graduated from high school with the ability to read only at a fifth-grade level. The suit contended that under California law the state is responsible for minimum educational standards and for establishing a system to turn out a student with these skills.[11]

Some people fear that advocating standards is dangerous and that rigidity may be the result, with schools taking an either/or approach, such as an extreme allegiance to mechanistic uses of behavioral objectives with almost total emphasis on "skills."[12]

Students will accept standards in the context of learning if there are also present the qualities of warmth, imagination, honesty, loyalty, empathy, and a sense of humor. Standards will be meaningful in programs that include faculty, students, and community in goal setting; that lead to true inquiry, insightful thinking, and aesthetic attitudes that respect both the knowledge of the past and the changing knowledge which forms the bridges to the future.

DIVERSITY

Adapting secondary education to widely diverse individual differences is a central problem. Presently individualistic and egalitarian trends are clashing. The American ideal of maximizing potential, when translated

[10] In "Barriers to Academic Achievement of Educationally Neglected Children," *Futures Conference: New Directions in American Education* (Proceedings of the ES '70 Conference, Washington, D.C., May 1972), pp. 107–116.

[11] "Can Schools Be Sued for Failing To Teach?" *Education U.S.A.*, May 14, 1973, p. 206.

[12] For further discussion of this point of view see Arthur W. Combs, *Educational Accountability beyond Behavioral Objectives* (Washington, D.C.: Association for Supervision and Curriculum Development, 1972), and James B. Macdonald, Bernice J. Wolfson, and Esther Zaret, *Reschooling Society: A Conceptual Model* (Washington, D.C.: Association for Supervision and Curriculum Development, 1973).

into economic terms, increases the gap between the elite and the common man. Schools are caught between the need to maximize the individual's talent and at the same time involve him in social processes and group dynamics in which each works for the good of all. A major "why" for innovation is the need to design secondary programs that will provide students with more awareness of their potentialities; create talents where none are presently evident; stimulate any spark of learning, no matter how faint, with rich educational experiences; broaden the options available to students, given current social conditions; find specialized capacities; and encourage and open expectations. Rigid predictions that freeze or lock a student into a narrow choice are to be avoided.

The student rebellion of the late sixties made it clear that many students, both "advantaged" and "deprived," viewed the rigidities of the system with disfavor. Emphasis, they said, was on prejudiced and slanted content, on conformity rather than creativity, or discipline rather than democratic involvement in decision making, and on a lock-step pattern rather than on flexibility that leads to action learning, discovery, and self-direction.

Ethnic Minorities

The painful truth is being faced that America's black, brown, red, and yellow citizens have been largely excluded from the mainstream in the schools and in society in general. No one can deny the seriousness of racial prejudice and ethnic conflict and the need to place top priority on the elimination of hostility between the races. Schools, either consciously or unconsciously, have tended to perpetuate undesirable racial attitudes and beliefs. Now minorities are more rapidly moving into leadership roles and demanding changes. Teachers are helping ethnic minority students to build strong self-concepts, to be proud of their own cultures, to develop political effectiveness, and to master strategies for liberating themselves from physical captivity in the ghettos and from the psychological oppression of dehumanizing attitudes and actions of other groups and individuals.

Ethnic content is rapidly being added to the curriculum in forward-looking schools. By studying the ways of other peoples, students learn more about their own values, perceptions, and prejudices. Students of more privileged groups are shocked to learn of the devastating and oppressing experiences of American Indians, blacks, and others in America. Educators of integrity are taking decisive steps to help create a truly pluralistic society in which people of all ethnic groups can live and work together in harmony.[13]

[13] See issue, James A. Banks (Ed.), "The Imperatives of Ethnic Education," *Phi Delta Kappan*, 53:265–343 (January 1972).

Selectivity versus Adaptivity

The climate of secondary schools has tended to seem selective rather than adaptive. Glaser observes that in a selective environment

> . . . the fixed or limited paths available require particular student abilities, and these *particular* abilities are emphasized and fostered to the exclusion of other abilities. In this sense, the system becomes selective with respect to individuals who have particular abilities for success—as success is defined and as it can be attained by the means of instruction that are available. The effectiveness of the system, for the designers of the system and for the students themselves, is enhanced by admitting only those students who score very highly on measures of the abilities required to succeed. Furthermore, since only those students who have a reasonable probability of success are admitted, little change in the educational environment is necessary, and the differences among individuals that become important to measure are those that predict success in this special setting.[14]

This view of the school cannot tolerate diversity, and justly invites vociferous objections from blacks and other minorities, women's liberation advocates, and sponsors of gifted and handicapped students.

In contrast to a selective mode, an adaptive mode of education assumes that the educational environment can provide for a wide range and variety of instructional methods and opportunities for success. Alternate means of learning are adapted to and in some way matched to knowledge about each individual—his background, talents, interests, and the nature of his past performance. An individual's styles and abilities are assessed either upon entrance or during the course of learning, and certain educational paths are elected or assigned. Further information is obtained about the learner as learning proceeds, and this in turn is related to subsequent alternative learning opportunities.

Compulsory Education?

Another expression of the need for recognition of diversity was the challenge of compulsory education laws by the Amish. On May 15, 1972, the Amish won a unanimous United States Supreme Court decision exempting them from state laws compelling Amish children to continue their schooling beyond the eighth grade. Although this was the first time in the history of America that compulsory education laws have been successfully challenged, the decision will undoubtedly have ramifications. A basic premise of the Amish case was whether social pluralism can be preserved

[14] Robert Glaser, "Individuals and Learning: The New Aptitudes," *Educational Researcher*, 1:6 (June 1972).

in this country if the inclusion of a group is compelled in a program whose inevitable effect is to mold opinion and values. The principle of individual freedom was strongly emphasized in the arguments of the case.

An NEA Task Force has asked for amendments to compulsory education laws to allow school systems to provide options for students of hours, days, and weeks required in attendance in school buildings. It has also called for legislation and policies to make it easier to leave and re-enter the schools, to increase work-study experiences for meeting credit requirements, to provide new curriculum content and teaching methods, experimental schools, and further exploration of alternative schools both within and outside present school structures.[15]

The question of compulsory education cannot be answered with a clean-cut yes or no. Countries that have not had some form of compulsory education are known to have higher illiteracy among the population. However, options can be devised within flexible requirements; these are illustrated in Chapter 4.

Recognizing that there may be a number of reasons why a student would choose to stay out of school for a period of time for community work or experiences outside of the school setting, Cunningham has advocated a proposal for delayed educational entitlement. Two interrelated policy changes would be required; the first, for allowed interruption in the normal kindergarten through twelfth-grade sequence would be linked with reducing the years to kindergarten through 11 or possibly kindergarten through 10. The second policy recommendation was for a one-year publicly supported educational experience for everyone in the society after age thirty. The resources saved by shortening the conventional attendance span would be redirected into dollars to underwrite delayed entitlement. A person wishing to take advantage of delayed entitlement would have extensive freedom in choosing ways to use his privilege. He may wish to return formally to school at an appropriate level, to select vocational training or retraining, or to design a program of independent study using libraries or television instruction, part-time on-campus work, or travel. Cunningham's suggestion would be a kind of GI bill for all people over thirty.[16]

Others have suggested that high schools should open their doors to serve the broader educational purposes of the entire community on a day and night basis, admitting adults to high school classes in the daytime and high school students to adult classes in the evening. In a few communities, efforts are being made in these directions and will be discussed in another section.

[15] *Education U.S.A.*, November 27, 1972, p. 75.

[16] Luvern L. Cunningham, "The Reform and Renewal of American Education," *Futures Conference: New Directions in American Education* (Proceedings of the ES '70 Conference, Washington, D.C., May 1972), p. 98.

Thus, among the most pressing reasons for innovation in secondary education is the educational need to nourish the diversity and pluralism of modern life. Finding ways to help the student learn how to live readily with differences—whether racial, academic aptitude, or whatever the differences may be—but keep his own integrity, are essential elements of effectiveness in education. How to release the learning energies and expand capacities of young students, and indeed of the entire population, are challenges to education.

QUESTIONS OF FINANCE

One of the most critical issues and one of the most potent for compelling schools to innovate is that of school finance. The relationship of quality education to the expenditures of the schools is rapidly coming under probing analysis.

A strong advocacy for educational reform is the final report of the President's Commission on School Finance. Major findings of the Commission include amply documented evidence that great disparities exist among school districts and among schools in the ability of local districts to provide financial support. The states have not been able to keep pace with the needs of the schools nor to reduce disparities. However, the relationship between cost and quality in education was found to be exceedingly complex and difficult to document. Numerous examples were provided of schools where increases in expenditure were accompanied by no discernible improvement in educational quality. Also, class size as an important determiner of educational quality could not be supported by evidence available at the time of the study. Special difficulties beset the urban schools and serious financial problems were reported among the nonpublic schools, particularly those sponsored by Roman Catholic institutions. The Commission urged that more fruitful ways be found to spend money to improve schools, to equalize educational opportunity, and to produce quality education for children. Educational reform was the theme of the Commission's report and a series of recommendations opened with an assignment of responsibility to the states:

> We recommend that each State assume responsibility for determining and raising on a statewide basis, the amount of funds required for education; for the allocation of these funds among the school districts of the State, and for the evaluation of the effective use of these funds.

> We also recommend that local boards of education be given wide latitude, within general State guidelines, to use resources provided by the State in ways that best meet their needs and demands. This should include choosing curriculums; employing, assigning and dismissing staff;

and defining local goals and objectives. Within this flexibility, local boards of education should be held accountable to local taxpayers, parents, students, and to the State.[17]

The Commission stressed the need for more effective standards and procedures for measuring the performance of our educational systems and, in particular, measuring the quality of school programs. Quality education was defined by the Commission as follows:

In schools where children are encouraged and guided toward healthy and useful maturity, the people, the purposes, and the procedures reflect certain common characteristics:

1. The concept that education aids greater fulfillment of the aspiration of man, and that the educational experience must provide each child, no matter how limited his potential, with a sense of accomplishment.
2. A pupil–teacher relationship reflecting concern, respect, and empathy.
3. Educational teachniques leading to the maximum development of each child, enhancing the prospect of responsible self-direction and self-control.
4. Pride in one's own culture and respect for the culture of others.
5. Flexible curriculums to motivate each child, that are adopted, modified, or discarded as empirical evidence dictates.
6. Mastery of basic communication skills such as speech, reading, writing, arithmetic.
7. Acquisition of cultural literacy—art, language, literature, music—and recognition of the value of natural and social environments and the need to protect them.
8. Acquisition of skills in both argument and objective inquiry through fact collection, discrimination, and selection.[18]

Quality education, the Commission stressed, must lend itself to substantive evaluation and educational accountability.

Schools are trying new ways to use available resources so that the best possible results are produced and so that an accounting can be made to the public for educational decisions and the results obtained. The substantial rise in teacher pay in recent years and the resulting financial pressure on many school districts have stimulated interest in various arrangements for paying teachers on the basis of competence, responsibility, leadership qualities, or other attributes that promote the quality of education and influence student growth effectively. When all teachers received low pay, it was necessary to center attention on raising the

[17] The President's Commission on School Finance, *Schools, People, and Money—The Need for Educational Reform* (Washington, D.C.: U.S. Government Printing Office, 1972), p. xiii.
[18] The President's Commission on School Finance, p. 16.

general level. Now that pay is much better in most places, practical questions arise. In order to give appropriate salaries to outstanding teachers, must the same salaries be given to all the rest? This question has led toward differentiated staffing and various other innovations for making the money go further.

EDUCATIONAL ACCOUNTABILITY

Greater attention to educational accountability is evidenced by increased involvement in needs assessments, goal setting, and assessment at federal, state, and local levels. The movement promises to become even more earnest and widespread. Implicit in the concept of accountability is the supposition that if the student has not learned the school has not taught. But the concept of accountability goes beyond this and concerns itself with all factors relating to learning input and outcomes. Although a multitude of definitions and partial interpretations have attached themselves to the word "accountability," its central implication is for goal-directed and performance-oriented educational leadership with analysis of feedback to focus more accurately on ways to reach objectives. The importance of the concept of accountability will stimulate cooperative school and community involvement in setting goals and priorities. More precise definition of the tasks of public education will result as evaluation and assessment become tied to objectives. However, the warning bears repeating that as schools develop measurable objectives, a sophisticated level of maturity will be required to prevent undesirable side effects of structural rigidity that stifle creativity and initiative. Far more humane outcomes must be required of the schools than those measured in standardized test scores.

A number of circumstances have led inevitably to the demand for accountablity: loss of public confidence in the schools stimulated by popular readings, taxpayer revolts, student unrest, neglect of various segments of the population, and demands for equity in school support.

At this point, assessment programs are in operation or on the drawing boards in almost every state department of education in the union. Some have passed legislation requiring educational accountability and have spelled out the steps to be involved. Colorado has developed a model for accountability, one of several states to do so. Colorado's 1971 Educational Accountability Act requires every district of the state to adopt an accountability program within the following year. The purpose of the act, as stated, is to define and measure quality in education, to help the public schools of Colorado to achieve such quality, and to expand the life opportunities and options of the students of the state. The act requires every school district to appoint an advisory accountability committee including both educators and lay citizens. Each committee is strongly urged to have student and minority groups represented.

The educational accountability plan for Colorado is composed of five sequential steps:

1. The local school community identifies its goals for education. This is accomplished by involving all parties who have an interest in the educational enterprise: pupils, parents, teachers, and other members of the community.
2. Priorities in goals are established, since everything cannot be done at once.
3. More specific objectives are then developed for each goal selected for action. This step is needed to get the goals into programs that can be implemented.
4. Implementation programs are developed for each objective. This includes the detailing of various activities and resources that are needed to make progress toward achievement of the objective.
5. At this point the entire program becomes the educational plan for the school community and is covered by a performance contract which the local board signs and submits to the state board of education as the basis for school accreditation. At the time of state board of education signature, the school is accredited by and under the contract.[19]

The accountability plans of other states and local districts are similar to this one although many variations are being developed. The process of developing goals through the mutual cooperation of many parties is an innovative process in itself in many localities. The progression that makes up educational accountability requires much time, thought, and effort: establishing goals, setting specific objectives, devising programs to meet the objectives, carrying out the programs, measuring their degree of success, comparing costs and performance under alternate programs, revising, and trying again. But with this process the American people can become more vitally interested in public education than ever before and, through this or similar means, financial support may be achieved for effective school programs.

FUTURE THINKING

By studying educational trends, predicted futures, and auspicious practices, educators can get ahead of the game of daily coping with immediate problems and plan on a long-range basis for the future. In this way, vigorous action can produce viable secondary school programs.

[19] See Rolland O. Powell, "Putting Goals to Work," *Educational Leadership*, 28: 608–610 (March 1971), and Donald D. Woodington, "Accountability from the Viewpoint of a State Commissioner of Education," *Phi Delta Kappan*, 54:95–97 (October 1972).

Curriculum guides reflect the diversity of programs in today's secondary schools.

Futurists are detecting movements that can be utilized in planning. Gibbons sees education moving toward greater freedom of choice for students, more personal and individual instruction, greater participation by teachers and students at all levels of decision making, diminishing emphasis on rules, requirements, and schedules (displaced by personal regulation and self-direction in study), and increasing interpenetration between the school and the community.[20] The School Management Study group notes similar movements in education: toward decentralization and pluralistic alternatives, more parent involvement, more options, more flexible structures, more choices for self-determination. Increasing interest is predicted in the areas of human rights, individualized learning, evaluation, change processes, community involvement, accountability, equity financing, affective learning, and negotiations.[21]

In a survey of reaction to possible educational futures, educators from among five occupational categories were invited to give thoughtful consideration to predictable future developments in education. Increasing emphasis was predicted in these areas that relate to secondary education: multimedia will replace the traditional monopoly of the textbook, the use of student tutors will be commonplace, increased time will be devoted to the expressive arts, social studies classes will come to grips with controversial issues, a twelve-month year and personalized programs will prevail, compulsory attendance laws will be revised, and differentiated staffing will come into general use. Team endeavors will replace the self-contained classroom and teacher education will be drastically modified to prepare preservice students to work in teams or partnerships.[22] If predictions become self-fulfilling prophecies, some or all of these could appreciably influence widespread change in education.

Irvine, rather than trying to predict what the educational system of the future will be, outlined specifications of what the system should be able to do. Broad specifications leave room for alternative solutions to be considered without focusing prematurely on a given solution or making an isolated innovation where there is no comprehensive plan for effective schooling. Irvine's specifications follow:

> The educational system of the future must be able to deal with large numbers of students.
>
> The system must accommodate itself to new and different population patterns.

[20] Maurice Gibbons, "Changing Secondary Education Now," *NASSP Bulletin*, 54:30–40 (January 1970).

[21] *SMSG Newsletter*, July 1, 1972 and August 15, 1972.

[22] Harold G. Shane and Owen N. Nelson, "What Will the Schools Become?" *Phi Delta Kappan*, 52:596–598 (June 1971).

The system must be capable of utilizing new technological developments for educational purposes.

The system must capitalize on the many other educational forces which exist in society.

The system must be able to bring learners in contact with a wide variety of realistic learning experiences.

The system must accommodate itself to changes in the natural resources available to man.

The system must be capable of coping with increased amounts of information.

The system must be concerned with economy of learning.

The system must emphasize the development of learning skills.

The system should progressively involve the learner in making decisions about his educational program so that ultimately the learner controls his own learning.

The system must develop broadly educated specialists.

The system must emphasize human relations.

The system must provide the means by which individuals can determine overriding purposes in their lives.

The system must help individuals break down the dichotomy between work and play.[23]

Whether these predictions and suggested specifications are the ones that should provide guidelines for educational innovation is not as important as the need for preparing reasoned plans. The educational system of the future can be shaped by educators, lay citizens, and students working together; it can become the victim of neglect or traditional practices; or problems and issues unsolved can set off an accelerated decline.

WHAT INNOVATIONS?

Whether to innovate or not is hardly a matter of choice for high schools. New needs, new conditions, and new thinking are demanding new responses. New responses from schools in all parts of the United States are described in the following pages under several general headings: the student, the curriculum, the organization, the staff, the media, the space. Chapter 8 describes processes of innovation. The authors have resisted any narrow definition of innovation that would preclude identification herein of practices considered promising by us and innovative and success-

[23] David J. Irvine, "Specifications for an Educational System of the Future," *Phi Delta Kappan*, 53:362–364 (February 1972).

ful in the schools using them. In general, we conceive of an innovation as the introduction of a novel factor, perceived as new by a given school and community, supported by a driving force, and implemented as a practical advance that deviates from established or traditional forms. We ourselves would accept and recommend use of such a series of questions as these in identifying and selecting an innovation in any sound process (see Chapter 8) of innovation:

1. Is the innovation not only consonant with the broad and fundamental purposes of contemporary secondary education but directed toward unique local needs, which have been assessed in a systematic, broad-based, and unprejudiced manner?

2. Will the proposed innovation provide a basis for decisions in making choices among alternatives? Is it concerned with valuation for setting priorities and allocating resources? Does it have utility for finding alternative ways to reach the broad goals of secondary education and not merely be introduced to satisfy an idle curiosity about an activity or situation?

3. Are there clearly discernible objectives which can be evaluated? Do the participants know what the objectives are and how they will be measured?

4. Can the innovative program be described or defined clearly and in advance of initiation not only in terms of the objectives of the program but in terms of staff qualifications and training, student selection and preinnovation performance, media, facilities that will be required, administrative support, and student and staff activities essential to successful implementation of the innovation?

5. Are the program objectives measurable and consonant with modern concepts of evaluation? Is evaluation utilized as a method of using evidence to improve learning and teaching, to aid in clarifying objectives and revising processes, and as part of a system of quality control to determine whether the school district processes are effective and whether the district's goals are adequate for contemporary times?

6. Will background work be provided in advance, including estimates of time and cost required, side effects that may develop, and a search of information and studies related to the innovation which can be found in the Educational Resources Information Center (ERIC) or other data sources?

7. Is the innovation directed toward fundamental and basic needs of youth? For example, are students being taught how to learn, how to acquire tools and processes for solving problems and acquiring knowledge, and how to grow attitudinally? Are there opportunities for pupils to assume responsibility? Are rational powers being developed, including the acquisition of skills and knowledge, critiquing of that knowledge, consideration of alternatives, formulation of values, and constructive ways of behaving?

8. Does the innovation provide a good learning environment with basic

principles of learning utilized, including motivation, interest, transfer of learning to new situations, goal setting, and so on?

9. Has substantial provision been made for individual differences? Will there be opportunities for the student to come into contact with a variety of types of learning experiences?

10. Are group dynamics given an important place in the program with considerable use of discussion and interaction, and opportunities for students to assume leadership roles and evaluate the productivity of their participation?

11. Does the innovation make explicit provisions for teacher growth as well as student growth? Will teachers find ways to be learners, to share ideas with other professionals, to engage in team efforts, to participate in observation, analysis, and self-evaluation to see how improvement is taking place?

12. Does planning for introduction of the innovation recognize that members of the organization may experience uncertainty, doubt, and anxiety at the outset? That they must constantly be kept informed of progress toward the objectives of the program with awareness of successes and setbacks? That through involvement in a problem-solving process they can find the means for constructive self-appraisal which leads to readiness for change, commitment to change, and ultimately the satisfaction of accomplishment?

13. Are resources to be used in imaginative ways, such as those provided in the community environment and by resource persons of the community? Will there be creative use of materials and equipment?

Certainly, there is no single best way or one panacea that should be sustained regardless of time and place. Many alternatives are being offered and some will succeed with one group and some with another. As educational values and goals continually change and develop so must responsive options continually be developed.

additional suggestions for further study

1. Browder, Lesley H., Jr., William A. Atkins, Jr., and Esin Kaya, *Developing an Educationally Accountable Program*. Berkeley, Calif.: McCutchan, 1973. In this exploratory study of the accountability process, an approach is offered with options for program development.

2. Frymier, Jack R., *A School for Tomorrow*. Berkeley, Calif.: McCutchan, 1973. Frymier and several other authors present here a series of propositions about what schools could be like in the years ahead and outline an alternative to the kinds of schools that exist today. Films, filmstrips, and audiotape cassettes are available as supplementary media.

3. Gorman, Burton W., *Secondary Education: The High School America Needs*. New York: Random House, 1971. A moderate response

to the severe critics of the high school is embodied in practical suggestions for change and reform.

4. Heath, Douglas H., *Humanizing Schools: New Directions, New Decisions.* New York: Hayden, 1971. The author makes a persuasive and compelling plea for educational change. Basing his conclusions on fifteen years of research, Heath presents a disturbing analysis of today's youngsters and how their schools are failing them. He offers a realistic framework for deciding what must be done and a thoughtful argument *why.*

5. Katz, Michael B. (Ed.), *School Reform: Past and Present.* Boston: Little, Brown, 1971. A compilation of readings on the recurring issues in public education provides perspective on current efforts to innovate.

6. Macdonald, James B., Bernice J. Wolfson, and Esther Zaret, *Reschooling Society: A Conceptual Model.* Washington, D.C.: Association for Supervision and Curriculum Development, 1974. Rejecting "the currently dominant model of schooling which emphasizes narrow predetermined ends and efficiency as a primary value criterion," the authors advocate and describe a model which emphasizes values and processes consistent with an explicit humanist ethical commitment.

7. The National Commission on the Reform of Secondary Education, Melbourne, Florida, sponsored by Kettering's Institute for Development of Educational Activities, is conducting a comprehensive study of secondary education and making recommendations for altering secondary schools to better serve the nation's young people. Reports are available.

8. Sarason, Seymour B., *The Culture of the School and the Problem of Change.* Boston: Allyn and Bacon, 1971. How schools work and what factors make changing them so difficult are analyzed. Provocative questions are raised regarding the traditional school culture.

9. Saylor, J. Galen, and Joshua L. Smith (Eds.), *Removing Barriers to Humaneness in the High School.* Washington, D.C.: Association for Supervision and Curriculum Development, 1971. Major barriers to implementation of humaneness in secondary schools are discussed as well as presentations on management, teaching, curriculum, and external factors related to humanizing secondary education.

10. Stufflebeam, Daniel L. and others, *Educational Evaluation and Decision-Making.* Itsaca, Ill.: Peacock, 1971. A substantive reference designed for the educational practitioner who must make decisions on ways of meeting educational needs, solving educational problems, and utilizing educational opportunities. In recognition of the paucity of information about program evaluation and the need for skills in employing evaluation procedures and techniques by those responsible for educational programming, Phi Delta Kappa sponsored a National Study Committee on Evaluation, whose work resulted in this volume.

11. Walberg, Herbert J., and Andrew T. Kopan (Eds.), *Rethinking Urban Education: A Sourcebook of Contemporary Issues.* San Francisco: Jossey-Bass, 1972. A series of lectures examine the problems of urban education, identify contributing factors, and suggest remedies. The central theme is the necessary adaptation to cultural and individual differences.

The Student:
New Opportunities
and Responsibilities

The wave of student unrest that erupted in the late sixties, later leveling
off, then declining, left its mark on secondary education. School leaders are
far more sensitive to the aspirations, desires, interests, and needs of
previously excluded or overlooked groups and individuals in the high
schools. Student-centered innovations in high schools have entered a new
era and adults find themselves listening more closely to student
concerns, involving students in planning, considering student rights and
responsibilities in a new light, and opening many more options and
alternatives in secondary education.

While apathetic or alienated students became a matter of concern in
the late sixties, activist students moved center stage during the height of
the disruptive period. Activist students range along a continuum from
moderate to radical. The moderate activists are more readily guided into
constructive activities. They want more voice in decisions pertaining to
curriculum and instruction, discipline, dress, grooming, and student
activities. During the rebellious era, radical activists initiated revolutionary
methods for satisfying their "demands" by disrupting the schools, defying

administrative authority, and gaining control of the school offices in some cases. Usually they claimed to be attempting to eliminate war, poverty, and prejudice but at times changed issues as tactics developed.

The alienated or apathetic students seem to reject the ethics of work and responsibility and usually appear withdrawn and passive in school. Glatthorn notes that "all across the country principals and pontificators are wringing their hands about the problem of student apathy," and suggests that apathy is of many sorts and of diverse origins. His typology includes (1) the student without purpose or interests, usually on drugs, who needs therapy and/or love; (2) the black student or blue-collar white student who feels doomed to a life of powerlessness in a larger society; (3) the bright student who figures the administration is merely playing games about involvement and chooses not to play along with the hoax; (4) the student who lacks skills or competencies the others have and fears that he might look stupid if he gets involved; (5) the student who has his own life to lead outside the school and doesn't care to waste his energies getting involved in things that don't really matter to him; and (6) those who are simply bored with inane and repetitive discussions and recitations.[1]

Other theorists have speculated on the causes of widespread, even worldwide, student unrest or apathy. Yankelovich, who has studied the revolution in campus values (reflected in the high school) since the mid-sixties, asks whether the student movement might conceivably harbor an idea of universal importance. He asks "Were we witnessing a new chapter in an authentic and serious movement in American cultural history or merely a nervous spasm elicited in response to the unsettling events of our time?" and refers to Alfred North Whitehead's comment that "Great ideas often enter reality in strange guises and with disgusting alliances." He finds three themes in the student movement: emphasis on the natural as opposed to the artificial; apparent anti-intellectualism, which he identified as the need to relate the abstract to direct experience; and the stress on new forms of community as a rejection of the loneliness and sense of isolation produced by the impersonality of mass society.[2]

New goals are needed to integrate the young into functional community roles with direct responsible activities that move them purposefully toward maturity. Coleman advocates the following: more liaison between schools and places of work; and replacement of the conception of full-time education up to a given age followed by full-time work, with a mixture

[1] Allan A. Glatthorn, "The Student as Person," *Theory into Practice*, 11:17–21 (February 1972).

[2] Daniel Yankelovich, "The New Naturalism," *Saturday Review*, April 1, 1972, pp. 32–37.

of work and education that begins at an early age and runs through adulthood.[3]

Participant observers in studies extending over many months have made "inside" reports of student and teacher behavior and have commented on institutional pressures and climate. Ruth H. Jacobs, a sociologist who engaged in a year of sociological participant observation in a 1600-student suburban high school, observed the effect of the mass impersonal situation of the high school when compared to the nurturing and valuing atmosphere of the modern elementary program. She noted the resistance of students who were pressured toward competitive achievement by teachers and parents. To competition and college-priming pressures, Jacobs attributed many of the serious drug, vandalism, sexual, and alcohol problems at the school in which she observed.[4]

However, another writer notes that disdain of competition can be overplayed. Students who scorn a highly competitive educational system may be confusing excellence with competitive success and creeping mediocrity can be the consequence. Self-worth must depend on fulfilling one's potential, not on winning over others. Or, as it has been phrased, "Intellectual excellence is unconcerned with power over men—its only interest is power over complex data and processes."[5]

Other studies have concentrated on the students' part in shaping the institution. For a six-month period, Philip A. Cusick, who had been a teacher and administrator, conducted a research study as a participant-observer in a high school of 1100 students. He attended classes daily, associated with students, and joined in their out-of-school social life. Cusick concluded that students' out-of-school group affiliations are of utmost importance as they provide what the organization denies. He observed that the school he visited seemed to deny students' freedom, keep them powerless and in a state of spectatorship with little human interaction. The school with its emphasis on teacher-initiated action, downward communication flow, routine, batch processing, and maintenance procedures was charged with consuming an enormous amount of time when students are actually required to do very little except be in attendance and be compliant.[6]

Perhaps the causes of student dissatisfaction have been caught by Komaridis who states that the principles of learning that are taught to

[3] James S. Coleman, "The Children Have Outgrown the Schools," *Psychology Today*, 5:73–76 (February 1972).

[4] Ruth H. Jacobs, "Focus on High Schools," *Phi Delta Kappan*, 53: 100–101 October 1971).

[5] Evelyn Shirk, "The Erosion of Excellence," *Intellect*, 101:23 (October 1972).

[6] Philip A. Cusick, *Inside High School* (New York: Holt, Rinehart and Winston, 1973), p. 214.

university students of education are found only in fantasy land. He suggests, tongue in cheek, that the "real" principles, those which are operational in most of our classrooms, are:

1. All learners are alike.
2. Students learn best in large groups.
3. Learning occurs at the level of recall and recognition.
4. Students learn best when the teacher is responsible for all the decisions regarding their learning.
5. Inactivity best facilitates learning.
6. Learning is best facilitated when feedback is limited or delayed.
7. Students learn best under aversive conditions.
8. The retention and transfer of learning results from minimal practice and application of the concepts and principles taught in class.
9. Creativity occurs only in the absence of all teacher influence.
10. The fundamental purpose of tests is to evaluate students.
11. The purpose of education is to reaffirm the normal distribution.
12. Humanistic education rests on the proper use of principles one through eleven[7]

MOVING TOWARD STUDENT-CENTEREDNESS

Komaridis' satire notwithstanding, many high schools are drawing upon the generalizations of theorists and upon feedback from students and are expressing new ideas in creative and innovative secondary school programs. Student-centered curriculum innovations are highlighted in Chapter 3. Illustrative of a student-centered school for present purposes is Shawnee Mission Northwest High School in Shawnee Mission, Kansas.

At this suburban Kansas City school, the student is in first place. Much of the instructional program is built around the concept of independent study and a media-oriented resource center. The school draws its major strengths from the involvement of students and parents, from the teachers' re-evaluation of their roles, from a flexible curriculum, and from the benefits of outstanding physical facilities. When the Northwest student registers, he indicates his preferences for a subject, the time of day for the class, and the instructor he wishes. Should a first-choice class become overcrowded, a second-choice will be honored. Evaluation is a two-way process. Evaluation and individual counseling take place in each classroom. Students are invited to weekly rap sessions with the administrative staff and they are given a voice in the hiring of teachers. In addition to the spacious and carpeted resource center well-equipped with

[7] George V. Komaridis, "The Real Principles of Learning," *School Research Information Service Quarterly,* 5:12–18 (Summer 1972).

electronic, film, and print resources, teachers are further aided by a ready supply of materials and student assistants. A parent-student-teacher association provides a unique and essential relationship. Students belonging to this organization have full voting rights, pay dues, and may be elected to executive positions. One of the organization's most important objectives is the encouragement of a close-knit family relationship.

Some students adjust to Northwest's freedom slowly or with difficulty. Unaccustomed to being responsible for their actions, a few find they are ill-equipped to discipline themselves for study, attendance, or personal behavior. But a student survey reflects success in achieving many of the school's goals. Students feel trusted, are proud of their school, and most of them feel they are learning more at Northwest than they would at a more traditional school.

Other high schools are earnestly seeking innovative ways to involve students in making plans and decisions about their schools. These innovations are detailed in this chapter. The most positive results are being achieved by principals and faculties who respect the intelligence, maturity, sense of responsibility, and the interest of students, and are expanding various means for involvement by individuals and groups in school affairs. Contrary to an alarm raised in some quarters during the period of widespread student revolt, principals are finding that sharing responsibility with students has not diminished the demands for their own administrative competence. Adults who are guiding secondary students constructively seem to recognize that the future of the world in ecology, government, business, and education demands answers that the present adult generation may not have. Since the youth of America have the greatest stake in the world of tomorrow, they need experience in finding answers to important questions.

CHANGES IN STUDENT ROLES AND OPPORTUNITIES

That student involvement does not mean student dissent is substantiated by efforts and statements by professional educational associations and organizations. NEA's Research Division reported in March, 1971 that students in numerous school systems are being asked for their opinions in areas that used to be reserved to administration. Protest is being turned into positive action and dissent is channeled into constructive criticism. A sixteen-student Task Force of Student Involvement that advises North Carolina's State Department of Public Instruction issued a statement declaring that "what students are saying is that they care; they want to be contributors to the educational process, not just recipients. Educators' greatest potential resource lies in taking advantage of this interest and in channeling it into responsible areas of activity." The National Congress of Parents and Teachers in 1971 recommended that local units include students in their membership and elected five students to national commissions in the organization. Pennsylvania's Chief State School Officer in 1973 appointed forty high school students, who had been selected by their peers from high schools all over the state, as a student advisory committee to meet bimonthly with him.

Since the student uprisings of the late sixties, at least four areas can be described in which students' roles and opportunities are changing: student rights, governance, curriculum, and teacher appraisal.

Student Rights

Administrators and teachers in secondary schools are being increasingly sensitized to students' rights as well as students' responsibilities. In the past decade, increasing numbers of students and parents, often encouraged by the American Civil Liberties Union, have been bringing and winning suits that spell out more specifically the judgment made by the Supreme Court in 1967 in the Gault case that "neither the Fourteenth Amendment nor the Bill of Rights is for adults alone."

In many high schools in which issues have developed and led into the courts, teachers and principals, to be sure, have not intended to disregard students' civil liberties but had honestly believed they were educating students for citizenship. Because of the way earlier generations were educated, teachers and principals viewed students' rights as decidedly

The Student Appeals Board in operation at Niles East High School, Skokie, Illinois. Reproduced with permission from the Chicago Daily News; *photograph by Don Bierman.*

limited and had not perceived the matter to be an issue. During the period of activism, students at all levels demanded closer scrutiny of their rights as human beings and challenged local rules and regulations or actions of individuals and organizations that infringed on their rights. A notable instance was the Tinker case in which the administration of the Des Moines Public schools suspended three students for wearing black arm-bands during the Christmas season in protest against the war in Vietnam. Carried to the Supreme Court, a decision was rendered in February, 1969 that students are indeed "persons" under the constitution and therefore have fundamental rights, which school authorities must respect. In essence the Court adopted the view that the process of education in a democracy must in itself be democratic, and the right to self-expression is an important part of the educational process.

More than fifty recent decisions rendered by state or federal courts on rights of public school students have been reviewed by the National Organization on Legal Problems of Education (NOLPE) which was organized in 1954 to provide an avenue for the study of school law problems. The fifty decisions reviewed did not reveal absolute rights or freedoms; however, the following rights or freedoms have been supported by the courts in relation to specific instances:

1. The freedom of symbolic expression (e.g., freedom buttons) as long as such expression does not cause disruption.
2. The freedom of written expression (e.g., underground newspapers) as long as such expression does not cause disruption.
3. The right to refuse to wear prescribed physical education clothing and the right to wear slacks to school.
4. The right of male students to wear long hair if the prohibitive rule is vaguely worded or too broadly drawn, if distraction is not shown, if the school regulation is arbitrary or unreasonable, or if length of hair does not involve a health or safety risk.
5. The right to public education free of religious overtones.
6. Freedom from racial discrimination.
7. Freedom from vague regulations.
8. The right to procedural due process, including notice of hearing, presence of legal counsel, cross-examination or confrontation of witnesses, and freedom from self-incrimination.
9. Off-campus freedoms, such as participation in civil rights activities and possession of personal articles.
10. The right of married students and unwed mothers to attend public schools.[8]

[8] Dale Gaddy, *Rights and Freedoms of Public School Students: Directions from the 1960's* (Topeka, Kans.: National Organization on Legal Problems of Education, 1971), p. 53. Also see related booklets in the *NOLPE Monograph Series*.

The above list by no means includes all of the rights and freedoms to which public school students are entitled. Also, several court decisions have gone against the student who is nonconformist in dress or grooming in support of the local school authorities' right to exercise considerable control over such matters.

Increased involvement of the courts in school-related decisions and the need for clarification of newly affirmed student freedoms has led the National Association of Secondary School Principals to issue a series of legal memoranda which advise its members on setting local guidelines. One of the most controversial areas is that of freedom of expression and publication. In these areas, the NASSP supports three major points:

1. Freedom of expression cannot be legally restricted unless its exercise interferes with the orderly conduct of classes and school work—provided also that students do not attempt to coerce others to their point of view.
2. School sponsored publications should be free from policy restrictions outside the normal rules for responsible journalism, but all students, including those who are not members of the publication staff, are also entitled to some access to its pages for their views.
3. Nonschool publications, if they follow the same rules of responsible journalism, also should be permitted, although their distribution may be subject to administrative restrictions as to time and place.[9]

Although the student press can be considered a learning device and not an official statement of the school, student publications continue to be a sensitive area with school administrators.

In general, however, progress is being made toward wider opportunities for students and increased recognition of their constitutional rights. This is not being accomplished without trauma. Students have seized upon their rights far more eagerly than they have accepted corresponding responsibilities. "Student rights" does not mean that the student has freedom to do as he pleases, but that by taking a more involved role in the functioning of the school, he can contribute to the improvement of the educational system, offer constructive criticism, help find additional means of improvement, and accept responsibility to obey school rules or policies until such rules or policies are revoked.

Numerous school systems are involving students in statements of the students' bill of rights and responsibilities. One of the most comprehensive district policies is that of the San Mateo Union High School District of California. The right of a student to due process and appeal in discipli-

[9] Robert L. Ackerly, *The Reasonable Exercise of Authority* (Washington, D.C.: National Association of Secondary School Principals, 1969). Also see the series of newsletters, *A Legal Memorandum*, from the same source.

Members of the San Mateo City Youth Advisory Council, Sally Tharp (Aragon High School) and Gene Robinson (Hillsdale High School), meet with their advisor, city administrative analyst Dennis Argyres. Members of the council, representing the four high schools within the city of San Mateo, are appointed by the City Council and serve in an advisory capacity similar to the other city boards and commissions. Photograph courtesy of the San Mateo Union High School District, San Mateo, California.

nary matters, to a voice in educational planning and evaluation are stated, as well as his responsibility in maintaining high standards of integrity, honesty, and morality. San Mateo's bill of rights recognizes the student's right to be heard and considered. The 55-page document was developed by representatives of the Union of Associated Student Bodies, the District administration, the Board of Trustees, and eventually the Negotiating Council. The statement thoroughly explains policy on attendance, student records, government and organizations, behavior, rights, and responsibilities. Responsibilities of students are outlined, including consideration for the rights of others. Guarantees of students' rights of free speech and assembly are clarified, and due process is described for disciplinary matters, including an appeal procedure and a review committee for hearings on appeals. Other school districts have developed similar policy statements, including San Francisco, Philadelphia, Evanston Township, and the Chicago Archdiocese.

Student Government

High school students are rejecting the old concept of student government embodied in a student council composed of the most popular and the "most likely to succeed" students whose main task was to arrange pep rallies and proms. In its stead, schools are developing variations of ad hoc student leadership or new kinds of representative government that involve high school students in decision making at the institutional level. A nontraditional student government is the Staples Governing Board of Staples High School, Westport, Connecticut. Composed of ten students, seven teachers, and three administrators, the board endeavors to give students a voice in cooperative educational decision making. The Staples Governing Board, subject to the general authority of the local school board, is authorized to legislate in a wide variety of areas including student behavior codes, curriculum, school–community relations, and extracurricular activities. The board finds itself dealing with such vital issues as offering pass–no record courses, the matter of allowing students to see their high school transcripts, and giving academic credit for extracurricular activities. Disagreements occur but the discussions have not broken down into factions, faculty versus students. For both faculty and students, however, a major problem is the amount of time self-governance requires. Other criticisms of this pioneering effort in student self-governance include the worries of some parents that students are running the school, although parents who have attended the meetings report that the intelligent way students talk through complicated issues has brought about the realization that the capability of young people for self-government has been underestimated in the past.

Numerous other examples indicate an increase in student involvement in school government. Massachusetts has adopted legislation which adds a student as a full-fledged, voting member of the state's board of education. The student is elected to the state board through a long process that begins in his high school. Each Massachusetts secondary school elects a representative to serve on one of fifteen regional advisory councils. Three members from each regional council are then elected to a state advisory council and the chairman of the state council also serves on the state board of education. Edina-Morningside, Minnesota, has a student board of education, some of whose members are elected and some student council-appointed, which meets just prior to meetings of the "senior" school board to present student concerns to their elders through the superintendent. Bay City, Michigan, sends student council members as ex-officio representatives to the board of education, where they cast votes recorded as "advisory." Twenty-two Anchorage Borough (Alaska) High School students form an official student advisory group to the Anchorage Borough School Board. The student advisory committee is composed of four students from each high school, of whom two are elected by popular vote and two are chosen by the student government.

Baltimore's city school board has added two secondary school students elected by their peers as nonvoting "associates." They will participate in all board discussions, public and private, except those dealing with personnel and site acquisitions. In a carefully detailed "memorandum of understanding" the Great Neck, New York, public schools have established regulations for including student delegates to the board of education. Procedures for election within the two high schools of the district are spelled out, as well as length of term, materials to be distributed to the student delegates, responsibilities of the student delegates for attendance, behavior, communication, and cooperative activities. The student delegates are given time to speak on given matters prior to discussion by the general public and consideration by the board of education at each meeting. Although student delegates serve in a consultative and advisory capacity without any voting rights, they have been granted an important avenue for discussion with the board regarding matters of direct student concern or of general educational interest to students.

Decision making, however, might be better regarded as a skill to be developed by students than merely a right to be granted, a recent study concluded. In an experimental setting sponsored by the Center for New Schools, Chicago, a research study concerning student involvement in institutional decision making found more enthusiasm among students for decision making related to personal concerns such as hair, grooming, dating, athletics, smoking, and lockers than they had for decision making concerned with the operation of the instructional program. That decision making is a skill to be developed was exemplified by the researchers' observations that the students generally saw their most desirable role in decision making not in terms of developing detailed programs and implementing them, but in terms of bringing complaints and problems to the attention of the staff, who would then have the responsibility to develop solutions. Development of student skills in decision making may progress through four levels of participation. At the lowest level, students engage in informal discussion and complaining within subgroups. At the second level, informal discussion and complaining to teachers may take place. At the third level, students begin to have limited involvement in specific activities of the government structure and at the most mature level, students are fully involved in the activities of the government structure of the school.[10]

Student Involvement in Curriculum Determination

Student participation in curriculum development is an innovation that manifests itself in a variety of ways in schools in all parts of the country. In some cases, students are paid for helping draft curriculum during summer work periods. Students in Buffalo, Atlanta, and San Diego have been paid stipends for working as members of curriculum writing and review teams. In University City, Missouri, high-school students were employed during the summer to work with teachers in developing a series of mini-courses in career education to be offered as electives for the entire school. In Pasadena, California, one high school has a student-parent-staff curriculum committee which meets once each month to provide an opportunity for student and parent reactions to the present curriculum and to the curriculum plans being developed. Dozens of eleventh-grade students were involved in Lubbock, Texas, in rewriting an American history course. Students who were currently enrolled in American history were surveyed for their response to the question "What do you think is worth knowing about American history?" Using the students' ideas, teachers worked with librarians to organize themes and related units. Students then assisted the teachers and librarians in searching out materials and readings that they viewed to be desirable for the course. Student enthusiasm for this type of participation was high and the cooperative effort of students, teachers, and librarians seemed to bring about unusually positive attitudes toward the American history course. Additional examples may be found in Chapter 3 of student involvement in curriculum planning.

Student Participation in Teacher Appraisal

Although students still remain mostly on the receiving end of evaluation, a few schools are taking small, cautious steps toward student appraisal of teachers. Student observations and appraisals, theoretically, are pointed toward helping teachers evaluate themselves and improve their instruction. Very few instances have been reported thus far of high schools who allow students to devise and administer a teacher evaluation form. One experiment was carried out on the East Campus of Pasadena High School in which a group of students, as part of a social studies assignment, devised

[10] Drawn from "Student Involvement in Decision-Making in an Alternative High School: A Preliminary Analysis" (multilith), a report of the Center for New Schools, Chicago, 1971.

and administered a teacher evaluation form. The form, approved by the school's administration, was administered to class sections taught by twenty-three teachers who volunteered for the project. The students later admitted that the voluntary aspect of teacher participation might have skewed their data, as the most confident teachers may have volunteered and selected their most successful classes for the survey. Results indicated that 87 percent of the students felt that the teacher graded fairly and 58 percent said they liked the teacher.

A more subtle and widespread type of teacher appraisal is the opportunity being given students in numerous high schools to select the course, the teacher, and the class time they want. An example is the "college-type" scheduling procedure used at North Reading High School, Massachusetts. Early in the spring, a preregistration is held when each student lists on a computer sheet the courses he wants to take the following year. The preregistration takes place in the homerooms after students have had an opportunity to consult their guidance counselors and the school's course description booklet. Later on in the spring, after the master schedule has been made up, registration is held in the cafeteria where computer cards are laid out on the tables in piles, one pile for each class period. The upcoming seniors have first choice of class time as well as teachers. The senior, junior, sophomore, and freshman classes register in that order, with members of each class drawing lots to determine who goes first. As each student goes through the cafeteria door he or she receives a card with his name and the preregistration list of courses he has selected. Then the student goes from table to table, picking up a card for each class period he wants. If the cards have run out for a certain teacher and/or period the student must make another choice. Teacher-advisors are assigned to each student and are available in the cafeteria during registration to answer questions. These people help solve the problems which inevitably arise when a student finds that the course he wants is already filled. However, all-elective programs in English and history for grades 10 to 12 give students a wide range of courses from which to choose. Similar procedures are followed elsewhere. Napa High School (California) follows a procedure similar to North Reading's. Miami Springs (Florida) Senior High School offers students the opportunity to select the teacher, the time, and the course from classes offered continuously between 7:00 A.M. and 5:00 P.M. with further options in the evening.

Teacher appraisal by students also takes place at the point of hiring in some schools. In University City, Missouri, and Mill Valley, California, students are included on interviewing teams when principals and teachers are being employed. Students have been found to ask the toughest and some of the most relevant questions of prospective school personnel.

THE CONTINUUM CONCEPT OF STUDENT PROGRESS

An educational continuum has been defined as "an unbroken flow of experiences planned with and for the individual learner throughout his contacts with the school."[11]

As more people opt for nonconventional kinds of education and for education as a life-long activity, "continuum" plans may be expected to proliferate in a wide variety of interpretations. Possibly the student of the future may not remain in school, college, and university in one uninterrupted span while pursuing a diploma and/or degree to "complete" his education. Instead he may periodically terminate his studies within the formal school environment while he works and continues to learn in another setting for a time, returning to an education institution when it would best suit his needs. Ideally, the continuum offered by the school would begin in early childhood and continue throughout adulthood. It would extend throughout the year, with exit–entry options for students to suit their individual needs. Failure, dropouts, promotion, and compensatory education are terms that will no longer apply when the continuum concept underlies the school's program. Schools are moving away from the concept that some students must fail and are giving them the option to leave school and re-enter, to attain early entrance to college, and to come to high school even though married or pregnant. Problem students are offered choices of instructional programs. Examples follow of innovations which put the continuum, or continuous-progress, concept into practice.

Miami Springs Senior High (Florida) has instituted a continuous progress program of instruction in a number of courses with the use of Learning Activity Packets (LAPs). The school's stated objectives for this approach to instruction include "to eliminate some of the more rigid conditions that sometimes exist in a traditional classroom and may hinder individual progress" and "to reduce the number of failures or dropouts from vital high school courses." The continuous progress units with individualized instruction are used within the framework of a class while representing a form of independent study. Each student progresses individually by working toward the objectives through use of the activities that make up the LAP, and moves to successive new units as often as he can demonstrate clearly that a high degree of learning has taken place. Only a mark of A, B, or C is awarded on teacher-evaluation of student achievement and these marks appear on report cards. If achievement for a given LAP is insufficient to warrant one of these marks then the student

[11] Harold G. Shane, "A Curriculum Continuum: Possible Trends in the 70's," *Phi Delta Kappan*, 51:390 (March 1970).

will continue study on a unit until he can demonstrate learning at an A, B, or C level. No mark is awarded until this takes place; in other words, there are no D or F grades. A student may continue his sequence in a following school term by picking up where he left off. Thus, he has not failed but may move faster or slower along the continuum.

The continuum concept can be said to award partial credit and emphasize accomplishments rather than failure. Partial credit mastery is awarded in courses like typing, mathematics, or other skill- or problem-oriented subjects at Archbishop Ryan Memorial High School, Omaha. Students may receive partial credit for a course rather than lose all credit for courses in which they are unable to meet all the performance criteria. Also students can "test out" of courses and receive credit for them. Spanish-speaking students who can effectively demonstrate mastery of the Spanish language according to course criteria, for example, may receive credit for two Spanish courses and then enroll in ninth grade in a third course if they choose. Students may also receive such credit in math, English, or any course that they already know. They may bypass part of a course and receive credit for the whole if they can demonstrate adequate competence. At the end of each semester, the school issues credit–no credit statements for each course, rather than letter, percent, or stanine grades. Transcripts list courses, credits earned, press-on labels from national tests, anecdotal data about educational performance and promise, a general rank from teacher consensus, and a statement of correlation between national test scores and actual performance in high school. Progress reports are issued to parents quarterly. The school leaders believe that a truly nongraded school that uses a progressive learning method in a highly individualized learning process should help students move through a program of studies by demonstrating their mastery of course objectives in terms of performance criteria that relate to "content achieved" rather than "calendar endured."

At Senior High School of Urbandale, Iowa, several innovations stimulate continuous progress. The curriculum is almost entirely elective. The only mandatory courses are those required by state rulings: government, American history, and physical education. All courses are nongraded, which means that any student of any age may elect to take any course offered, so long as he can demonstrate sufficient preparation and ability to succeed in it. Individualized projects in lieu of classes and credits for world-of-work jobs provide other means for keeping students moving along the continuum of lifelong learning.

A unique program in Clark High School, Las Vegas, Nevada, is designed to assist students in moving ahead at a rate of speed, degree of difficulty, and by alternative learning activities best suited to each student. From a wide-ranging program of 212 courses organized by achievement level rather than grade level or age, a student who uses Clark's index system may predict in advance of registration his chances of success in classes that depend on prior achievement in math, reading, or English. The index is also used in constructing matching courses. The student's index predictor is a score of 1 to 10 derived from a statistical formula that considers numerous test scores. For example, Bill may have index scores for the previous semester of 6 in math, 5 in reading, and 5 in English and Jim may have 8, 10, and 9 in these respective areas. The course descriptions not only provide narrative information but also state that a given course, for example, American Literature and Composition, is within an index of 5 to 7 reading level, 5 to 7 English level, and math, not applicable. Bill could predict success for himself in this course while it would probably be too easy for Jim, who could select a similar American literature and composition course offered at an 8 to 10 index level. The index is designed to provide continuing success and challenge, not to exclude students from courses. A student is permitted to take the risk of enrolling in a more difficult course than his past semester's index score suggested or even in an easier course. However, to qualify as an honor student, he must receive an A or B grade at his index level or above, and then is eligible for independent study and other honor privileges.

Arrangements for students to accelerate in all subject areas along the continuum is provided by the John Dewey High School, Brooklyn, New York. By utilizing DISKs (Dewey Independent Study Kits) students may take self-contained courses outside of the formal classroom. Department advisors are available to help and guide students working on DISKs. Students can get course credit by passing examinations (written, oral, or laboratory) designed to determine mastery in a DISK. The John Dewey High School has one of the highest number of subjects taken per student in the city, which means that many students will graduate early or will be in a position to take additional electives.

In a number of secondary schools, junior high school students may take advanced courses at the senior high school, and senior high students may take courses at nearby colleges and universities. The Advanced Placement Program of the College Entrance Examination Board also continues to attract accelerated students in more formal ways.

Other interpretations of the continuum concept leave the continuum open for students to leave school and re-enter. In Burlington, Vermont, the Burlington High School sponsors a program known as ASPIRE, which offers an opportunity for disenchanted high school students to spend a year apart from the pressures and formal requirements of the standard school system at the tenth-grade level. ASPIRE students are involved in the community, working with skilled adults, assisting teachers in an aide program, and in a great deal of learning outside the school such as partici-

pating in camping, field trips, mountain climbing, and other student-
planned educational experiences. Students, in cooperation with a guiding
teacher, usually prepare in advance a contract or agreed-on plan of action
which defines the work and evaluation standards to be completed by the
student in meeting the objectives of a unit of study. Similar examples are
given in Chapter 4 in the discussion of alternatives.

Students with serious behavioral or out-of-school problems are also
encouraged to continue their educational progress. In Washington, D.C.
public schools, even a student who has been suspended for disciplinary
reasons must be provided with educational services while he is awaiting a
hearing, according to the federal district court decision of Mills versus
Board of Education. Detailed procedures must be followed by teachers
who plan to suspend, transfer, or expel a student, and no student may be
suspended for more than two days without a hearing. During the time
that he is suspended the school system must provide an alternative form of
education.

Not only are high schools dropping the practice of expelling pregnant
girls from school but they are offering special courses of education for
young parents. Court decisions in Maryland and Massachusetts have
declared that a public school education is a basic right of a pregnant
student. Some state departments of education, for instance that of Pennsylvania, have ruled that even part-time education programs, such as
instruction in the home, are violations of the pregnant pupil's constitutional right to attend school. Special programs have been developed by
some school districts for pregnant students. In the Niagara Falls (New
York) School District, the Center for Young Parents has been developed
by coordinated community effort to meet the comprehensive needs of the
adolescent unwed mother. Both single and married mothers between the
ages of twelve to twenty-one years who have dropped out of school are
enrolled. Many of the students keep their babies and the Center for
Young Parents expects to expand its services to include a day-care center
for these infants, a health development component for parent and child,
and a child-care training program for the young parents. Students are
motivated to continue their high school education and become financially
independent. The curriculum includes most academic subjects offered in
junior and senior high school with special courses in health, home economics, business education, and reading skills. Individual and group counseling
is intended to help the young mother understand herself so that she will
be better prepared to make good decisions regarding her life situation.

Such programs are positive reactions to the general tone and trend of
recent court decisions: That the right to an education is a fundamental
property right not to be denied unless an overriding public interest is
served.

GRADING AND EVALUATING STUDENT PROGRESS

The student's credits, grades, and marks continue to be matters of much interest and concern. Although innovative forms of grading and reporting are increasing, traditional grading practices are still firmly entrenched in most high schools. Grades, in the traditional mode, are usually assigned in some arbitrary manner to about five categories of student performance. This custom dates back to the early 1900s when "grading on the curve" became popular. In other words, 2 percent of the students should qualify for an A grade, 23 percent for a B, 50 percent for a C, 23 percent for a D, and 2 percent should fail.[12]

Bloom has suggested that the distribution of a teacher's grades on a normal curve shows that the teacher has not taken individual differences into consideration. Bloom and others advocate using diagnostic procedures and alternative methods and materials to supplement group instruction. These teaching and learning strategies not only recognize individual differences but also bring a large proportion of the students to predetermined standards of achievements.[13]

Reporting practices are changing to reflect new philosophies, but many schools have found that there is much more involved in evaluating and reporting student progress than substituting some other kind of grading system for A, B, and C. Changing from a traditional to a modern system of reporting involves serious reconsiderations of educational philosophy, school board policy, teaching methods, relations with students, and relations with parents and the community. These were among the conclusions of an extensive study by a twenty-seven-member committee of students, parents, teachers, and administrators appointed by the Superintendent of the Montgomery County, Maryland, Public Schools.[14] The committee recommended that, in order to provide meaningful and adequate evaluation reporting of student progress, it was important for every student to know what would be expected of him, learning activity by learning activity, or unit by unit, before his instruction began. This requires a definition of objectives in behavioral terms and the development of coordinated teacher guides and evaluative procedures. It was also

---

[12] Walter F. Dearborn, *School and University Grades* (Madison: University of Wisconsin Press, 1910), reported in *The Encyclopedia of Educational Research* (New York: Macmillan, 1960), p. 784.

[13] Benjamin S. Bloom, J. Thomas Hastings, and George F. Madaus, *Handbook on Formative and Summative Evaluation of Student Learning* (New York: McGraw-Hill, 1971), pp. 43–57.

[14] "Venturing toward Change: An Unfinished Story," *Grading and Reporting: Current Trends in School Policies and Programs* (Arlington, Va.: National School Public Relations Association, 1972), pp. 15–22.

considered important that every student in every classroom should know how he was doing unit by unit so that prompt attention can be given to problems. The Montgomery County Committee encouraged its secondary schools to experiment with pass–fail systems for courses in which credits are not required by state law for graduation. In addition, all secondary teachers and administrators were urged to give more emphasis to comprehensive, evaluative dialogues between individual students and teachers, to work toward improving school–community communication regarding reporting policies and practices, and to involve students in the development of new practices and procedures. It was recommended that the grading curve be rejected since the goal is to have as many students as possible be successful. When relatively large numbers of low ratings are earned, the instructional program is to be re-examined to find ways of improving the learning experience. New ways of evaluation and reporting were to be encouraged if these practices were clearly stated, understood, thought out, and if the faculties and school communities were willing to accept them.

College Admission

The difficulty of installing grading and reporting systems other than the traditional A, B, C system was underlined by a 1972 report of a study by the National Association of College Admission Counselors. Responses to a questionnaire were received from 63.6 percent of all NACAC college and university members. The 617 questionnaires returned represented 273 private independent, 222 private church, and 122 public colleges and universities. The report concluded that a majority of the colleges will require from applicants objective data, with rank-in-class still considered to be the most important item. Written evaluation by teachers ranked in second place of importance, test scores in third place, with rating sheets of students' academic ability, motivation, and interest considered acceptable.

However, other types of data were becoming more acceptable. On invitation to respondents to state their personal opinions of pass–fail or other nontraditional grading systems used by high schools as they affect their institutions' admissions decisions, only 23 percent gave a totally negative response, with another 16 percent expressing themselves as reluctant to accept nontraditional reports. The remaining majority ranged from a positive reaction to a high school pass–fail concept to willingness to accept, providing other information is available. In general, private colleges and universities were more cordial toward nontraditional reporting systems than public colleges. The most common objections given by college admissions officers to pass–fail grading systems included: lack of objectivity, lack of college manpower to evaluate nontraditional applicants individually, and lack of realistic preparation of students for future life experience. The survey, nevertheless, strongly indicated a trend toward establishing policies regarding acceptance of nontraditional transcripts.[15]

Pro and Con

Unfortunately, arguments against traditional grading systems often lack positive alternatives and frequently do not follow a sound theoretical rationale which includes a comprehensive approach to education. Many of the writings in opposition to grading are quite readable but they often represent opinions rather than comprehensive studies. Nevertheless, the reasoning against grading is impressive. One summary includes the arguments that marking practices are variable, subjective, contaminated, capricious, create a condition of unfair competition, reflect an aristocratic rather than democratic attitude, preoccupy students and their parents, deny the psychological principle of individual differences, tend to influence teaching in the direction of memorization and regurgitation at the expense of concept formation and creativity, encourage student dependence, and frequently have an emotional impact that is at variance with good mental health practices.[16]

Even though arguments against traditional grading and reporting systems are impressive, innovations will lack quality unless the purpose of evaluation as an important part of the learning process is emphasized. Evaluation must be based on stated goals and objectives and involve the teacher and student in working together by sharing information and feedback, identifying strengths and weaknesses, and planning steps toward improvement. Evaluation of student progress falls into two broad categories: the personal or private evaluation between the teacher and student, and communicating with parents so that they can be helpful. It is also necessary to make available to prospective employers or educational institutions summary data concerning the student as he leaves the high school. Kirschenbaum and others have identified eight alternatives to traditional grading that may be shared with the home and with parties outside the school. These include written narrative evaluations; self-evaluation by the student, either in writing or in a conference with the teacher; recording grades but not telling the students (inform them in general terms of their progress); contract plans which automatically produce a

[15] John Startzel, "Collegiate Attitudes toward Pass/Fail Courses," NASSP Bulletin, 56:107–117 (September 1972).

[16] Richard Kindsvatter, "Guidelines for Better Grading," Clearing House, 43:332 (February 1969).

given grade if a student does a certain type, quantity, and quality of work; the mastery approach or performance curriculum plans; pass–fail grading; credit–no credit grading; and blanket grading in which everyone in the class who does the required amount of work receives the blanket grade, usually B. Each of these has advantages and disadvantages.[17]

Pass–Fail

The concept of pass–fail appears to be spreading in secondary schools with each high school modifying and adapting it to its own conditions. Some call it credit–no credit; others report to the student that his work in the course has either been satisfactory or unsatisfactory. Around 1966 and 1967, only a scant number of high schools were experimenting with pass–fail; in 1971 more than 9 percent of all high schools responding to an NEA research survey reported that they used the system. Representative high schools having successful experiences with pass–fail or credit–no credit plans include Longmeadow (Massachusetts) High School, Horton Watkins (Ladue, Missouri) High School, Cottonwood (Salt Lake City, Utah) High School, Athens (Ohio) High School, and Niles Township (Skokie, Illinois) High Schools.

A typical procedure for offering pass–fail options is that of Athens High School. Students have the option of taking one elective course each semester on a pass–fail basis. A student wishing to enter a course on this basis must inform the instructor when he enters the class; in other words, it is usually not permissible for a student to change his mind mid-course and decide to receive traditional grades instead. Neither "pass" nor "fail" are counted toward class rank.

A research study on pass–fail was completed in the Niles Township High Schools in 1970. All students were given the option of taking one course of their choice per semester on a pass–fail basis except Advanced Placement courses. The rationale was to allow students to take courses out of their usual areas of interest, or difficult courses they might otherwise have passed up for fear of jeopardizing their grade-point averages. Poor students were found to do better when the threat of low grades was removed and high-achieving students did as well in these courses or almost as well as usual. The study led to the conclusion that motivation was not reduced in courses that were graded on a pass–fail basis. Both parents and students recommended expansion of the option for the following year.

[17] Howard Kirschenbaum, Sidney B. Simon, and Rodney W. Napier, *Wad-Ja-Get? The Grading Game in American Education* (New York: Hart Publishing Co., 1971), pp. 292–307.

The Mastery Approach

Learning for mastery is a concept used in connection with a performance-based curriculum and requires an entirely different approach toward teaching and learning. It may be practiced by one class, one department, or an entire school. In one sense it is a refined version of the traditional grading system. The mastery approach begins with operational, performance, or behavioral objectives for the students. Learnings are organized into units arranged in a logical sequence with each unit leading to the next. For each unit, designated levels of mastery or proficiency are stated. Students may master the course content in various ways by utilizing resources the teacher has provided, such as learning packages, programmed texts, films, tapes, speakers, field trips, and so on. Each student proceeds at his own pace and asks to be examined when he thinks he has completed a unit.

Such a "Learning for Mastery" concept for reporting student progress is used by the John Dewey High School of Brooklyn, New York. Dewey students do not receive traditional numerical grades but receive M (for mastery) indicating sufficient mastery to move into the next phase of work; R (for retention) indicating need to repeat the course due to a failure to achieve mastery; MI (for mastery in independent study) indicating mastery utilizing the Dewey Independent Study Kits; and MC (for mastery with condition) indicating marginal mastery with specific areas of weakness. Students receiving MC or R also receive a prescription for helping them overcome deficiencies. At John Dewey High School, the mastery approach to reporting is part of a broad program. Students elect to attend this high school but there is no special examination for admission. A broad spectrum of student ability levels is represented and the school population is typical of Brooklyn high schools. Other features of the total program are an eight-hour day, independent study, flexible modular scheduling, cyclical programming (five seven-week cycles with an optional sixth summer cycle), a broad array of course offerings, an extensive guidance program, and various innovations in teaching techniques including team teaching, interdisciplinary courses, and community involvement activities outside of the school.

Viewpoints on New Practices in Grading and Reporting

Two seemingly opposite viewpoints seem to underlie innovative practices in reporting and grading. The first concept calls for the use of performance or behavioral objectives. It may emphasize skills and academic subjects, sometimes organized in mechanistic terms. The second concept embraces self-motivation, self-education, pass–fail plans, and other programs which emphasize wide freedom for the student to pursue education for the sake of learning with low emphasis on marks and grades. This second concept is advocated by people who fear that an overemphasis on behavioral objectives, academic achievement, and grading may develop negativism toward school learning. They would stress the importance of psychological processes, human relations, positive mental health; they believe in the student's setting his own goals, selecting options (including how his progress is to be reported), learning how to work toward goals, and developing persistence in spite of occasional failure.[18]

Ideally, regardless of the type of evaluation system used, whether traditional or innovative, the following elements should be included in the evaluation process between student and teacher:

1. Learning objectives should be clearly understood in advance, with criteria for measurement and levels of performance.
2. The teacher should communicate meaningfully either in written or oral form to the student in discussing with the student his strengths, weaknesses, and suggestions for improvement with respect to the objectives of the course.
3. The student should be involved in self-evaluation of strengths and weaknesses, and should plan improvement in meeting the course objectives as well as his own learning goals.
4. Time is needed for the teacher and student to share perceptions and engage in a discussion of each other's evaluations.

OPTIONS FOR STUDENTS

The availability of options is the most wide-ranging current innovation in secondary education. This is perhaps the chief difference between today's high school and the high school of the past. Reacting in part to the student movement and also recognizing at last that individual learners have to be nurtured through opportunities for choice, schools have greatly increased their options for students. Now, innovative programs are not confined to affluent suburbs but include urban, rural, small town, and suburban students; all levels of ability and of socioeconomic backgrounds; and white, black, and other ethnic groups. Chapters 3, 4, and 6 are filled with examples: program variety in curriculum content and teaching/learning styles, alternative organizational modes, and a wide range of media and other resources to draw upon.

Today, high schools are determined to provide a variety of learning methods to reach all students' needs. Recognizing that in the past, instruction has often been geared to a hypothetical average student rather than

[18] See Alfred S. Alschuler and Allen Ivey, "The Human Side of Competency-Based Education," *Educational Technology*, 12:53–55 (November 1972).

to individual students with different backgrounds, attitudes, needs, interests, and abilities, new ways of learning are being created. These range from options for students within the school itself, to community involvement, and even to visiting or living in other countries. Innovative projects and programs are designed to reach students who have become frustrated and uninvolved in the work of the conventional high school. Options are intended to make learning more interesting, realistic, and meaningful to students. New ways of approaching the academic disciplines, more personal relationships with students, and imaginative learning activities are being invented.

Matching Learning and Teaching Styles

That there are many styles of learning and many styles of teaching and that one is not any better or more nearly "right" than the other is the premise illustrated by an innovative program of the Douglas (South Dakota) High School. Options under the title of the "XYZ Program" are designed to provide for the full range of student abilities and interests. The differences in the three programs X, Y, and Z are not in the nature of the content or in the proficiency level that can be reached, but in the way of approaching content and materials. For example, one student may learn biology through regular class lectures and standardized laboratory experiments. Another may be engaged with a small group for a full day or part of a day in learning biology by dissecting a rabbit and studying its basic body systems, then presenting the research findings to the group as a whole. Another student may be engaged in a completely independent project in which he grows different varieties of grains and notes the development and growth patterns of each. All three are engaged in a study of biology; however, the difference is in areas of interest, approach, and possibly depth.

The student in the first instance was enrolled in the X program, which is a traditional program, teacher directed and evaluated. The group that dissected the rabbit was in the Y program, which is based on a flexible schedule allowing students to pursue a topic in depth rather than on a fixed hourly schedule. In the Y program, approximately 100 students and four or five staff members work together in deciding on topics, schedule, and methods of study. A student involved in this program would include on a typical day a combination of several kinds of experiences. He may spend half an hour working on reading improvement, an hour on a science experiment, a half hour in a folk music group, an hour in a discussion of current events, then lunch, followed by a half hour viewing a film to reinforce a previously learned concept, one hour learning horseback riding skills, and one hour in a group studying math with a teacher. No two days are exactly alike.

The students in the third setting are enrolled in the Z program, which consists of independent or contract study of topics chosen by the student with the teacher-advisors assisting him with advice, conferences, and analysis of the study. Program Z is designed for the student who is able to direct his own learning in a very independent way. This program can meet the needs of students who wish to go beyond the usual offerings and explore areas that Douglas High School is unable to offer in the regular curriculum. Those who wish to pursue a talent or topic in great depth, and those vocational education and work-study students who need blocks of time are provided for in this Z program.

Another example of ingenuity in creating many types of options within one school is the varied program of the William H. Hall High School, West Hartford, Connecticut. Here students may choose numerous nonclass-time options utilizing the cafeteria space, media and dial-select center, town libraries, study areas, supervised resource centers, and guidance facilities. In addition, teacher and counselor conferences are available as are review sessions, study projects, and auditing of courses on request. Students may also assist as aides for teachers and counselors.

The school provides a directory of minicourses, short-term informal courses open to all students on nonclass time and occasionally to parents. Each minicourse meets once a week for a definite period and no credits or grades are given. Options include: Introduction to Broadcasting, Electronic Music, Organic and Natural Foods, English Grammar, Standardized Test Review, Basic Photography, Astrology and the Psychic World, Bridge Instruction, Consciousness Raising for Young Women, Introduction to Nursing, Motor Vehicle Emergency Situation Seminar, and others. Except for nonclass time, students are expected to be in their regular classes, where attendance is taken and recorded each quarter on report cards. Most students use nonclass time in educationally sound ways, with freedom of choice based on each person's interests and aptitudes. With parental permission, students have the privilege of late arrival (coming to school in time for their first class), early dismissal (leaving school after their last class), and may leave the campus during periods they are not scheduled for classes. However, the administration reserves the right to revoke these privileges if abused. Failure to return a signed permission slip from parents means that permission has not been granted to leave the school grounds.

Some unique examples of exemplary and innovative programs are designed to meet difficult problems. In Chicago, the East Woodlawn Academy Program serves 150 male students between the ages of twelve and sixteen whose problems are chronic absenteeism, severe lack of discipline, and overage nonpromotions. The program is nongraded and semi-individualized and uses programmed methodology, creative arts, instrumental and vocal music, work-study programs, and emphasizes the development of skills. Students are given personal assistance to help them overcome negative actions and teachers are re-educated on the causes and effects of student problems. In another project in Chicago, an urban Indian village center provides a program intended to meet the educational needs of 100 American Indian youths to help overcome their feelings of prejudice, frustration, and anger by contributing to the dissemination of American Indian culture and skills.

Students as Aides, Tutors, and Teachers

From the principle that teaching is also a way of learning have sprung countless innovative programs across the country in which high-school students, and other students as well, tutor younger children or their own peers, teach groups of children, or serve as aides to other teachers than their own. The high schools of the Los Angeles City Schools have launched a tutorial project to test the hypotheses that the process of teaching is an effective method of learning, that one's sense of power and worth is enhanced by success in a teaching role, and that this success will motivate behavior suitable for maintenance of a more positive self-image and improve performance in school.

Westchester High School has more than seventy-five student tutors instructing at eight area elementary schools in Los Angeles. San Pedro High School sent fifty high-school students to tutor in twelve elementary schools. Ninth graders at Griffith Junior High School may apply for an elective called Cross-age Teaching in which each ninth-grade student is responsible for one seventh-grade student for an entire semester, with lessons conducted outside of the younger student's regular classroom in available areas throughout the school. To become a tutor, a high school student spends two weeks learning various teaching techniques. During these two weeks he learns from experienced tutors some of the problems he will encounter and how to cope with them. Classroom responsibilities are emphasized. After this brief orientation he is ready to begin tutoring. Students aid others in all subject areas (art, arithmetic, etc.) and assist handicapped children and Spanish-speaking children, among others.

In Great Neck, New York, South Senior High School, eleventh- and twelfth-grade students receive credit for working as teacher aides in the elementary schools. Students are expected to spend three afternoons a week in an elementary school and are assigned to areas of their personal interest when the elementary program permits; but final placement rests with the elementary school administrator. Student aide activities include small group instruction, one-to-one tutoring, arts and crafts instruction, teaching of games, dance instruction, and working with children having special learning difficulties. An appraisal report of the program noted that the students performed outstanding service and exhibited considerable responsibility and commitment.

In Pasadena, California, high school students receive two and a half units of credit each semester for teaching two hours per week at a nearby elementary school. The students do not serve as classroom aides or tutors, but actually construct a course of study and teach a particular skill to a selected group of elementary students. Some of these minicourses, such as sewing and art, are taught on the high school campus, thus allowing elementary students to avail themselves of the specialized equipment of the secondary school.

Students are involved similarly at several levels in the Cherry Creek, Colorado, High School. There students may begin as participants in the Students Assisting Teachers (SAT) Program in which they spend a minimum of four hours a week in an elementary or junior high classroom aiding teachers with clerical and supervisory tasks; but they are not responsible for any instruction. A student may move from this level to the Mutually Aided Learning Project (MAL) in which he becomes a Learning Assistant. The program has these objectives: to give the high school student some actual teaching experience so he can make a career decision; to help a student be of service to others; to give the elementary students more individual help in the content areas; to place them in contact with committed adolescents; and to assist the elementary classroom teacher. Learning by teaching, learning by doing, and learning by sharing, are specific objectives of the program. Its distinguishing features are its comprehensive planning and involvement of elementary and high school teachers and students in new kinds of partnerships which include workshops and summer curriculum development periods. (Also see "Cross-age Tutoring," Chapter 5.)

Involvement in the Community

Imaginative ideas for off-campus learnings are being generated in high schools and localities of all types. Students of the Snohomish High School, near Seattle, Washington, run a drive-in restaurant for other students as part of the district's vocational education program. At the drive-in, students prepare and serve the standard fare of hamburgers, cheeseburgers, French fries, malts, and soft drinks at prices comparable to other "burger havens" in the area. The drive-in restaurant attracts about 200 to 250 students daily during two 30-minute lunch periods. It operates only during limited hours and is one of several choices other students have at their lunch periods.

At Portland High School, Michigan, high school students have reopened the school cafeteria, which had been closed because of financial troubles, and it has become self-supporting with all bills paid from the income, including hourly pay for one teacher's aide who oversees the operation. Students earn class credit and nominal pay. All of the workers take turns at the jobs, rotating among cooking, dishwashing, and other tasks.

In Evanston Township High School, Illinois, volunteer students enrolled in a new course called the Community Service Seminar, give public service. Many work with mentally and/or emotionally disturbed children as well as with normal children. Others work in day-care centers, hospitals, and the police department.

Juniors and seniors of Lincoln High School, Portland, Oregon, are participating in a unique social studies intern program which takes them into actual professional career situations in governmental and private agencies. Students have been assigned to one or more agencies, including a public interest research group, county offices, a community college, the American Civil Liberties Union, a university, a metropolitan youth commission, hospitals, the city planning commission, and an architectural firm. Specific activities have covered environment, police science, theater arts, freeway and airport studies, law enforcement, domestic relations, urban studies, corrections, parole, education, and medical research. The purpose of the course is to allow students to learn about career possibilities in the social sciences and develop greater insights into urban institutions.

In Los Angeles, high school students have been invited to attend classes sponsored by various industries on their sites to introduce students to industrial careers. Opportunities have been made available in the areas of computer programming, stenography, engineering, photography, and aircraft related industries among others.

Other innovative plans to help students gain more information about the adult world are being practiced. Rochester High School of Rochester, Vermont, sets aside a week in May of each year for students to engage in a community-oriented program. Choices include studies of farming and related occupations, housing construction, forestry studies, Indian reservations, governmental agencies, and others.

An environmental control program of Katahdin (Maine) High School is part of a broader plan for community involvement. Students enrolled in an environmental control course are released from two to four hours each day for learning activities at various sites in nearby forests and state parks. The course involves about 110 hours of instruction and grants one high school credit. A sequential curriculum includes an introduction to the need for environmental improvement, studies of woods fire control, woods safety, entomology, woodlot management, and the work of game biologists, park rangers, state wardens, and the forest service. Trips are made to fish stream projects and wilderness waterways. The course culminates in a five-day wilderness trip.

Traveling Students

Although student exchange programs are not new, Cherry Creek (Colorado) High School's program is probably unique in two aspects: the extent to which students are involved in operating the program, and its comprehensiveness. An active student committee of about thirty members identifies schools for exchange, publicizes the program, and works out many of the details. The exchange program is broad in scope, involving about 200 students each year in some kind of exchange program, lasting from one day to a week or more. Exchanges are arranged with several kinds of schools: within Colorado, out-of-state, and in other countries. A definite attempt is made to arrange mutual exchanges with schools much different from Cherry Creek so that students will have opportunities to broaden their backgrounds.

Students of Craig High School, located on the west coast of Prince of Wales Island, Alaska (having a total enrollment of 110 in the entire school district), engage in several new techniques and approaches to education which involve students both in the community and far afield. A three-week exchange program sent students from the small Indian community to visit a variety of communities in the mainland forty-eight states; in exchange, stateside students spent three weeks at Craig High School.

Elsewhere, exchange programs continue to expand. The American Field Service, Youth for Understanding, and the Experiment in International Living select students from all backgrounds for varying lengths of time ranging from ten days to a year in which they are placed with foreign families carefully selected from equally varied backgrounds. Host families in America and other countries make the exchange programs possible.

A new traveling school in New York, the Trailside Country School, takes about twenty teen-aged students, boys and girls, on a high-school accredited, one-year camping and study trip throughout the United States. The student travels by school bus and studies geography by hiking down into the Grand Canyon, biology by digging for fossils in Utah, sociology by living with Indians on a reservation, and American history by touring colonial New England. Each new class, outfitted with sleeping bags, pack frames, and hiking boots, is accompanied by two or three staff members, young men and women with experience in both teaching and camping.

Travel-study programs abroad continue to combine serious summer study with the experience of living and traveling abroad. With scores of new organizations and agencies operating in various parts of the world, study tours seem to be growing by leaps and bounds. Usually students are housed at a university or a secondary school and may study a foreign language and/or literature, comparative government and culture, art history, Spanish or Roman civilization, Bible history, Oriental civilization, and others. High school teachers accompany the students and assist native teachers in conducting the programs. The study tours, once reserved for relatively few college students or socioeconomic classes have become available to many high school students for a modest fee.

Thus, private schools and agencies continue to perform their historical function of providing various alternatives to the public school system. It is only recently that options have been provided extensively within the public schools.

additional suggestions for further study

1. Baughman, Dale, *What Do Students Really Want?* Bloomington, Ind.: Phi Delta Kappa Foundation, 1972. The author has written his considered judgments of what youth wants from home, school, community, peers, employment, and society at large.
2. Coyne, John, and Tom Hebert, *This Way Out.* New York: Dutton, 1972. Alternatives are suggested for students who want more education but less tradition. Possibilities for independent study, pointers for parents, and other topics are included.
3. Gattegno, Caleb, *The Adolescent and His Will.* New York: Educational Solutions, 1971. Beamed toward educators and parents, the book deals with the need to make the adolescent aware of his original creativity, and proposes this as an approach to educational reform.
4. James, Charity, *Young Lives at Stake: The Education of Adolescents.* New York: Agathon Press, 1972. The author emphasizes the importance of human relationships in the school and the essentialness to learning of the small group in which teacher and students work together. Concerns about the isolation of individualization in American schools are expressed by this British author, with suggestions for designing diversity without divisiveness.
5. Nelson, Jack L., Kenneth Carlson, and Thomas E. Linton (Eds.), *Radical Ideas and the Schools.* New York: Holt, Rinehart and Winston, 1972. Essays by Marcuse, Theobald, Carmichael, Roszak, Huxley, Zinn, and others examine relationships between school and society, and among science, technology, and human values. Strategies for humanizing the schools are suggested.
6. Pearl, Arthur, *The Atrocity of Education.* St. Louis: New Critics Press, 1972. The author discusses the lack of relationship between education today and the real world with illustrations of why students are alienated by the system. Going beyond a description of the problem, however, he presents imaginative, workable proposals that offer equal freedom to all students in choice of careers, equip students for democratic decision making, permit ethnic diversity, and promote responsible individuality.
7. Popham, W. James, *Criterion-Referenced Measurement.* Englewood Cliffs, N.J.: Educational Technology Publications, 1973. An explanation is provided of new forms of student assessment geared to individualized instruction rather than group norms.

8. Segal, Rebecca. *Got No Time to Fool Around: A Motivation Program for Education*. Philadelphia: Westminster, 1972. Specific help for teachers and school administrators trying to provide quality education for poorly motivated students, and encouragement for parents whose own children need motivation to learn. A step-by-step story of the Motivation Program in Philadelphia high schools, problems and pitfalls, remarkable successes, and techniques for instilling confidence and a desire to achieve.

3

The Curriculum: Student-Centered Innovation and Renewal

Although the high school curriculum continues to be characterized by courses and classes, the 1970s seem to be a transitional period from the 1960s' updating of the academics to a more comprehensive curriculum reformation. The new trend is toward matching individual student needs with appropriate learning opportunities. How long this revolution may take, or even whether it will be completed, we cannot predict, but it is occurring.

In this chapter we therefore give particular attention to these student-centered emphases as they can be identified in the common academic areas of English, mathematics, science, and social studies; in the other established areas of the curriculum; and in various less easily classified efforts to match new curriculum objectives with new and emergent programs.

INNOVATION IN THE COMMON ACADEMIC AREAS

Increased options for students that characterize student-centered curriculum innovations (see Chapter 2) still have not reduced enroll-

table II

Course Enrollments in Subject Areas, and Percentage These Enrollments Are of Total Pupils Enrolled in Grades 7 to 12 of Public Secondary Schools: United States, 1948–49, 1960–61, and 1970–71

SUBJECT AREA	1970–71 pretest		1960–61*		1948–49*	
	Number	Percent	Number	Percent	Number	Percent
total pupils, grades 7–12	18,406,617	100.0	11,732,742	100.0	6,907,833	100.0
English language arts	25,852,165	140.5	12,972,236	110.6	7,098,770	102.8
Health and physical education[1]	22,193,800	120.6	12,081,639	103.0	7,794,671	112.8
Social sciences	19,659,790	106.8	11,802,499	100.1	6,981,980	101.1
Mathematics	14,137,090	76.8	8,596,396	73.3	4,457,987	64.5
Natural sciences	12,772,195	69.4	7,739,877	66.0	4,031,044	58.4
Music	6,559,452	35.6	4,954,347	42.2	2,484,201	36.0
Business education[2]	7,314,194	39.7	4,667,570	39.8	3,186,207	46.1
Industrial arts	5,397,074	29.3	3,361,699	28.7	1,762,242	25.5
Home economics[2]	5,282,850	28.7	2,915,997	24.9	1,693,825	24.5
Foreign languages	4,729,282	25.7	2,576,354	22.0	1,234,544	17.9
Art	4,350,685	23.6	2,383,703	20.3	1,219,693	17.7
Agriculture[2]	789,102	4.3	507,992	4.3	373,395	5.4
Vocational trade and industrial education[2]	1,141,638	6.2	344,704	2.9	369,794	5.4
Distributive education[2]	295,633	1.6	38,363	.3	(3)	(3)
Other[2]	232,736	1.3	106,467	.9	111,053	1.6

[1] Includes driver education and ROTC.
[2] Includes in 1970–71 occupational programs as well as individual courses. These programs may represent enrollment in 2 or more courses.
[3] Not reported separately in 1948–49.

* Source: U.S. Department of Health, Education, and Welfare, Office of Education, Subject Offerings and Enrollments in Public Secondary Schools, 1965.

Note—Percentages exceed 100.0 because a pupil may be enrolled in more than one course within a subject area during the school year.

From Dianne B. Gertler and Linda A. Barker, Patterns of Course Offerings and Enrollments in Public Secondary Schools, 1970–71. Washington, D.C.: U.S. Government Printing Office, 1972, p. 10. DHEW Publication No. (OE)73–11400.

ments in the common academic areas. Graduation requirements and tradition still keep these areas in priority position. The accompanying table, taken from the United States Office of Education report of a preliminary survey of course enrollments in public secondary schools in 1970–1971, shows that English, mathematics, science, and social sciences more than held their ground from 1948–1949 and 1960–1961 to 1970–1971. Indeed, in percentage of the total school enrollments, these subjects counted for greater enrollments in 1970–1971 than in either of the preceding surveys. Although this fact is partially explained by the overrepresentation of junior high schools in the sample of secondary schools included in the pretest (a report of the full-scale survey made in 1972–1973 is not available as our book goes to press) it is also true that the trend toward multiple, short-term courses has also been pronounced in these areas. Hence many students are enrolled at any time in more than one course in these areas, especially English and social studies (and also physical education, with all three areas consequently showing enrollment percentages above 100 percent of the total enrollment). The multiple enrollment was explained in the survey report as follows:

> Another finding of the pretest is that a multiplicity of *short courses* have been introduced into the curriculum. The average number of courses per pupil rose from 6.4 in 1960–61 to 7.1 in 1970–71. The *higher number of courses* taken by the average pupil during a school year has undoubtedly been made possible by a lengthened school day and by flexible class scheduling plans in a number of schools.[1]

In addition to their continued and increasing high enrollments and their development of many short courses, the common academic areas are becoming generally more responsive to student needs for relevant content and appropriate learning aids. The emphases that came with the national curriculum project movement beginning in the late 1950s, on structure rather than isolated facts and principles, on modes of inquiry and inductive learning, and on the use of a wide variety of materials and media, greatly influenced curriculum content and instructional strategies in these (and other) areas. Schools were at first slow to adopt the new curriculum programs after the Sputnik-stimulated curriculum development movement began to produce them. But by the 1970s the new programs, especially in the academic areas and beginning with science and mathematics, had probably reached more American high schools more rapidly than had usually happened with innovations in education.

[1] Dianne B. Gertler and Linda A. Barker, *Patterns of Course Offerings and Enrollments in Public Secondary Schools, 1970–71.* DHEW Publication No. (OE) 73–11400 (Washington, D.C.: U.S. Government Printing Office, 1972), p. 8.

Schools throughout the country are tending to move away from such limited objectives as covering a body of factual information toward helping students acquire the skills of continued learning. However, the introduction of innovations in curriculum content raised problems in the beginning. The curriculum projects erred in their preoccupation with a single-principle basis for curriculum development, the structure theory.[2] Many of the new projects were initially aimed at the academically interested and able student and missed a large segment of the student population. New materials were misused in many instances because teachers lacked orientation or interest in them. Processes for adapting projects to local needs and collecting feedback were ignored. The emphasis on separate subjects tended toward fragmentation and little serious attention to design of the curriculum as a whole. These problems are resulting in other innovations, including massive efforts to produce learning systems and materials adapted to all high school students. More conscious attention is being given to curriculum and instruction objectives, and students are more frequently involved in developing their own objectives and in providing feedback about learning experiences.

Some of the significant efforts to relate the common academic areas to student needs and interests are identified and briefly illustrated in the following sections on these areas.

English

Although the English program had long been studied by committees of the National Council of Teachers of English and other groups, the development of a "New English" in the 1960s was slower and less dramatic than the changes in science and mathematics. Indeed one leader in English education wrote in 1968 that "What is really new in English is the increased support being given to in-service education of teachers of English and the extraordinary attention that English is receiving in curriculum centers and school systems throughout the country."[3] He did note the impact of the new linguistics emphasis in grammar, but observed that "grammar (as distinguished from reading, speaking, writing, and listening) constitutes a relatively small part of the school subject called English."[4] A major move toward change in English was called for at the Dartmouth Seminar of 1966, attended by teachers of English from the

[2] See Glenys G. Unruh, "Beyond Sputnik," *Educational Leadership,* 30:587–590 (April 1973) for an evaluation of the curriculum project movement. This issue of *Educational Leadership* features several articles on the theme "Whatever Happened to Curriculum Content Revision?"

[3] John J. DeBoer, "The New English," *The Educational Forum,* 32:394 (May 1968).

[4] DeBoer, p. 394.

United States, England, and Canada.[5] Noting that the thrust of the Dartmouth agreements "puts the learner in a central position," Shuman observed that "education is becoming less subject-centered and more student-centered," with this trend "especially true in English."[6] He further reported that the Dartmouth Seminar and its publications had caused many English teachers to re-examine their practices and predicted that "as more teachers are able to participate in international meetings and to see schools abroad and in various parts of their own country in operation, self-examination and healthy self-criticism will increase."[7]

Reports from high schools indicate that innovations are reflecting these emphases upon student interest and involvement, toward less regimentation and more internally motivated reading and composition. Heterogeneous groupings in high school English classes are bringing together students of a wide range of abilities and experiences in which group processes and sharing of backgrounds and ideas are stimulating vitality and creativity. The poor reader, formerly sent to remedial classes, is becoming a first-class citizen who learns through a variety of media other than the printed page only. He receives supplemental individualized instruction for short intensive periods as needed and as an adjunct to the regular English program. Innovative courses of the John F. Kennedy High School, Fremont, California, include "Literature and Films: Mass Communication" and "Individual Reading and Communications." In the former, the impact and uses of mass media are emphasized; the latter is designed to reach the student whose interests in school are minimal and who has not learned to like reading. Students in the course are given the opportunity to choose their own reading material and have freedom in selecting writing topics.

The most widespread trend in innovative English programs is the increase of electives and the corresponding increase in short courses. The semester elective program at Tempe, Arizona, High School is a two-year program for juniors and seniors that is ungraded, differentiating only between regular or extra-challenge courses such as literary criticism. Some twenty-four semester electives are offered from which students may choose freely; these electives were selected from among fifty-three possible course offerings, and planned in detail during a two-year planning period before the program was implemented. The Pocatello, Idaho, High School has reorganized its English program from the traditional survey courses

[5] Albert H. Marckwardt, "The Dartmouth Seminar," *The Bulletin of the National Association of Secondary School Principals*, 51:104–105 (April 1967).

[6] R. Baird Shuman, "The Teaching of English in the Decade Ahead: The 1970's," Ch. 1 in *What Will Be Taught—The Next Decade?* Mark M. Krug (Ed.) (Itasca, Ill.: Peacock, 1972), p. 27.

[7] Shuman, p. 27.

to a broad range of shorter, more concentrated units of study from which students may make their own selections. The five areas of the program are: I. Literature, II.Writing, III. Speech, IV. Drama, and V. Visual. The student must take to meet the two-year (four semesters) credit requirement: two nine-week or one-semester course from Area I; one nine-week course from Area II; one nine-week course from Area III; and he may choose the other four nine-week courses from any of the areas so long as not more than two of the four are from Areas III, IV, and V. During 1972–1973 the offering included ten semester courses, and fifty-five nine-week courses. Indicating the appeal to student interests are the titles of a sample of nine-week courses:

"Gulliver's Travels Is Not a Story for Children"
"Some Titillating American Classics"
"Cultures—Old, Foreign, Mixed, and New"
"The Ghastly Gothic"
"Who Done It? Where? When? Why?"
"Red, Yellow, Black, and White"
"Did You Hear the One?"
"Getting To Know You"
"Be a Better Reader"
"Folk-Rock Poetry"
"Agonizing Research Writing"
"With Pen in Hand"
"Stop! Look! Write! and Spell!"
"Group Discussion and Conference Leadership"
"Read and Lead"
"Media Investigation"
"Television—A Variety"

Most high schools require some core of English courses and offer electives to complete or exceed the total requirements. Anniston (Alabama) High School, for example, requires three twelve-week courses ("Oral and Written Communication," "Survey of American Literature," and "Survey of English Literature") and students must take one of these and elect two additional twelve-week courses each year. The electives include: "The Play's the Thing," "Contemporary Media," "Man in Conflict," "Composition," "Pleasures of Reading," "Myths and Legends," "Creative Writing," "Ethnic Literature," "Group Dynamics," "Twentieth-Century Authors," and "Vocational English." Another approach is described in this statement from the Shawnee Mission, Kansas, Northwest High School:

Each sophomore student is required to take a one-term sophomore English course. Each fulltime English teacher has one or more sections of sophomores. The course's main purpose is to make sure that each student knows and is known by at least one teacher. During this time the student and his teacher begin to define the student's objectives and needs, and to plan a language arts program for him. The teacher will continue to serve as language arts advisor for his sophomore students unless, of course, the student later gets to know a teacher with whom he is more comfortable.

After this orientation course, we attempt to provide as many ways as possible for a student to meet the state language arts requirements. Only through coincidence, or by their choice, will any two students follow the same program. We offer a variety of courses from very traditional literature courses to very untraditional mass media courses. Other courses, such as writer's workshop, TV production, or actor's studio, attempt to meet individual needs and interests. There are courses which take place mainly outside the school; for example, one based on attending live drama and one involving tutoring in a lower school. Students who don't want or need a classroom atmosphere or who have unusual interests may choose either independent or directed study. There are interdisciplinary courses developed with teachers in other departments. There is now a course for students who need work in specific communications skills such as spelling or sentence construction.

Some types of phasing or other grouping by interest, ability, or achievement are frequently used, although the less rigorous applications suggested by the Dartmouth Seminar are widespread. For example, this phasing policy of the Cottonwood High School, Salt Lake City, Utah, introduces a description of forty-six "selective" nine-week courses:

> Courses are designated by phases (1, 2, 3, 4) to aid you in determining the difficulty of each one. Phase 1 courses are designed for students who feel the need for further work in the skills areas. Along with relatively easy reading materials and assignments, these courses will offer you opportunity to improve your reading, writing, and speaking. Phase 2 courses encompass literature within the scope of most students. Emphasis will be on enjoyment of these works for their own value. These courses are designed for students who are ambivalent about pursuing a college career. Phase 3 courses will emphasize critical reading and evaluation of the material presented in class and will give you preparatory background for college courses. Phase 4 courses are designed for students particularly interested and strong in English and who plan to attend college.
>
> You are not limited to any phase; you may register for any course which interests you (only three require teacher approval). The purpose of phasing is to help you choose the level at which you learn best.

More electives and shorter courses do not guarantee students that their English instruction will always be relevant, functional, and interesting, but they do involve a competition of courses and teachers that is responsive to student demand. The fact that students will choose teachers who answer their needs, added to that of the competition for English-teaching jobs in a period of over-supply, supported by the increased preparation and in-service education of teachers of English may point to a new trend. The evidence may mean that such predictions about future developments in English instruction as the following are indeed coming true:

> If the fruits of the Dartmouth Seminar and the Vancouver Conference are harvested, if the warnings of Kohl, Dennison, Silberman, and a host of other keen observers are heeded, English teachers will move away from the formal classroom and schools will move away from the formal regimentation which now so often characterizes them. In doing this, the chief emphasis will be on the student and on learning theory rather than on rules and structure.[8]

> Through such developments as the Dartmouth Conference and the visits to British schools, we may hope to find a corrective to the current trend toward formalism in American high school classes in English. They may not bring us a "new" English, but they can restore some of the flexibility, irreverence, and wonder that characterized earlier periods in our educational history, and—who knows—may relax some of the tensions we are creating in so many of our high school students.[9]

Mathematics

Mathematics reform had a pre-Sputnik origin and initiated the first national curriculum project, precursor of hundreds since, that of the University of Illinois Committee on School Mathematics in 1951. Prior to that event, the creation of the first high-speed electronic computer in 1946 had alerted educators to the need for enabling students to learn mathematical skills that would constantly change and grow with changing demands. After 1957, federal funds were poured into the improvement of mathematics content and teaching methods, producing the "new mathematics."

Common characteristics emerged in mathematics programs sponsored by various curriculum centers.[10] Emphasis shifted from "how" to "why,"

---

[8] Shuman, p. 34.

[9] DeBoer, p. 402.

[10] For information on the early curriculum programs and projects in mathematics, see Robert B. Davis, *The Changing Curriculum: Mathematics* (Washington, D.C.: Association for Supervision and Curriculum Development, 1967), and Warren C. Syfert (Ed.), *The Continuing Revolution in Mathematics* (Washington, D.C.: National Council of Teachers of Mathematics, 1968). See also for a more recent evaluation of the new math Vincent J. Glennon, "Current Status of the New Math," *Educational Leadership,* 30:604–608 (April 1973).

on how to learn and use mathematics rather than to memorizing it. Practice, or drill, was not excluded but made more meaningful. Components of the new programs included both new subject matter and new ways of teaching students. Sets, functions, and patterns became unifying trends in mathematics, and old sequences were greatly modified so that by high school the mathematics program could concentrate on mathematical structure.

Calculus, once considered the final goal of secondary school mathematics, was augmented by computer science and probability and statistics. Many school systems offer mathematics courses involving the computer (see Chapter 6). Through hookups to large computer centers by means of time-shared terminals and telephone connections, even by traveling computer math vans, students are using the computer to solve problems and to learn computer science. For example, the Garfield High School in Los Angeles has two programs in computer science, one an off-campus, job-oriented program, and the other an on-campus program of two classes, beginning and advanced. The beginning on-campus class works on solving elementary problems in mathematics which are designed for the study of logic and other techniques required for more advanced programming, and the advanced class, composed primarily of gifted students, deals with number theory, matrix algebra, probability, statistics, and elementary linear programming. The off-campus program, supported by the IBM Corporation, includes a two-hour daily class at the IBM Basic Systems Center. This program, called the "equalizer," requires only one semester of elementary algebra. Each student is assigned a particular system and permitted to operate the system on his own so far as possible. The school also has a terminal used in the advanced placement calculus class.

The computer is also used to build motivations for learning mathematics. For example a report from Skyline High School, Idaho Falls, Idaho, states:

> We did not attempt to push the use of the computer to learn computer science but rather to motivate students in math. Just the fact that the little black box in the corner was a computer stimulated curiosities. Then as they began to play with it, interest began building until they started to write simple programs to execute. Some simple computational programs became a snap and the question was "What can I do next?" Many students found that their math background was meager and could see a real need for learning more math. This caused many to go on to Independent Study to learn more mathematics or to do some research on a particular concept.

But not all of the new mathematics instruction worked as successfully as had been hoped for in the national projects. In his 1972 assessment Bell noted the accomplishments of the reform movement, capsuled somewhat in his statement that "the reform decade produced considerable agreement on *what* should be taught, if not on how or when," but noted the subsequent disillusionment because the programs had less effect than hoped for: "Larger numbers of students were taking more and more mathematics (hence the initial reform aims were being met) but for most people the school mathematics experience was still very poor."[11] The reform movement was a subject matter revision, albeit an overdue and very significant one. But the new textbooks, with teachers still more conversant with the old mathematics, did not always work despite massive efforts at in-service education, and there is continuing innovation in mathematics.

Some national curriculum projects continued after their first plans were completed, to revise materials and develop new programs to meet the deficiencies of the early ones. The School Mathematics Study Group completed its set of texts in 1966 for the entire range, kindergarten through the high school, and immediately initiated the development of a new flexible, sequential program for grades 7 through 12. The primary emphasis was on a new junior high school curriculum, *Secondary School Mathematics,* for completion by capable students within three years. The distinguishing characteristics of this program, of which publication was completed in 1971, were stated by SMSG as follows:

(1) this curriculum is devoted solely to these mathematical concepts which the SMSG planning and writing groups believe all citizens should know in order to function effectively in our society;
(2) the usual grade placement of mathematical topics is ignored; instead, topics from arithmetic, algebra, and geometry are introduced in a logical sequence and in such a way as to provide mutual support;
(3) certain topics new to the junior high school curriculum are included; in particular, functions, coordinate geometry, rigid motions, computer mathematics, probability, and statistics;
(4) a strong attempt is made to make clear to the students the relevance of mathematics to problems of the real world.[12]

The follow-up course, *Secondary School Advanced Mathematics,* is designed for students who elect additional mathematics after completing the junior high sequence and is intended to prepare them for a variety of courses: analytic geometry; elementary functions and calculus; algorithms, computation, and mathematics; matrix algebra; and probability and statistical inference.

[11] Max S. Bell, "Mathematics Education for the Next Decade—New Emphases for the Next Decade," in *What Will Be Taught—The Next Decade,* p. 147.

[12] School Mathematics Study Group, *Final Report on a New Curriculum Project,* Newsletter No. 36, (Stanford University, Calif.: SMSG, February 1972), p. 3.

Another program designed for motivated students is the Comprehensive School Mathematics Program being developed by the Central Midwestern Regional Educational Laboratory, Inc. A series of thirteen books was being used in 1973 with about 1000 students in several states, for the Elements of Mathematics program in secondary schools. The program goals include understanding of the basic ideas and techniques of modern mathematics, the use of the axiomatic method, the role of abstraction in mathematical theory, and the processes involved in model building. There is also an elementary program, with both the elementary and secondary based on the thesis stated in a 1973 announcement that "the mathematical potential of children has hardly been tapped."

Many developments relate to the problems of the nonmathematically interested or inclined, variously called "slow," "underachieving," "remedial," and so forth. A 1970 review of the problems of program development and instruction for these students, estimated by some to have been as high as 80 to 90 percent of the entering students in some high schools, described the problem in these terms:

> While program developers had virtually neglected low achievers prior to the early 1960's, teachers have been vividly, if not painfully, aware of their presence. Since the new mathematics was apparently out of step with the cadence of these students, it became apparent to many teachers that a different drummer, or at least a different rhythm, would have to be found for them.[13]

Among the various efforts to provide better and more successful learning experiences for these students are more relevant content and everyday problems, more concrete teaching materials, more teachers interested and competent in teaching slower learning students, individualized instruction. The latter seems to be the most widely used since it attempts to provide for *each* learner, not just the fast or the slow. Various innovations for individualized instruction usually include some type of tutorial assistance with a set of materials that can be worked through individually. For example, a program for over 300 students, most of them underachievers two or three grades below grade level, in Jordan High, Los Angeles, aims at mastery learning through (1) defining a set of terminal performance objectives, (2) setting a standard of mastery at the 80 percent level, (3) using diagnostic tests for each unit of instruction, (4) providing additional instruction for students who do not achieve mastery on the first instruction, and (5) allowing students to progress at their

[13] John W. Ogle, "Unfinished Revolution: Mathematics for Low Achievers," *The High School Journal*, 53:298–299 (February 1970).

own rates. This program provides two teacher assistants and one student assistant to assist the regular teacher, and utilizes tape cassettes, film strips, slides, programmed instruction, and other printed material. Similar patterns of specific programming and individualized instruction are widely employed. Predicting further increased use of this pattern of individualization, Bell voiced a marked limitation. He noted that it is based on published materials "rather than on the laboratory experiences and activity that would be far more fruitful," seeing danger "that in the name of 'individualization,' small group and classroom group work may virtually disappear, with possibly serious consequences, including further isolation of children and dehumanizing of the educational process."[14]

Special materials for low achievers are also resulting from national and other curriculum projects.[15] Thus the School Mathematics Study Group has produced a *Special Edition of Secondary School Mathematics* for seventh- and eighth-grade low achievers, presenting the same general content as the first two years in the regular program described above, but rewritten to appeal to students with low mathematics achievement. The quantity of reading and the reading level are reduced, and addition and multiplication tables and flow charts for computational algorithms are provided.

Science

Science, like mathematics, was a subject field of great ferment in the late 1950s and 1960s, and remains one of continuing study and revision. National concern for improvement of science education following Sputnik (1957) became somewhat hysterical, but actually had a rational beginning. Years before Sputnik, the science crisis in the United States had been identified, and reports to the President of the United States had urged federal support of scientific research and development, and stressed the need for training more scientists and strengthening science education in schools and colleges.[16] The National Defense Education Act of 1958, appropriations for the National Science Foundation, and other legislation made available millions of dollars in federal funds to improve science teaching in schools, and many national curriculum projects were launched with a mass of new programs and materials made available during the

---

[14] Bell, p. 171.

[15] See Ogle, pp. 306–307 for lists of these materials and further references.

[16] See Vannevar Bush, *Science: The Endless Frontier* (Washington, D.C.: U.S. Government Printing Office, 1945), and John R. Steelman, *Manpower for Research*, Vol. IV of *Science and Public Policy* (Washington, D.C.: U.S. Government Printing Office, 1967).

1960s.[17] In the new science programs, the processes of science were emphasized, with process and knowledge considered inseparable. Conceptual schemes in science are the unifying themes, and many concepts and principles are introduced that were not included in traditional programs. Much descriptive and irrelevant material has been eliminated. The new programs are laboratory-centered, with opportunity for students to approach frontiers of science, to investigate unknowns. Serious attempts are made to develop skills of inquiry and investigation.

But in the beginning the new programs also had weaknesses. In the first place, they were individual, usually one-year, courses in biology, chemistry, and physics, without a consistent sequential development. Also, many of the early programs were designed for college-bound students, and average or below-average students were neglected until more recently. Further, significant and relevant problems that were related to the student's own environment and interests might be crowded out by the conceptual approach. Summing up the situation as the 1960s ended, one reviewer made these comments:

> In education the pendulum that marks periods of change has swung from side to side; we have been through a decade when scholars in science have dominated curriculum reform and school programs have benefited. Now the pendulum may be in transit to a pole where focus on students and their learning capacities will be central in science curriculum design. There is an acute need for training new curriculum workers who have sufficient competence in science to maintain the gains achieved through the contributions of scientists and who can add a new dimension of instruction technology and learning theory to improved curriculum designs. Those of us who have cast our lot to the field of science education must accept this as the major challenge in the improvement of school science teaching.[18]

The increased focus on students and their learning capacities as Novak forecast is occurring through the many approaches to individualization in the science program. Inquiry is emphasized, but with many alternative opportunities for its practice. Illustrative of an individualized science program is the individualized chemistry program at the P. K. Yonge

[17] See for information on the curriculum projects of the 1960s, Paul Blackwood, "Science," Ch. VII in Glenys G. Unruh (Ed.), New Curriculum Developments (Washington, D.C.: Association for Supervision and Curriculum Development, 1965); and Richard E. Haney, The Changing Curriculum: Science (Washington, D.C.: Association for Supervision and Curriculum Development, 1966). Also see for a more recent evaluation of the science projects, James A. Rutledge, "What Has Happened to the 'New' Science Curricula?" Educational Leadership, 30:600–603 (April 1973).

[18] Joseph D. Novak, "A Case Study of Curriculum Change—Science Since PSSC," School Science and Mathematics, 69:383–384 (May 1969).

Laboratory School, University of Florida. This program, originally developed by chemistry teachers at the school for their own classes, in 1973 was used in twenty-three high schools in Florida and had been extensively pilot and field tested. Chemistry is divided into five major units which are further broken up into twenty basic instructional units. Each instructional unit has a guide sheet and related materials, including a time contract, and there are thirty-six laboratory experiences in the main unit structure plus ten options or enrichment laboratories. Each student must complete Unit I (self-paced) and any two (or the equivalent in optional projects, of two) units of the remaining four units (self-selected and self-paced) to receive credit in chemistry. The guide sheets provide for pre-testing, study questions, problems, laboratory activities, and reading references, as appropriate. Comparative evaluations done of the program indicate "that students achieve more in chemistry, as measured by the ACS–NSTA Chemistry Test, and have a more positive attitude toward the study of chemistry in the experimental, individualized chemistry classes than in traditional chemistry classes used in this study."[19]

New programs in environmental education to be described later also aim to relate science education to the student's own interests and environment. The two other major weaknesses of the early science revisions—neglect of the general high school population and lack of sequential development in a total science program—are being attacked through the emphasis in the 1970s on "unified science." Jerrold Zacharias, father of the PSSC physics program, had written as early as 1964 of the need for such a program:

> The division of science at the secondary school level into biology, chemistry, and physics is both unreasonable and uneconomical.
> Ideally, a three-year course that covered all three disciplines would be far more suitable than a sequence of courses which pretends to treat them as distinct. Today such a three-year course would be difficult to fit into the educational system, but much of this difficulty might be overcome if such a course existed. . . .[20]

The NASSP report of December, 1972, reported that such a course did exist "in secondary schools of all sizes and types from coast to coast—and abroad as well." In fact the National Science Foundation supports a

[19] Paul A. Becht, *Individualized Chemistry: A Program Designed to Personalize Instruction* (Gainesville, Fla.: P. K. Yonge Laboratory School, University of Florida, January 1973), p. 18.

[20] Cited in *Putting It All Together, Curriculum Report*, Vol. 2, No. 1 (Washington, D.C.: National Association of Secondary School Principals, December 1972), p. 1. Also see the NASSP *Curriculum Report*, Vol. 2, No. 2 (February 1973) for reports of additional science projects.

clearinghouse for information about developments in this field, the Center for Unified Science Education, at Ohio State University. This Center maintains a directory of unified science programs in operation or being planned, a comprehensive file of unified science instructional materials, a "response system" for use of the Center's resources, and distributes a quarterly newsletter (*Prism II*) about developments in the field.

The NASSP newsletter describes unified science programs in operation at the following high schools:

Lincoln-Sudbury Regional High School, Sudbury, Mass.
Monmouth Regional High School, New Shrewsbury, N. J.
Villa Angela Academy, Cleveland, Ohio
Moose Lake High School, Moose Lake, Minn.
Monona Grove High School, Monona Grove, Wisc.
Moline High School, Moline, Ill.
Dunbar High School, Dayton, Ohio
St. Louis Country Day School, St. Louis, Mo.
Catlin Gable School, Portland, Oregon

The following characteristics of these programs are noted:

1. Unified science courses are not just upgraded general science courses.
2. Most of the present unified science programs are essentially "homemade."
3. Unified science courses can be used satisfactorily with students of different degrees of academic competence and at many different grade levels.
4. Most senior high schools that have introduced unified science courses continue to offer traditionally organized science courses as well.
5. These programs offer adequate college preparation ("It's good college preparation, too").
6. Most unified science courses are built around a family of major themes or "big ideas," not as subject-matter sequences.
7. Many courses employ a flexible, modular design.[21]

Social Studies

Although projects were slower to develop in the social studies than science and mathematics, by 1967 Michaelis could identify some fifty different social studies projects.[22] These were organized in a variety of ways, were financed by a variety of agencies, and seemed to have a multiplicity

---

[21] *Putting It All Together*, pp. 2–5.
[22] See John U. Michaelis, "A Directory of Social Studies Projects," *The Bulletin of the National Association of Secondary School Principals*, 51:104–105 (April 1967).

of aims. Some projects devoted their efforts to preparing a single course for a single discipline; others prepared materials drawn from anthropology, economics, sociology, or other disciplines, which could fit into existing courses; still others proposed to develop K through 12 curriculum sequences; and some sought to isolate principles and develop a rationale upon which social studies programs could be built. The chief contribution of these projects has probably been the infusion of much new content, especially from the various social sciences other than history, into the social studies programs.

During the years since the appearance of the projects Michaelis listed, others have appeared and many of the original ones have published their materials and terminated. New social forces and conflicts have produced other demands on the social studies, and there continues a determined search for a more relevant and influential content.[23] Krug summarized in part the state of the use of the project materials in 1972 as follows:

> And yet in spite of the accumulation of the new teaching materials, relatively little progress can be observed in the social studies classrooms. The difficulty seems to be with the social studies teachers. The task of a social studies teacher who is trying to teach the New Social Studies is formidable, if not impossible. In most schools, the new materials in sociology, anthropology, geography, and economics have been grafted into the existing curriculum which is centered on the United States and world history. Social studies curricula across the country present a veritable hodgepodge of history, social sciences, courses of study based on the search for a structure in history and in the social sciences, on concepts, or on a search for broad generalizations. Still others postulate skills of inquiry and critical thinking (whatever is meant by these ambiguous terms) as their main objectives. . . . To teach on the basis of units prepared by the anthropology, geography, or sociology projects, teachers need more, not less, grounding in the social science disciplines and a great many new teaching skills. And yet, few schools or school districts have made provisions for the training or retraining of teachers before the new social studies curricula have been introduced. The result of this failure is that many teachers make half-hearted attempts to introduce some project materials and then abandon the effort because of total unfamiliarity with the material, or because of the formidable methodological problems encountered.[24]

[23] ERIC at Boulder, Colorado, provides information about social studies materials, and occasionally provides consultants through the Social Science Education Consortium.

[24] Mark M. Krug, "The Social Studies—Search for New Directions," Ch. VI in *What Will Be Taught—The Next Decade*, pp. 200–201. Also see a slightly more optimistic view regarding the results of the projects, John Jarolimek, "In Pursuit of the Elusive New Social Studies," *Educational Leadership*, 30:596–599 (April 1973).

Despite such appraisals and the facts that underlie them, many innovations in individual high schools have incorporated new directions. Perhaps Jarolimek's commentary is correct that "the curriculum efforts of the 1960s were necessary in order that social studies programs might at long last begin moving in the 1970s to teach young human beings how to live with each other peacefully, compassionately, and above all, charitably."[25] Thus, the national concern about minority groups has been reflected in a flood of materials and courses dealing with particular groups and multiethnic and multicultural roles and problems. Black studies came into prominence in the 1960s, with the Detroit school system probably the first to include special Afro-American history units in the curriculum and to write its own texts to begin teaching the subject in 1963. New York City, Washington, D.C., Chicago, Columbus and Cincinnati, Ohio, and Pittsburgh and Philadelphia were among the first cities to incorporate Negro contributions into the social studies curriculum on a broad scale. By 1970 an *Education U.S.A.* survey reported that the addition of black studies programs or of material about blacks to regular history courses was so widespread that "the conflict over whether the nation's elementary and secondary schools should teach black studies seems to be over."[26] Similar efforts have been made to develop special courses on Indians, Mexican Americans, Puerto Ricans, and other minority groups. For example, a course on the history of the American Indian at Everett High School, Lansing, Michigan, was described by its teacher in these words:

> The course is primarily a survey which touches on the various geographical areas of the continent, the types of Indians that lived in the respective environments, and their social values and languages. To balance the survey approach to the Indian, students are assigned a semester project to study one particular tribe in depth. There are approximately three hundred tribal names from which to choose, so each student can study independently. The idea of being an "expert" in one tribe appeals to them.[27]

Whether the emphasis on the various social cultures and groups in America, their contributions, problems, and status will be typically approached through special courses or through more emphasis in broad courses on multiethnic and multicultural content remains a moot issue. Currently

[25] Jarolimek, p. 599.

[26] *Education U.S.A.* Staff, *Black Studies in Schools*, Special Report (Washington, D.C.: National School Public Relations Association, 1970), p. 3.

[27] James W. Faulkner, "American Indian History," in *Social Studies in Michigan* (Lansing, Michgan: Michigan Department of Education, 1972), pp. 83–84.

there are many efforts in both directions, with the one certain trend being the emphasis on effective cooperation and participation of all Americans in a pluralistic society. Somewhat similar emphases also underlie the trend that has lasted several years to a world view in the social studies. Many courses on individual areas of the globe were developed; also world history and other courses changed markedly to include civilizations outside the West. Fraser summarizes this trend as follows:

> Another feature of new social studies programs is a strong emphasis on nonwestern studies and world affairs. Traditional social studies programs were oriented almost exclusively to the study of the United States and western Europe. During the 1940s and 50s this situation began to change slowly. The experimental projects of the 60s have accelerated the movement by producing units, courses, and materials for both elementary and secondary levels that stress world cultures and international affairs. . . . The increasingly popular secondary school courses in culture area studies, comparative economic systems, and comparative governments treat nonwestern as well as western peoples and nations.[28]

However, it does not appear that high schools have generally added specific programs in international studies. A survey in 1970–1971 noted that such courses as existed, frequently titled "international relations" or "politics," were "taught almost exclusively in the eleventh and twelfth grades to students who are likely to go to college, are above average in ability, and are from other than the lower socioeconomic class."[29] These authors commented that "there seems little reason to believe that more than 10 percent of the total population has been exposed to international studies at either the precollegiate or collegiate level."[30]

One way of increasing the numbers of students exposed to new content and providing alternative opportunities for relevant social studies is the use of short electives and minicourses. The movement in this direction has been especially pronounced in the social studies field. For example, the "Student Selective Series," initiated in September, 1971, at Flint, Michigan, Northwestern High School, was a battery of forty-three one-semester course offerings, including such innovative ones as "American Historical Myths and Legends," "World Religions," "You and the Law," "How To Make a Million," "Administration of Justice," "American Radicals, Reformers, Reactionaries," "Man's Struggles for Peace," "Reconstruction and Its Impact on the Negro," and "U.S. Historic Vacations."

[28] Dorothy Fraser, "Social Sciences," *Nation's Schools*, 84: 34–35 (July 1969).
[29] James M. Becker and Maurice A. East, *Global Dimensions in U.S. Education: The Secondary School* (New York: Center for War/Peace Studies, 1972), pp. 15–16.
[30] Becker and East, p. 26.

Brandywine High School, Wilmington, Delaware, offered in 1972 a two-week "interim program" featuring a variety of intensive short courses including "Asian Humanities," "The Bible," "Consciousness III," "Controversy," "Culture of Appalachia," "Dissent in America," "Egyptian Civilization," "Ethnic Problems," "Group Counseling." Thomas McKean High School in Wilmington offers nine-week, one-quarter credit electives including "History Through Photography," "Poverty in America," "Art History," "Environmental Problems," "The Under-18 Citizen." Northern University High School, Cedar Falls, Iowa, had a "Social Inquiry" elective comprising a series of four-week inquiry modules in which students examined persistent and crucial social problems originally identified through a survey of student interests. The Patchogue-Medford, New York, schools offer ten-week minicourses, those in grade 12 including Anthropology, Black and Latin Studies, Comparative Religion, Psychology, Sociology, Consumer Economics, Political Science, and International Studies.

Two other closely related emphases in current social studies programs relate to the eighteen-year-old vote and community participation. The New York City Office of Instructional Services has developed for use throughout the schools a recommended procedure and suggested plan for a voter registration campaign; a checklist of practices in mobilizing registration efforts; and strategies to use in large groups, small groups, and class activities relating to the political process. The Edgewood School District, San Antonio, Texas, has developed guidelines for students' registration and campaigning. The Shawnee Mission, Kansas, schools developed a year-long action program on youth and the political process, involving 2000 students in a mock political convention, with other related curriculum activities in social studies, language arts, foreign languages, science, math, and music. A pilot project in Hudson Bay High School, Vancouver, Washington, involved 100 students in assessing the relevance of their school learnings to their community. Students at the Mount Saint Joseph Academy, Rutland, Vermont, do volunteer work for academic credit in public and private social service agencies. A "mini-mester" course in government at Monte Cassino High School, Tulsa, Oklahoma, features field trips to government offices and institutions, and related individual projects.

The continuing efforts to improve social studies instruction generally emphasize values and valuing, conceptual structures, and social processes rather than accumulation of facts and details as ends in themselves. Values are treated rationally and analytically, and directed toward the development of responsibility for self and others, with somewhat sophisticated group processes introduced to resolve conflicts.

INNOVATION IN OTHER ESTABLISHED AREAS

To varying extents the other established areas of the high school curriculum were also affected by the curriculum reform movement beginning in the late 1950s. Our reference here is to the curriculum categories or areas that are commonly provided by high schools but usually on an elective basis.

Activity Programs

Once the major, in some schools the only, innovation in the high school curriculum, the activity, or "extracurricular" program, has probably changed least in the last two decades. In part because of the lack of evidence of "significantly changed student activity programs or practices" in the literature, a survey was initiated in March, 1971, with support of the National Association of Secondary School Principals, to determine what was happening in the student activity programs.[31] Some developments considered promising by the director of the study were noted:

> Increased involvement of students in activities related to pressing problems of society and students—such clubs as Ecology, Anti-Pollution, Students for Peace and Freedom, Minorities Council, World Affairs, Women's Liberation, Drug.

> Reduction or removal of academic restriction for participation in student activities, especially for student governance.

> Increased involvement of students of all abilities and backgrounds in student governance activities.

> Innovative activities such as "student leadership" courses required of students elected to the student council; "fireside chats" by the student council; establishment of a "free speech area"; interschool visitations.

But the survey also revealed conditions indicative of the need for further innovation in the activity programs.

> The ratio of activities added to those dropped was approximately four to one in schools of all sizes.

> Of schools identified by the officers of the state principals' associations as having exemplary activity programs, 30 percent reported no significant innovations since 1965 in new activities, policy changes, or administrative procedures.

[31] See Robert L. Buser, "What's Happening in Student Activities in the Schools of the Seventies?" *The Bulletin of the National Association of Secondary School Principals*, 55:1–9 (September 1971).

A considerable percentage of schools identified as above, reported that they had to curtail their activity programs since 1965: small schools, 17 percent; medium, 18 percent; large, 24 percent.

There was an apparent lack of faculty commitment to student activity programs in some schools.[32]

In view of the success of activities in some schools, of the excellent opportunity they provide for the exercise of student governance and leadership, and of their relation to the development of special and enduring interest, the lack of innovativeness in this area seems a major point of weakness in secondary education.

Business Education

The survey of enrollments (see Table II) shows that the percentage of business education enrollments of the total enrollment dropped over 6 percent from 1948–1949 to 1960–1961 and was holding at the latter point in 1970–1971. The earlier drop was probably due to the increasing options available and also the pressure in 1960–1961 on students to take more academic subjects, especially science, mathematics, and foreign languages. Within the business education area, discernible trends include the increasing provision through various schedule devices (early and late hours, summer school, variable periods) for typing for personal usage; introduction of data-processing instruction; and innovations in office occupational education.

Instruction in the computer and data-processing techniques occurs in mathematics and elsewhere as well as in business education, and there continues the issue of whether this instruction is appropriate for high school level students. But many high schools do introduce at least an orientation to the uses, opportunities, and limitations of electronic data processing, with visits to data processing installations.

Innovations in office education and other aspects of the business education field have aimed toward more functional learning opportunities, especially through work experience, and toward individualized instruction. Office practice and machines laboratories have been established in many schools, and business simulation methods are used in instruction. Particular effort has been made through federally funded and other special programs to reach disadvantaged and potential dropout students. For example a report of the Integrated Business Program (IBP) at Waterford-Halfmoon High School, Waterford, New York, aiming to attract and hold the potential dropout, described this "4-year continuum for grades 9 through 12" as follows:

[32] Buser, p. 8. Also see Philip A. Cusick, *Inside High School: The Student's World* (New York: Holt, Rinehart and Winston, 1973).

Each student electing IBP in the ninth grade will take two consecutive periods (total time 100 minutes) each day for four years—yielding eight Carnegie units toward graduation.

The student is pretested for shorthand, English, mathematics aptitude plus general business understanding before beginning the program. Then the student is allowed to begin self-paced study of the topics using packets of materials to guide his progress. The initial introduction to each topic is led by the teacher but the student completes work and requests examination in the topic when ready. Individual profile sheets are sent home periodically throughout the year, but report cards use H for honors and regular A, B, C, D, and F. It is expected that the students will be prepared adequately for any Regents or school examination in the topics covered at the completion of the program. There have been no difficulties with students transferring into or out of the program.

The project has used the regular facilities of the business department with the addition of audiovisual equipment and necessary wiring for self-pacing materials, including slide/filmstrip projectors, cassettes, tape players, tape recorders, camera and mounting stand, and cassette duplicator.[33]

Fine Arts

The enrollments table (see Table II) shows that the percentage enrollments in music were almost the same in 1970–1971 as in 1948–1949, there having occurred a decided decrease from 1960–1961 to 1970–1971. Art, on the other hand, increased substantially from 1948–1949 to 1960–1961 and again to 1970–1971. There is no complete explanation of these changes, but one possible explanation is the addition of art courses in many high schools not previously offering them, as a part of the revival of interest in the arts of the past decade. By 1970–1971, over 60 percent of the high schools of the United States offered a first-year course in "General or Fine Art I" as listed in the United States Office of Education survey, and this course enrolled over one-tenth of the total enrollment; neither band nor chorus, each offered by more schools, enrolled quite as many students as the first high school art course, and the music enrollments were undoubtedly swollen by the inclusion of grades 7–8 band and chorus. The increasingly popular theater arts area is not separately reported in this enrollment survey, and is usually subsumed as dramatics in the English enrollments or still exists as an extrainstructional activity.

The trend toward an introductory general arts (or music) course followed by various electives and independent study is illustrated by this statement of philosophy of the Shawnee Mission Northwest High School, Kansas:

[33] New York State Education Department, *EPIC*, 1:2 (Fall 1971), Project #906.

The primary goal of the Northwest art department has been to develop a flexible program which will allow the individual student to build his art curriculum according to his skills and interests. The courses range from Art I, a prerequisite course offering a foundation in the basic principles and techniques of art, to a wide range of one-term electives, many of which are followed up by advanced courses in those specific areas. We also offer an independent study program which was developed for the more advanced student who has had a background in related areas of art and needs a prescribed program designed to deal with his specific problems and needs.

The electives in art at Northwest include beginning and advanced drawing, functional design, decorative design, oil and acrylic painting, and water color in the two-dimensional area; and beginning and advanced sculpture and jewelry, textiles, printmaking, and ceramics in the three-dimensional area; mixed media, and photography. Humanities, taught in conjunction with the art, English, drama, and music departments, is taught in a two-hour block, with one credit given in English and one in fine arts.

Three recent major movements in the arts have been identified as aesthetic education, humanities, and related arts, said by Marantz to have in common "a reaction to the almost monolithic position maintained by studio art in the secondary schools."[34] Although the studio program remains prevalent, many programs include the development of aesthetic perception as well as the development of studio competencies. The historical-critical program is oriented toward the development of a critical appreciative power and historical understanding of art in the human culture; studio activities are employed from time to time. Another type of program emphasizes the acquisition of creative design skills. Students are taught to perceive by using media to solve visual problems that for them are strikingly new. Interesting three-dimensional designs, unusual uses of photography, and multisensory art forms are within the scope of this program.

The humanities-based program intends to enable students to experience the several arts, to view them as a product of an age, to recognize not only the statements artists have made but also the questions they have raised. One proponent of interdisciplinary humanities courses, Charles R. Keller, wrote that they were "one of the most interesting and significant developments in secondary education" and described their possibilities in part as follows:

[34] Kenneth Marantz, "Visual Education and the Human Experience," Chapter II in *What Will Be Taught—The Next Decade*, p. 71.

Humanities courses give students chances to wonder, to do creative work, to find new interests. So much good reading, looking and listening can be part of these courses. And art and music get a deserved new position in the curriculum. Education can be deep involvement rather than superficial exposure. Education can become the kind William James liked, "knowledge by acquaintance," rather than the kind he disliked, "Knowledge by description."[35]

An innovation made widely with Title III funds is that of bringing cultural resources, especially in the arts, to schools and students in communities lacking these resources. For example, a Sullivan County, New York, Festival of the Arts brought performances, with preclassroom and post-classroom sessions, by personnel from Lincoln Center for the Performing Arts, the Metropolitan Opera Studio, the Julliard School for Music and Dance, the Lincoln Center Repertory Theater, the New York City Ballet, and Maximillian Productions. Students were involved, too, when forty-seven students combined with the Julliard Chamber Orchestra to present solos on small symphony programs. In another project, a coordinated fine arts program was provided in the rural setting of Livingston, Steuben, and Wyoming Counties, New York, by the cooperation of the State University College at Genesco. Programs were offered for hundreds of students in both elementary and secondary schools, in art, dance, drama, and strings. The arts, too, are affected by social conditions, and changing society requires changing aesthetic experiences. A music educator described the implications of social needs for his field in these words:

In the face of rapid change, the information explosion, and the power of the media, music educators must help students evaluate the world of sound around them. It will make little difference whether students "appreciate" the symphonies of Beethoven or the nuances of a Haydn string quartet if they are imprisoned in a world plagued by noise pollution —be it Muzak or jets. Music educators must help students recognize the aesthetic problems of their times. Music education, which helps students make sense out of their environment, helps them deal with a complex world, and equips them to solve some of the artistic problems which they will face, can be viewed as relevant not only to the individual learner, but to the needs of society as well.[36]

[35] Charles R. Keller, "Interdisciplinary Humanities Courses—A Needed Challenge to the Present Separate-Subject-Dominated Curriculum," *Today's Education*, 57:19 (January 1968).

[36] Roberta Newman, "Music Education: The Need for Change," *School Review*, 79:446 (May 1971).

Foreign Language

American post-Sputnik efforts to strengthen our international position brought a long-needed renovation and expansion of foreign language education. Outmoded textbooks were cast aside and replaced by modern materials supported by electronic aids and institutes for training teachers in the audiolingual approach. Enrollments in languages increased markedly, and students were encouraged to begin a language earlier and study it longer. New languages were added to the fairly usual offering of Latin, French, and Spanish. In 1970–1971 one or more languages were offered in 70 percent of our secondary schools, with nearly 50 percent offering French and Spanish, and with 22.5 percent offering first-year German (as compared with 9.3 percent in 1960–1961), the latter surpassing the percentage still offering Latin. Although still small in enrollments, Russian and Italian were offered by more than twice as many schools in 1970–1971 as in 1960–1961.[37] Kaulfers' 1970 review of the field cited the "marked increase in the percentage of the total high school population enrolled in foreign languages" as "one of the most distinctive trends in American secondary schools since 1955."[38] Table II shows this percentage to have increased almost 8 percent from 1948–1949 to 1970–1971, the actual enrollments being almost four times greater in 1970–1971. Another reviewer, however, in 1972 reported "a crisis in foreign language education"; and that "enrollments seem to be contracting."[39] The "crisis" to which he referred, however, was more in terms of the dropping of foreign language requirements by colleges and universities, and the uncertainties as to methodology. It may be that the enrollments of 1970–1971 do represent a high point and that there may be a period of somewhat stabilized, even slightly dropping, enrollments.

Undoubtedly the chief innovation in foreign language education of the past two decades has been the swing to the total communications objectives of listening, speaking, and writing in addition to reading. The first change was the introduction of the audiolingual approach, aided greatly by the purchase of electronic equipment made possible in many schools by the National Defense Education Act of 1958. The term *audiolingual* implies a priority to listening comprehension and the spoken language. It means that the initial learning of a modern foreign language is through the ear, not the eye. Thus, the student is first introduced to a period of oral instruction without use of books or printed material for a

[37] See Gertler and Barker, pp. 6–7, for further enrollment data.

[38] Walter V. Kaulfers, "High School Foreign Languages—Developments and Prospects," *The Educational Forum*, 34:384 (March 1970).

[39] See Robert L. Politzer, "The Foreign Language Curriculum: Present Problems," *School and Society*, 100:15 (January 1972).

time that may last from a few weeks to several months. Once the student has mastered the sound system of the language and has memorized several dialogues, he is introduced to reading. But problems arose by misuse of the foreign language laboratories with overreliance on drill, and inadequate attention to all forms of communication. Politzer observed that "one of the main drawbacks of the audiolingual curriculum was simply that it imputed the same motivation (e.g., attainment of oral proficiency) and the same aptitudes (e.g., audio-modality preference) to all students" and saw as the challenge ahead, "to create curricula which allow enough diversification and individualization to meet the goals and interests of the largest possible number of individual students."[40] Kaulfers' assessment of the situation produced a somewhat similar, optimistic conclusion: "The re-evaluation of the linguistic approach, already underway, will in time lead to a better balanced, less mechanical, and more creative approach in secondary schools."[41] This balanced approach may also include more frequent offering of courses in other disciplines through the medium of a foreign language, already provided in some schools in such forms as Russian literature, art, music, and history all in the Russian language, for example.

Meanwhile the objective of foreign language study for aid in understanding the culture of peoples of the world should take priority in an era in which intercultural understanding is so greatly needed. Study of one's own language may even help in understanding its cultural backgrounds: A class at Burlingame High School in San Mateo Unified School District, California, is described as "Spanish for the Spanish-speaking" to serve as "a bridge between cultures." Most of the students learned Spanish from their infancy in such places as Cuba, San Salvador, Argentina, Mexico, and Texas. The emphasis of the class is on "the literature and civilization of Spain, and the comparative values of Spanish culture in Spanish America and North America."[42] In the same school another teacher has groups of students studying Latin, Hebrew, and Italian, working in the same classroom, and another teacher has four levels of German instruction in the same room. As schools continue to move away from a single-method approach and only one or two languages that seem to assume a standardized type of student, and begin to draw fully upon their resources in personnel of the community and the technology possible, they should help produce citizens better able to cope with national and international problems.

[40] Politzer, p. 18.
[41] Kaulfers, p. 393.
[42] San Mateo Union High School District, "Burlingame's Language Program," *PULSE*, 2:3 (March 1972).

Home Economics

Despite some fall in enrollments in the post-Sputnik period, Table II shows that by 1970–1971 home economics enrollments were almost 30 percent of the total secondary school enrollment, a substantial increase over the comparable figures for 1948–1949 and 1960–1961. This area has become somewhat distinctly separated into general and specialized education, categorized by the Vocational Education Act of 1968 as Consumer and Homemaking Education and Occupational Home Economics. A further breakdown of courses offered in 1973–1974 by the high schools of a large urban county school district into three "paths," is shown in the accompanying table.

table III
Program Paths—Home Economics*

CAREER EDUCATION	PRE-TECHNICAL	PRE-COLLEGE
Child Care, Guidance and Services	Child Care, Guidance and Services	Child Care, Guidance and Services
Child Development	Child Development	Child Development
Clothing Management	Comprehensive Home Economics	Comprehensive Home Economics
Comprehensive Home Economics	Cooperative Child Care Services	Family Economics
Cooperative Child Care Services	Cooperative Food Management	Family Living
Cooperative Food Management	Family Economics	Food Management
Family Economics	Family Living	Food and Nutrition
Family Living	Food Management	Home Economics, Guided Studies
Food Management	Food and Nutrition	Housing and Home Furnishings
Food and Nutrition	Personal, Family and Social Relations	Personal, Family and Social Relations
Food and Nutrition for Boys	Textiles and Clothing	Textiles and Clothing
Home Furnishings Equipment and Services		
Housing and Home Furnishings		
Personal, Family and Social Relations		
Textiles and Clothing		

*Courses are arranged in alphabetical order and not in order of difficulty or in the sequence in which students would progress.

From Cecil D. Hardesty, Superintendent, Catalog of Course Offerings in Duval County Senior High Schools, 1973–1974. Jacksonville, Fla.: Duval County Schools, 1973, p. HE–3.

Few areas in the secondary school curriculum adjust as readily to innovation and change as does home economics, whether vocational or homemaking. Many alternatives can be offered students for meeting their individual needs. Large group instruction can make use of specialists, television, visual aids, role playing, and other thought-provoking presentations. The laboratory method offers opportunities to apply principles, to develop manipulative and managerial skills, to apply the processes of decision-making and the ability to think, plan, and evaluate. The resources of home and community can be closely related. Also, home economics is an area that can be and is especially responsive to multidisciplinary approaches described more fully later in this chapter.

Possibly the most significant innovations in the home economics program are: (1) the various courses relating to education for family life, preparation for parenthood, and child development, frequently using experience working with young children; (2) the specialized courses such as shown in the pretechnical grouping for specific job preparation; (3) the occupational home economics work-experience programs; and (4) a wide variety of short-term and also longer courses aimed at developing consumer competencies. High school students assist in Headstart and child care programs to gain practical experience and insight. Child development laboratories in some high schools serve as nursery school and child care centers for the community, and also as classrooms and laboratories for high school students.

A full offering in home economics includes a variety of courses, for credit and noncredit, short-term or long-term, for boys as well as girls, for the academically able and the disadvantaged, and courses intended to help students find solutions to particular social problems. Noncredit, non-graded minicourses assist students in buying clothing, spending money wisely, selecting food, understanding children, being socially acceptable, and preparing for marriage. More technically oriented courses prepare students to work in child care centers, beauty parlors, dry cleaning establishments, tailoring shops and departments, laundry services, food services, bakeries, florist shops, gift shops, department stores, drapery shops, and various other service occupations.

Industrial Arts

Confusion continues as to the definition of industrial arts in relation to such terms as "career education" (see pages 94–97), "industrial education," "occupational education," and "vocational education" (see pages 92–93). The following definition and explanation to us represents the most desirable purpose of industrial arts courses as usually offered in grades 7 to 9:

Industrial arts in education is the study, in shops, laboratories, and drafting rooms, of industrial tools, machines, materials, processes, products, and occupations, for purposes of general and specialized education. In the upper grade levels, it is confused with vocational-industrial education. But it is not vocational education; it does not aim to prepare youth for specific trades. Rather, it should serve, among its other purposes, to provide exploratory and prevocational education.[43]

Thus, industrial arts is career education in the 1970s usage of this term, and it is *pre*-vocational, *pre*-occupational, and *pre*-industrial education.

The career education emphases are indicated in such products of the Industrial Arts Curriculum Project (a joint effort of The Ohio State University and the University of Illinois) as "The World of Work," "The World of Construction," and "The World of Manufacturing" series of materials developed for use in grades 7 to 9. These programs stress career exploration in industrial arts, presenting contemporary industrial technology with emphasis on occupational orientation. Such emphases offer students in general more knowledge of our industrial society and are prefatory to work experience and specific occupational training for some youth. The modern industrial arts program is thus much more than: (1) the original manual training emphasis on hand skills with tools; (2) the succeeding, but still limited, manual arts emphasis that added the construction of well-designed, useful articles; and (3) the type of industrial education that is scarcely distinguishable from a vocational program designed for immediate job entry.

Innovations in industrial arts utilize wherever possible facilities that are far more complex than the old shop with its large room for machines and tools, the adjoining "finishing room," and area for storage. New shop-laboratories have auxiliary classrooms in which the light can be controlled so that overhead, film, and filmstrip projectors, and various types of media can be used in instruction. Attention is given not only to lumber and woodworking tools, but also to machines, metals, plastics, graphic arts, applications of electricity and electronics, and design and drafting, and to the use of research in the production of industrial products. More instructional aids of all kinds are in use. Several programmed booklets on such topics as the interchangeability of parts are available. Ingenious printed and graphic materials for instruction are increasing. More field trips are made as part of the study of industries of the community. New aids reduce the amount of disproportionate construction activity formerly necessary to apply small bits of knowledge; for example, kits

[43] H. H. London, "The Place and Function of Industrial Arts in Preparing Youth for the World of Work," *Theory into Practice*, 9:295 (December 1970). This entire issue is devoted to "Industrial Arts and/or Vocational Education."

in which the student is able to assemble selected components of an electrical system and dismantle them without injury to the parts can be reused by other students.

Continued innovations in the industrial arts area offer much hope for the success of the career education movement, with its emphasis on orientation to clusters of occupations and to some beginning acquaintance with the tools and skills in the industrial arts area. The use of independent study projects beyond the orientation type of classroom activities helps to identify students whose interests can be the bases of more specialized education.

Physical, Health, and Safety Education

Despite some efforts in the late 1950s to find room for more academic subjects by reducing requirements in physical education, this area has gained, not lost enrollments. For 1970–1971, the percentage that health and physical education enrollments was of the total secondary school enrollment accounted for the largest of all subject enrollment percentages; it showed a marked increase over 1960–1961, after the post-Sputnik drop, and even over the 1948–1949 statistic. This fact reflects the continued requirements of physical education in almost all grades and also the inclusion in the enrollment figures of the increasingly common separate courses in health education and driver education. With today's great need for increased reduction of automobile accidents and of health abuse through drugs and other social problems, we see no reduction of emphasis on the latter courses.

The chief trends in this area seem encapsulated in the terms "individualized" for physical education and "practical" for health and safety education. As to the former, an interesting description of physical education in a hypothetical "Would-You-Believe High School" in 1975 incorporates the best of present innovations and trends in the three program elements:

1. Varied opportunities for developing understanding and appreciation of movement, including movement as expression and communication as in dance or games, and movement in society as in neighborhood activity programs.
2. Physical fitness, including muscular strength, cardiorespiratory endurance, and survival aquatics.
3. Competence in lifetime sports.[44]

The organization of such a program indicates the individualization characteristic:

---

[44] Ann E. Jewett, " 'Would-You-Believe' Public Schools 1975," *Journal of Health, Physical Education, and Recreation*, 42:41–44 (March 1971).

All students are individually programmed. Except for the initial assessment module, one expressive movement module, one movement in society module, and the lifetime sports orientation module, students may select any activities for which they meet the basic entry qualifications. Physical education is a required sophomore subject; juniors and seniors who have demonstrated the required competence are not required to continue in the physical education curriculum, although most students elect additional units.[45]

The attention to individual differences, independent study, self-direction, and other aspects of the student-focused curriculum movement of the 1970s finds many applications in the physical education program. Timberland Regional High School, Plaistown, New Hampshire, offers an independent study option in the activity areas, with these three requirements as to the choice:

1. The student must have genuine interest in the activity.
2. The activity must have realistic carry-over values.
3. Participation in the activity must provide an opportunity for a goal-centered learning experience.[46]

The aims of such a program at Ridgewood High School, Norridge, Illinois, were stated as follows:

> The program at Ridgewood High School is geared to enable the student to enjoy an activity and not be forced into it. The student makes his own choice and, because of that, he works harder and tries to get as much out of the project as possible. Students learn to structure themselves and to become active. The physical education department has high hopes that this approach will make for a definite carry-over in physical education after graduation and that the training so received will become an important part of students' lives.[47]

At Ridgewood, independent study projects were offered in: adaptive activities, apparatus, archery, badminton, baseball, basketball, bowling, camping skills, cheerleading, exercise program, fencing, first aid, football, golf, indoor recreation, judo, modern dance, outdoor recreation, personal defense, pom pom, soccer, softball, tennis, therapy, track and field, trampoline, tumbling, volleyball, weight training, wrestling, Yoga. The elective physical education course for grades 11 to 12 at Silverton, Colorado, High

[45] Jewett, p. 44.

[46] Carolyn L. Stanhope, "Independent Study Option," *Journal of Health, Physical Education, and Recreation*, 42:24 (September 1971).

[47] Gregory M. Sadowski, "Flexible Modular Scheduling Allows for Student Choice of Independent Study Units," *Journal of Health, Physical Education, and Recreation*, 42:25 (September 1971).

School, was planned by the students to include such activities as skiing, backpacking, fly fishing, and mountaineering, involving weekend trips:

> The weekend trips, on a volunteer basis, included a cross country ski tour in the high country above Aspen, a backpacking expedition to the isolated Havasupaid Indian Reservation 11 miles into the Grand Canyon (where physical education goals were integrated with social studies projects like studying federal aid to Indians) and a weekend of harvesting crops with migrant workers in the San Luis Valley.[48]

Individual progress in prescribed activities is normal in physical education. It is aided by the use of learning packages or contracts as "phy-paks" in the Omaha, Nebraska, public schools. The "phy-pak" has these parts:

1. Content classification (task or concept)
2. Purpose
3. Learning objectives
4. Diagnostic test or pretest
5. Taxonomy category (based on Bloom's taxonomy, with a coding system "to enable the transcriber to determine the complexity, class, and degree of difficulty of each contract")
6. Learning activities
7. Self-test
8. Final test
9. Challenge activities (assisting or teaching someone else)[49]

Health education has been greatly affected by the problems and issues concerning drug education and sex education (see later sections on these topics in this chapter). Public concern about these matters has produced considerable controversy and some legislation; for example, a November, 1972, summary of recent legislative action cited state laws affecting health education in Nebraska (requiring a comprehensive health education program but specifying only the one item of drug use, misuse, and abuse); Montana (required secondary school health education course to include instruction on drug and alcohol education and abuse); Florida (a comprehensive K through 12 program on drugs); Illinois (specified twelve content areas for inclusion in all elementary and secondary schools); Michigan (ten areas required). Most common areas of health education are included in the latter two legislative enactments, these being the twelve in Illinois: (1) human ecology and health; (2) human

[48] George Pastor, "Student-Designed," *Journal of Health, Physical Education, and Recreation*, 42:31 (September 1971).
[49] Robert D. Shrader, "Individualized Approach to Learning," *Journal of Health, Physical Education, and Recreation*, 42:33 (September 1971).

growth and development; (3) prevention and control of diseases; (4) public and environmental health; (5) consumer health; (6) safety education and disaster survival; (7) mental health and illness; (8) personal health habits; (9) alcohol; (10) drug use and abuse; (11) tobacco; and (12) nutrition and dental health.[50]

Innovations in health education include the creation of programs designed to evoke the emotional and intellectual commitment of high school-aged people. *Resources for Youth,* a publication of the National Commission on Resources for Youth, reported in 1972 that their files included descriptions of more than 100 programs in which teen-agers were helping each other in health fields; illustrative reports included:

Two-weeks summer service by high school volunteers at a state hospital in California;

Sponsorship by a Philadelphia organization, "Students Concerned with Public Health," of puppet shows and other activities by teen-agers to teach nearly 22,000 elementary school children over a two-year period about alcoholism, drug-addiction, smoking, venereal disease, and tuberculosis;

Service by more than 100 New York City teen-agers, some paid by Neighborhood Youth Corps, in helping doctors test more than 3000 children for lead poisoning;

Collection for the Air Resources Laboratory of data about air pollution by six South Harlem teen-agers;

Operation by teen-agers, with much assistance from lawyers, doctors, nurses, and others to whom referrals are made, of a HELP referral service.

Both physical and health education include some aspects of safety education such as first aid, but the dominant aspect of high school safety education remains driver education. Continued state legislation, insurance reductions for driver education graduates, and driver licensing regulations mandate wide provision of driver education programs and a substantial investment in the equipment required and increasingly available (see Chapter 6). In addition to the somewhat standard driver education course, using both simulation and actual driver training cars, some high schools offer more advanced courses for students who already have their driver licenses. The course on defensive driving may use the Defensive Series offered by the National Safety Council.

Vocational Education

Long-smoldering dissatisfaction with vocational education erupted in the early 1970s into a major movement toward the "career education" espoused by the then United States Commissioner of Education, Sidney

[50] See Dean F. Miller, "Legislative Action, Health Education, and Curriculum Change," *The Journal of School Health,* 42:513–515 (November 1972).

P. Marland, Jr. Since we consider this a much broader concept than the vocational education it includes rather than replaces, we treat career education as a separate, emergent area in the next section of this chapter.

In addition to the phases already considered in this section—home economics, industrial arts, and business education—vocational education in the high school characteristically includes agricultural education, distributive education, health occupations, trade and industrial occupations, and occupational experience programs. In addition to their regular courses and work experience activities, these programs actively sponsor various youth organizations such as Future Farmers of America, Distributive Education Clubs, Future Homemakers of America, Future Business Leaders Associations, and others. Many of the innovative efforts in these fields have been spearheaded by the youth organizations.

Under the spurs of the Vocational Education Act of 1963 and the Vocational Education Amendments of 1968, the federally aided vocational programs introduced many innovations. Illustrative of new developments at the high school level are these:

Aeronautical science course for high schools in California;

An airport and airline operations program for a new high school near Kennedy Airport stressing airline occupations (pre-pilot training, pre-stewardess training, air traffic control, meteorology, purchasing, ticket sales, executive management);

Nautical occupations courses, such as "Sea Ed" in Ketchikan, Alaska, featuring field experiences in a former Coast Guard ship and a leased fishing vessel, and a student-operated fish hatchery for students of Ocean Beach and Naselle-Grays River School Districts, Washington;

Project ABLE at the Quincy, Massachusetts, Vocational-Technical School providing individualized instruction on a skills ladder basis in eleven curriculum clusters: business education, computer data processing, electro-electronics, foods preparation, general piping, general woodworking, graphic and commercial arts, health occupations, home economics, metals and machines, and power mechanics;

A Work Opportunity Center in Minneapolis, Minnesota, which had graduated 3300 students since 1966 and offered highly individualized programs with a built-in reward system in electronics and electricity, small engine repair, machine work, office skills, home economics, health care, marketing and merchandising, food service, and auto mechanics and service station occupations;

A training hotel-motel facility at Nelsonville, Ohio, for adults taking classroom work there and high school students having academic training at their high schools half-days and hotel training at the facility half-days.[51]

[51] See *Education U.S.A.* Staff, *Vocational Education: Innovations Revolutionize Career Training* (Washington, D.C.: National School Public Relations Association, 1971), pp. 35–41. See also "Exemplary Projects," pp. 56–62.

Curriculum developments in vocational education feature especially the relating of training programs to new occupational needs, the use of individualized instruction approaches (probably introduced in vocational education much earlier and more widely than in other curriculum areas), and work experience programs. Thus the Northwestern High School, Detroit, with funding from the Chrysler Corporation and the cooperation of four local hospitals, developed a medical health career program involving work experience in the hospitals and instruction in the school, with additional field trips to nonhospital facilities related to health and medical occupations.[52] The Crestmoor High School in San Mateo Union High School District, California, offers an all-girl auto shop, justified by the teacher on this basis: "The boys usually start off knowing so much more, because they work around cars with their fathers. The girls would really be at a disadvantage in the same class with the guys."[53] However the instructor found the girls to perform so well that his expectations for their progress were revised. Most specific vocational education programs are developed for particular groups of learners, and the focus on disadvantaged and potential drop-outs is especially common. The state of Hawaii, for example, developed in the early 1970s a "Pre-Industrial Preparation Program" designed "primarily for the underachieving disadvantaged student to help him see the importance and usefulness of academic skills for performing a job task," and an "Occupational Skills Program" offered "to the limited ability learners in the high schools" and team-taught by the special education teacher and the occupationally competent instructor.[54] In Florida a project focusing on thirteen- to eighteen-year-old disadvantaged and handicapped students established a special education center in each participating county to provide a nongraded occupationally oriented curriculum, related academic work, intensive vocational counseling, and a social motivation program. A diversified-satellite occupations program in the Granite School District, Salt Lake City, Utah, included a special bilingual-bicultural program for Mexican-Americans, and an intensive drop-out identification program at the sixth-grade level.

Although it is federal support for vocational education and innovations therein on which schools have generally relied, many innovations have come through the support of industry and philanthropic foundations. The school–industry partnerships have been especially pronounced in the vocational education field, where industry can supply the training labora-

[52] See Joshua Geller, "An Exploratory Program in Health Careers," *The Bulletin of the National Association of Secondary School Principals*, 54:90–103 (March 1970).

[53] San Mateo Union High School District, "Crestmoor's All-Girl Auto Shop," *PULSE*, 2:1 (January 1972).

[54] Emike I. Kudo, "An Outline of the Restructured Vocational Technical Education Program for Secondary Schools" (Honolulu, Hawaii: State Department of Education, September 1972), mimeographed.

tories as well as employ the trainees. Foundations help, too; for example, a 1972 statement by Harold Howe II, then of the Ford Foundation and a former United States Commissioner of Education, cited Ford Foundation contributions to these vocational education programs in the schools:

> The Richmond Plan which offered students in two Richmond, California, high schools basic technical training leading to employment and at the same time helped them to continue their education;
>
> Production of new texts and materials by the Education Development Center, Newton, Massachusetts, for introducing vocational education at the junior high school level and carrying it upward to the junior college;
>
> Development in the New York City schools of an academic vocational curriculum to replace the "general" program for noncollege-bound students;
>
> The School Without Walls program of the Parkway School, Philadelphia;
>
> Alternative school programs in Berkeley, California, including work and community experience projects;
>
> The Urban Center in San Francisco established by the Athenian School and offering programs for high school students, including four-week internships in business, government, social agencies, media and cultural institutions, schools, and labor unions;
>
> "The City as School" experiment in a Brooklyn high school involving learning in all the city's resources.[55]

The emphasis on individualization which will be further commented on in a later section, is not really innovative in vocational education, for even the original apprenticeship training was basically tutorial and individualized. Further, the vocational education program probably provides for more students in need of special attention than any other area of the curriculum. Indeed one vocational educator argues that vocational education is "where humanization works":

> Because much of the work in vocational education is done either on an individual basis or in small groups, the instructor must often interact with students as unique individuals. This provides the opportunity for the essence of humane teaching—the chance for the teacher to show his acceptance of the student for what he is. No other area in the curriculum provides the opportunity for as much one-to-one interaction between student and teacher as does vocational education. Through this continuing opportunity to contact the student on an individual basis, the teacher can show the student that he is concerned about him as a person, concerned about his feelings, his values, and his attitudes.[56]

[55] Harold Howe II, Schools and the World of Work, a Ford Foundation reprint (New York: Ford Foundation, 1972).

[56] Harold E. Zirbel, "Vocational Education: Where Humanization Works," The Bulletin of the National Association for Secondary School Principals, 56:86 (February 1972).

EMERGENT OBJECTIVES AND MOVEMENTS

In addition to the developments in the common academic and other established areas we have described in this chapter, the high school curriculum of the 1970s is considerably influenced by certain emergent but pervasive objectives: career development, drug abuse, the environment, and family life and sex education, in particular. All areas of the curriculum are affected by movements to break away from the disciplines to more interdisciplinary and multidisciplinary approaches as such objectives as those just listed demand. These movements also result in providing students with many options for individualization, and in basing many curriculum plans on performance objectives. Each of these emergent objectives and movements is briefly described and illustrated in this concluding section of Chapter 3.

Career Education

The impetus given career education in the 1970s is generally credited to Sidney P. Marland, Jr. As Commissioner of Education in 1970 Marland called for a widespread reform of vocational education and indeed general education with an emphasis for all students on career development. In a speech made in January, 1971, to the National Association of Secondary School Principals, Marland suggested that "we dispose of the term vocational education, and adopt the term career education" and stated that "true and complete reform of the high school, viewed as a major element of overall preparation for life, cannot be achieved until general education is completely done away with in favor of contemporary career development in a comprehensive secondary education environment."[57] Marland was really voicing the long-standing discontent of many educators and citizens with vocational education; but he was also calling for a revival of national concern for developing work motivation and preparation on the part of all youth. Policies of the United States Office of Education reflected this concern and wide federal support for career education programs undoubtedly stimulated the plethora of approaches that emerged. Many of these have been criticized as "old wine in new bottles," such criticism being geared to preserve former programs of vocational education; but reports of the new programs do suggest a considerable enlargement of opportunities for high school youth to be counseled and instructed in careers and career development. Some two years after his first pronouncements on career education, Marland, by then Assistant Secre-

---

[57] For the complete text of this speech, see William M. Alexander, *The Changing High School Curriculum: Readings*, 2d ed. (New York: Holt, Rinehart and Winston, 1972), pp. 191–199.

tary for Education, Department of Health, Education, and Welfare, noted his satisfactions with the subsequent developments:

> What is truly remarkable about the past two years is the ground swell of enthusiasm and support for career education that has come from nearly every segment of our national life. In my conversations and correspondence with state and federal legislators, with business, industry, labor and civic leaders, with ethnic and women's groups, with college presidents and professors, and with students themselves, I have noted a genuine, almost urgent, sense of commitment. It is as though everyone had arrived independently but simultaneously at the same conclusion. I am pleased to have had the opportunity to give that concern and commitment a national focus and, in financial terms, a federal thrust that now runs to considerably more than $100 million a year.[58]

Innovations for career education have been of many types, although the United States Office of Education has underway research and development activities on four national career education models: school-based, employer-based, rural-residential, and a "home-community effort which would use TV and radio announcements to encourage unemployed adults to take advantage of local retraining programs."[59] Characteristic of most local programs is the extension of career guidance activities, the involvement of community planning and work experience, and the increased provision of career exploratory and training options. For example, the Portland, Oregon, Schools' Office of Career Education described the activities required for developing a comprehensive offering of occupational preparation programs in grades 10 to 12, preceded by orientation to occupations in grades 1 to 6 and occupational exploration in grades 7 to 10, as the following:

a. Assessing the programs and program resources presently available.
b. Continuously assessing the various interests, ability levels, and aptitudes of students as they progress through the career development program.
c. Determining current and projected manpower needs and employment opportunities.
d. Establishing and maintaining strong links with business and industry.
e. Evaluating on-going occupational programs.
f. Developing exemplary programs.

[58] Sidney P. Marland, Jr., "The School's Role in Career Development," *Educational Leadership*, 30:204 (December 1972). Also see Marland's "Career Education: A Report," *Bulletin of the National Association of Secondary School Principals*, 57: 1–10 (March 1973).

[59] See Peter P. Muirhead, "Career Education: The First Steps Show Promise," *Phi Delta Kappan*, 54:370–372 (February 1973) for a brief identification of the models and other USOE programs.

A basic group of curriculums will be developed in each of the high schools and, in addition, a variety of special programs, designed to meet special needs, will be offered in one or more schools or as special district-wide programs.[60]

The Dallas, Texas, schools offer a different approach in the comprehensive "magnet" Skyline High School. Students from the entire city district may apply for Skyline (4000 students applied in 1971–1972 for 2000 openings in the Career Development Center). Skyline is three schools in one: a comprehensive senior high school for students in its area; a Career Development Center in which students from other high schools spend three hours per day in one of twenty-eight career clusters of related courses; and a Center for Community Services offering a full program of continuation and evening courses. The Career Development Center was described in a popular article as making Skyline "significantly different from most other high schools."[61]

Even at the high school level much career education is of a highly exploratory nature. For example, the Oxbow High School of Bradford, Vermont, developed a "Career Life Investigation Program," which allows students to work a half-day a week in any occupation at no pay for the purpose of investigating what the career offers him. This program is not intended to train a student for a vocation but to expose him to a possible occupational area. After two years of the program, about one-fifth of the school population had been involved in this program in such areas as X-ray, dentistry, butchering, various professional offices, and teaching.

One of the major challenges in career education is the marshalling and coordinating of the many resources available in media, community, and school that can contribute to career development. For example, a listing of published printed materials, films, filmstrips, slides, tapes and transcriptions, and other materials nationally available on career education for grades 10 to 12, required fifty-four pages in a 1972 publication.[62] Add to this the local materials and agencies related to careers in general and to specific careers, and one has a mass of resources to be checked, screened, related, utilized, and evaluated. Some skepticism about programs of career education make the evaluation phases especially important. For example, the National Urban League in 1972 devoted the Vol. 1, No. 1, issue of its publication *EPIC* to career education, noting its "potential threat to the educational options open to America's Black and urban poor." Cer-

[60] Office of Career Education, Portland Public Schools, A *Program of Career Education in Portland Public Schools* (Portland, Ore.: The Schools, June 1971), p. 8.

[61] See "Skyline: The School with Something for Everyone," *Saturday Review*, 55: 37–40 (November 11, 1972).

[62] See Harry N. Drier, Jr. and Associates, *K–12 Guide for Integrating Career Development into Local Curriculum* (Worthington, Ohio: Charles A. Jones Publishing Co., 1972).

tain key questions suggested by this publication to be asked about career education programs are shown in the excerpt.

Analysis of Educational Programs: How It's Done

Below are key questions you should ask as these programs are being planned and implemented in your community. It is important that all programs be carefully monitored if they are to mean improved educational opportunities for our children.

A. THE PROGRAM
1. Who is planning the program?
2. What are the realistic alternatives to this kind of program for minority students?
3. Who will direct the program?
4. How will the program be evaluated?

C. THE STUDENT
1. Will the program meet the needs of minority students? How?
2. What part will a student play in planning his program schedule?
3. What can a student expect at the completion of the program? A degree? A diploma? A job?
4. What are a student's alternatives: (pre- and post-program entrance)?

B. THE SELECTION PROCESS
1. What process will be used to identify the needs of the target population? Who will do the identifying?
2. What process will be used to recommend the eligible students? Who will do the recommending?

D. ANALYSIS
1. What does the sponsor have to gain? Lose?
2. What are the implications for response from concerned community residents?
    (a) immediate
    (b) long-range

From The National Urban League, Inc., "The Crisis of Career Education," EPIC, 1:6 (Summer 1972).

Drug Abuse Education

Critical social problems have long been finding their way into the school curriculum when legal and extralegal pressures cause the creation of a new focus in existing subjects, or of a new subject, or of a group of activities that compete with, or in rare cases supplant, existing subjects and/or activities. Career education tends to be an enlargement and expansion of existing programs of vocational education. The critical problem of drug abuse in the United States has long been reflected in various laws pertaining to the teaching of units or other types of instruction about drugs, but no consistent, successful pattern of drug abuse education was known when the drug use situation in the country came to be widely recognized as a critically important problem in the late 1960s. Such teaching as was done about drugs had been a unit here and there perhaps in science or an occasional assembly program. The mounting public interest and concern that led to the Federal Drug Education Act of 1970 and many new state statutes and regulations could not be satisfied by renaming some existing program. The millions of dollars to be spent for drug abuse education must be put to use in new and better ways.

And so the schools and all the groups concerned, from parents to law enforcement agencies, continue searching for answers to an old but currently acute problem: how to develop personal attitudes that will prevent drug addiction. One answer, of course, is to teach the young the facts about drugs, their use and abuse; a somewhat moralistic approach to the subject has been the traditional way of handling it. Authoritative groups have sought to develop superior curriculum guides and teaching materials to implement the factual approach. For example, an especially well-developed guide, *Teaching About Drugs, A Curriculum Guide, K–12*, was prepared by the American School Health Association and the Pharmaceutical Manufacturers Association (first edition, 1970; second, 1971), and promoted with the cooperation of leading professional education associations. The point of view stated in the introduction to this material indicated clearly that the authors understood the limitation of educating by teaching facts alone in dealing with the drug problem:

> . . . it is imperative that accurate scientific information be made available to those who are charged with the education of youth. Educators need a clear understanding of the facts in order to make the unbiased presentation of these facts their classroom objective. At the same time, it must be realized that knowledge alone will not change behavior. Actual behavior, particularly with respect to drug use and abuse, will always be influenced profoundly by individual personality, attitudes and values.
>
> Therefore teaching about potentially dangerous drugs or other products should start in the early school years and continue throughout the school experience. Effective education in the constructive use of drugs can be assured only by conscious planning to integrate the subject with the total health education program. In this way, the pupil can receive, with the proper emphasis throughout his entire school life, the necessary comprehensive instruction about the relation of drugs to total health.[63]

This guide provides, in a four-column arrangement, objectives, contents, learning activities, and resources and materials, for the lower elementary years, middle elementary years, early adolescent years, and later adolescent years. Objectives for the later adolescent years are:

A. To understand the widespread use of drugs in modern living.
B. To know and appreciate that a healthy person usually does not need drugs as an aid to performing daily activities.
C. To recognize that drugs, when misused or abused, cause serious problems.

[63] American School Health Association and Pharmaceutical Manufacturers Association, *Teaching About Drugs: A Curriculum Guide, K–12* (Kent, Ohio: American School Health Association, 1971), p. xiii.

D. To know and employ resources against illegal and unwise use of drugs.
E. To realize that drug control is complicated by many factors and considerations.
F. To comprehend the need for qualified personnel in drug control.
G. To know that individual responsibility is an important factor in effective drug control.

Undoubtedly the materials developed through such processes as involved in and recommended by this guide are very useful in high schools whose personnel are seriously attempting carefully planned programs including, but aiming at more than, information about drugs and drug abuse. Schools' experience with drug abuse education fully confirms the point of view that information alone does not achieve the behavior sought; this is emphasized in "Facts Alone Are Not Enough," the title of an article on drug education in *Learning* for February, 1973. This article commented favorably upon programs which aimed to build the self-image of children rather than "simply giving the facts about drugs, simply trying to frighten kids away from experimenting," and cited as such programs those in Newington, Connecticut; Montague, Massachusetts; Coronado and Orange County, California.

An excellent review of "The Ups and Downs of Drug-Abuse Education," also confirming the more-than-facts-needed argument, offers these suggestions from extensive experience in the New York City schools, as to school modifications that "have worked in New York and are worth pursuing":

1. Providing situations ["sanctuaries"] different from the normal school environment, "where students have a chance to focus on their own concerns and problems, work out alternative ways to handle them, and receive the support they need to implement these alternatives" [rap sessions and temporary alternative schools cited as examples].
2. Using such noncertified teaching personnel in the drug prevention program as former drug users.
3. Giving students themselves major responsibility for drug education programs: "The content of student-led programs seems less important than the extent to which the process of student involvement creates a kind of 'counter-peer' pressure against the use of drugs and generates student initiative in developing alternatives to drug abuse."
4. Creating "positive alternatives" to drug abuse, "ranging from Yoga and other ways of achieving mechanical 'highs' to programs that taking a clue from the Black Panthers, emphasize political and economic action as an alternative to drug abuse."[64]

[64] Richard H. de Lone, "The Ups and Downs of Drug-Abuse Education," *Saturday Review of Education*, 55:27–32 (November 11, 1972).

A report of the program at the Carmel, California, High School, also emphasized the more-than-knowledge approach, stating that at Carmel the idea of an "instant, easy answer" was abandoned, and this clue adopted: "That to dredge drugs out of the schools' systems and the students' systems, you have to concentrate not on the *drugs*, but on the *students*—on their needs, problems, pressures, and hangups."[65] This report emphasized as the crucial actions at Carmel which reversed the drug tide there, first, "a bold long overdue revamping of the school administration so that students were afforded a true voice in decision-making at every level of school government," and, second, the employment as community counselor, of "a man equipped to educate students, teachers, parents, and all segments of the community about every aspect of the drug culture." Among the changes at Carmel were: elimination of the dress code; increased responsibility to student councils; institution of new courses wanted by students and teachers; making the last two years of high school entirely elective; proliferation of sports (as alternative to drugs); initiation of many new noncompetitive activities; operation of a huge pottery shop; elimination of film material on drugs; holding community meetings with parents; adoption of a community-wide drug education program, emphasizing teacher education.

The great interest in drug education has resulted in the commercial development of many drug education programs, kits, and packages, as they are variously called. Especially in view of the sensitive nature of this curriculum area, and of the possible costliness of instruction and of the materials, local groups considering the introduction of new programs would do well to make careful analyses of the available materials. A product development report by the American Institutes for Research, of the Creative Learning Group Drug Education Program is a useful model of such an analysis; this report includes a description of the product, explanation of its origins and development and own evaluation, if any, and a description of its diffusion and adoption.[66] The report also includes a statement as to the possible future of the product and a recapitulation of the critical decisions made in its development. No evaluation is given by the analysts, but the data provided should facilitate judgments by readers as to the usefulness of the program in their own situations.

[65] Barbara Lewis, "How One High School Licked Its Drug Problem," *Family Circle*, June 1971, p. 46.

[66] See Lorna J. Thompson and Daniel W. Kratochvil, *The Creative Learning Group Drug Education Program Developed by the Creative Learning Group*. Product Development Report No. 6 (Palo Alto, Calif.: American Institutes for Research in the Behavioral Sciences, December 1971).

Environmental Education

Mounting concern in the 1970s over such problems as pollution, depletion of natural resources, increasing world population, and others considered as "the population/environment crisis" were reflected, as social problems are inevitably reflected, in demands for more and better educational programs—especially in ecology or environmental education. Certainly much of the relevant content had long been included in such approaches as nature study, conservation education, outdoor education, biology, and population studies. But the new demand was for meaningful and better-coordinated programs that would result in understanding of and changed behavior toward the problem, defined by one writer in these terms: "When we speak of the overpopulation/environment crisis, we are really referring to a concept of biological 'carrying capacity'—how many people can our world-wide ecosystem support at what level of material affluence for how long?"[67]

A publication of the United States Office of Education reviewing various approaches to environmental education took this position:

> The challenge for formal education is the establishment of curricula with relevant ecological content, presented in a way to meet the present high motivation of students. This means that we must take advantage of all opportunities to relate learning experiences to actual environmental improvement and problem solving in the community (frequently referred to as "issue orientation").
>
> The school must divorce itself from the traditional classroom concept and expand its frame of reference to make full use of all community resources in the curriculum. Environmental study areas, museums, libraries, local businesses and industries, and local governmental agencies all have a role to play in formal education.[68]

This publication considered as "less desirable" at the primary and secondary level, new courses called environmental studies. However, the 1970–1971 United States Office of Education survey of secondary school enrollments noted the impact of interest in environmental problems on creating such courses:

> This concern with the environment and its protection was reflected in new courses entitled Environmental Problems, Ecology, and Environmen-

---

[67] Richard L. Harriman, "The Ecology Backlash: How Close to the Brink Are We?", *Phi Delta Kappan*, 53:229 (December 1971).

[68] From *Environmental Education: Education That Cannot Wait* (United States Office of Education, 1971), quoted in Cornelius J. Troost and Harold Altman (Eds.), *Environmental Education: A Sourcebook* (New York: Wiley, 1972), pp. 262–263.

tal Sciences, with 5.5 percent of schools offering at least one of these courses. In addition, the percent of schools offering earth science increased from 5.2 in 1961–62 to 29.8 in 1970–71. The pretest study did not measure the extent to which schools also offer environmental education as individual units within traditional natural or social science courses.[69]

Observation suggests that the most frequent approach to environmental education remains the individual unit within an existing science course. Troost described the provisions in several national curriculum projects for ecology content: Intermediate Science Curriculum Study; Educational Research Council of America—Life Science; Engineering Concepts Curriculum Project; Biological Sciences Curriculum Study; Population Curriculum Study of the University of Delaware; Earth Science Curriculum Project; and various activities of the American Association for the Advancement of Science.[70] There is also a national curriculum project, Environment Studies Project, headquartered at Boulder, Colorado, aiming to develop materials that can be used at any level and in any subject.

The use of field trips and local resource studies is critical in environmental education. The entire 813-square-miles watershed of the Cuyahoga River in Ohio is being used for exploration of ways to stem the steady advance of pollution. Environmental studies using this watershed were reported in early 1973 as involving student–teacher teams in the following school districts: Cleveland, East Cleveland, Beachwood, Akron, Kent, Independence, Middlefield, and Burton. Also participating in these studies were two private schools, University School in Hunting Valley, and Western Reserve Academy in Hudson; one Catholic school, St. Patrick's Elementary, Cleveland; and Cleveland's South Euclid-Lyndhurst Community Environment Center.[71] This project, funded by the United States Office of Education under the Environmental Education Act and managed by the Cleveland-based nonprofit Institute for Environmental Education, is regarded as a model for training teachers and developing curriculums to teach "how the urgent problems of a disintegrating environment might be solved."

Illustrative of other approaches toward specific aspects of environmental education which also use local resources is the Mercer Island, Washington, organic gardening project in which each student gets a 9 x 9-foot plot to plant and tend, with all students cooperatively cultivating three acres

[69] Gertler and Barker, Patterns of Course Offerings and Enrollments in Public Secondary Schools, 1970–1971, p. 6.

[70] Cornelius J. Troost, "Curriculum Projects with Ecology Content," in Environmental Education: A Sourcebook, pp. 346–350.

[71] See Walter Wood, "Ecological Drums along the Cuyahoga," American Education, 9:15–21 (January–February 1973).

of gardens, a cornfield, an orchard and flower beds, and tending compost and mulch piles. In Kanawha County, West Virginia, fourteen high school drop-outs started growing organic foods on a 3.5-acre plot given them by the county school system. The Staten Island Institute of Arts and Sciences serves children living and attending school in New York City; some 33,000 to 40,000 elementary school children have an opportunity at the Center to participate in natural laboratory lessons, field demonstrations, and improvement programs from grounds, trails, and structures. For the benefit of its students and those from other schools, the Musselman High School in Bunker Hill, West Virginia, maintains a museum of preserved biological specimens; a center for culturing, photographing, studying, and shipping living biological specimens to other schools; a two-acre environmental study area and outdoor classroom; and a consulting service for elementary teachers.

Family Life and Sex Education

Despite strenuous objections from some groups and even sporadic controversy after programs were introduced with widespread community participation in their planning, sex education plans had become generally accepted in many school districts by the early 1970s. Mounting divorce rates (especially from teen-age marriages), illegitimacy, and venereal disease made these plans seem essential to many citizens and educators. A Special Report, *Sex Education in Schools*, by the editors of *Education U.S.A.* included in a section on "What's Happening Now in Sex Education" reports of the development of state board policy statements in sixteen states, and brief illustrative descriptions of plans in process or being implemented in the Virgin Islands; Chicago; New York City; Baltimore; Washington, D.C.; Kansas City, Missouri; San Diego; Hayward (California) Unified School District; Evanston, Illinois; Keokuk, Iowa; Anne Arundel County, Maryland; Flint, Michigan; Moorestown Township, New Jersey; Fayette County, Michigan; Arlington County, Virginia; and Summit County, Ohio.

Sex education programs generally start earlier than high school, but the high school years may well be the "last chance," according to Dr. Mary Calderone, a well-recognized authority in this field:

> The upper grades, says Dr. Calderone, offer the "last chance" to arm the student with sound knowledge and attitudes about his sexuality. Once he gets into college it is too late, for he will take with him "his misconceptions, his incomplete information, his preconceptions, his experiences uninterpreted to himself whatever his sexual experience has been.[72]

[72] *Education U.S.A.* Staff, *Sex Education in Schools*, Special Report (Washington, D.C.: National School Public Relations Association, 1969), p. 25.

That the sex education programs had not yet reached most youth is confirmed by a 1970 study of young men in high school and beyond. Of the sample included, just over one-third said they had sex education in high school although the overwhelming majority wished they had been given such an opportunity.[73] At the high school level the approach seemingly best accepted is a course related to family life. Such a year course is required in the secondary schools of Dade County, Florida, with specific prescription only of venereal diseases instruction in grades 7 and 8. The family life course usually includes units on dating, marriage, and day-by-day family life, and parenthood. In one Dade County school, Miami Springs Senior High School, more than three-quarters of the students received sex education in a six-week program meeting one period per day; parents and community organizations were involved in planning and in maintaining the course.

The family living course (usually without "sex education" in its title) may be offered in home economics, sociology, or other departments or on an interdepartmental basis. "Family relations" was offered as a home economics course in 1970–1971 by more high schools than offered any other specialized home economics course—5853 or 22.3 percent of all secondary schools, although only 1.6 percent of all pupils enrolled were enrolled in these courses.

The most recent emphasis in family life education is education for parenthood. Data supporting the need for this emphasis include:

The national divorce rate for those married in their teens is three to four times higher than that of any other age group.

Among girls 17 and under, approximately 210,000 gave birth in the United States last year.

One in every ten 17-year-old girls in the country is a mother, and 16 percent of these girls have at least two children.[74]

The United States Office of Education and Office of Child Development are cooperating in a national program of Education for Parenthood, planned to be operating in at least 500 school districts by September 1973. Kruger's description of this program stated its objectives as follows:

Called Education for Parenthood, its immediate goal is to encourage the establishment of well-organized, expertly planned instruction in at

---

[73] Jerald G. Bachman, *Young Men in High School and Beyond: A Summary of Findings from the Youth in Transition Project* (Ann Arbor, Mich.: Institute for Social Research, The University of Michigan, May 1972), p. 36. Mimeographed.

[74] W. Stanley Kruger, "Teaching Parenthood," *American Education*, 8:25 (December 1972).

least 500 school districts by September of 1973 and . . . to continue to expand the coverage until parenthood education has become an integral part of secondary-school instruction in many schools across the Nation. The long-range objective is to help strengthen the family as the funda-mental unit in the American society by assuring that every youngster graduating from high school has received training in child development and parenthood. The program is also seen as having the ancillary purpose of serving as an introductory course for attracting more young people into careers as child care workers.[75]

A description of a course already in operation in the Montgomery County, Maryland, schools in 1972–1973, stressed the experience high school students have in caring for children three to five years old. Field sites included child development laboratories in the schools as well as child care centers. The report observed that "the small children themselves seem to be enjoying their early school exposure thoroughly," explaining further:

Classrooms are sometimes like a three-ring circus, with decorations and devices they may never see again in a school. Many of these are designed by the teen-age "parents" themselves—posters, mobiles, and even improvised "books" that teach the youngsters how to zip, fold, button, and tie.[76]

More extended and specific child-care training courses are also provided as a career education program. McGavock High School, Nashville, Tennes-see, for example, started a three-year course in 1971–1972, to prepare high school students for jobs in child-care service. A nursery school is operated at the school for the program, which includes classroom study, lab observa-tion and lab work in the nursery, field trips, and internship experiences in local child-care centers.

We see as a desirable trend the emergence of emphasis on the study of human development, including sexuality, as a replacement for isolated lessons on human reproduction, venereal diseases, dating, marriage, and child care. Each of these areas needs to be treated, and treated fully and carefully, but their sequencing on the continuum of human growth and development can make for a more balanced program of family life and sex education than occasional, unrelated units. Such a continuum can be developed with reference to the various school levels and subjects and its phases assigned therein for curriculum planning.

[75] Kruger, p. 26.
[76] Constance Stapleton, "Teaching Youngsters To Be Parents," *Parade*, March 11, 1973, p. 25.

Other Interdisciplinary and Multidisciplinary Programs

In addition to the four interdisciplinary areas just discussed, individual high schools offer a variety of courses that select and combine material from several disciplines. Especially common are *humanities* courses, offering various combinations of disciplines, selections of topics, and cooperative teaching arrangements.[77] Irrespective of the approach, however, the common focus of the courses is the study of man. Students are guided through these courses to examine the ideas of man, his modes of expression, and the forces influencing him. At Franklin-Simpson High School, Franklin, Kentucky, the course is a semester elective for juniors and seniors called "The Human Quest: Today's Issues," organized around these five thematic units and utilizing selected works from literature, religion, philosophy, music, art, and the theater:

    I. Man Is Emotional and Rational
    II. Contemporary Man Is Emotional and Rational
    III. Greek Man Is Emotional and Rational
    IV. Renaissance Man Is Emotional and Rational
    V. Re-evaluation of Contemporary Man

A course developed for two high schools in Council Bluffs, Iowa, was organized in these units:

    I. Man's Conflict with His Fellow Man
    II. Man's Conflict with Himself
    III. Man's Conflict with Nature
    IV. Man's Conflict with God[78]

The Crow Creek Reservation High School, Stephan, South Dakota, serving Indian students of Crow Creek Reservation and administered by a tribal school board appointed by the Fort Thompson Tribal Council, introduced in 1971–1972 an interdisciplinary course for freshmen and sophomores. A team of five teachers—in social studies, music, science, art, and language arts—organized the course around four themes: love, freedom, violence and nonviolence, and the mysterious.

A national curriculum project, "Exploring Human Nature," is being developed by the Education Development Center, Cambridge, Massachu-

[77] See Austin F. Droden, "The Second Coming of the Humanities," *Educational Leadership*, 30:612–614, for an evaluation of these courses and other provisions for the humanities.

[78] See Harold L. Chappell and John T. Metz, "Planning and Teaching a High School Humanities Course," *Bulletin of the National Association of Secondary School Principals*, 55:35–46 (March 1971) for a description of the development and implementation of this course.

setts, for a year course for juniors and seniors, that will be "cross-discipli-nary, cross-species, and cross cultural"; the themes of the course are:

I. The Roots of Human Behavior
II. The Family and Its Social Context
III. Coming of Age: Managing Maturity
IV. Cooperation, Conflict, and Competition

In February, 1973, the course was reported as being used on a pilot basis with about 1500 students, and Unit III was to be ready for general dis-tribution by 1973–1974.[79]

Among many examples of other innovative interdisciplinary programs, only a few can be cited here. The Whitmer High School, Toledo, Ohio, offers a multidisciplinary "General Studies Survival Curriculum," focusing on problem-solving processes and using a three-hour block of time and a four-member teaching team. The concept areas involved include psychol-ogy, consumer economics, environment, law and society, religion and values, ethnic studies, applied aesthetics, creative studies, occupations, futurisms, and patterns of life. The Browne and Nichols School, Cam-bridge, Massachusetts, one of the schools participating in the National Humanities Faculty three-year program on authority, offers a course in this connection called "The Limits of Law," described in the school catalogue supplement as:

> . . . a study of the relationship between the laws of society and the conscience and freedom of the individual. A number of recent court deci-sions will be studied, along with selections from Sophocles, Plato, and Mill.

A "Law and You(th)" program in the School District of the City of Niagara Falls, New York, is described by the district as "a course of study for high school students utilizing the area law enforcement agencies at all levels to inform, educate and improve the understanding of the law for the young adults in our community" and as "an effort to build a bridge of communication between some of the interested youth and the law enforcement agencies of our community."

"Deciding" is a program being developed by the College Entrance Examination Board to help secondary school students learn more about themselves and the personal, educational, and values choices open to them, and to develop skills of decision making. The program, first tested in grades 7 to 9, but planned to be extended to other levels, aims to help students, according to the CEEB announcement:

[79] See *NASSP Curriculum Report*, "At the Edge and Still Cutting," 2:2–4 (Feb-ruary 1973).

evaluate and utilize different sources of information

identify their values and translate these values into clear objectives

discover existing alternatives and possibly create new ones

recognize which decisions will have long-range significance

estimate risks and outcomes

learn more about themselves

identify and use decision-making strategies

gain practice in applying decision-making skills

Among other interdisciplinary areas represented by courses in some high schools are consumer education, aerospace, population studies, war and peace, and education itself. Some of these fields are aided by various national and regional agencies. For example, the continuing interest of the National Association of Secondary School Principals in consumer education is reflected in its publication, *The Consumer Educator*, a newsletter reporting many materials, projects, and other developments in this field. The Diablo Valley Education Project, Orinda, California, supported by the New York-based Center for War/Peace Studies, provides curriculum development and other services to develop and test curriculum materials and plans on war, peace, conflict, and social change. A grant from the South Dakota Department of Education enabled the Rapid City, South Dakota, schools to develop a three-week supplement to social studies classes on public education. The minicourse is based on a booklet developed in the district, entitled "Project Public Information," describing the role of various groups in education: the division of responsibilities for educational administration; school financing; and curriculum development.

Disciplines taught at the university level also find their way into the high school both in such interdisciplinary ways as illustrated in this section and as separate courses. A one-semester course entitled "Patterns in Human History" has been produced by the Anthropology Curriculum Study Project, as well as various materials useful in other courses. Psychology courses are becoming more common in high school; in 1970–1971 psychology was taught as a separate course in 140 Florida secondary schools.[80] A course in philosophy was introduced in ten Chicago area high schools in 1968.[81]

Many of the interdisciplinary programs, as well as many other cur-

---

[80] See Robert J. Stahl and J. Doyle Casteel, *The 1970–71 Study on the Status of Pre-College Psychology in the State of Florida: A Final Report* (Gainesville, Fla.: P. K. Yonge Laboratory School, University of Florida, November 1972). Mimeographed.

[81] See Donald D. Reber, "Philosophy—A Course for High School Students," *Bulletin of the National Association of Secondary School Principals*, 55:47–53 (March 1971).

riculum innovations described in this chapter, have aimed toward the goals of education influenced by the diversity of cultural, racial, and ethnic strands of our society. Recognizing the special demands these goals have placed on secondary schools and the multiplicity of curriculum, instructional, and other provisions made by the schools, the National Study of School Evaluation published in 1973 *Evaluation Guidelines for Multicultural-Multiracial Education*. Its justification is stated in this introductory paragraph:

> Every school within our nation's context has an imperative mission: To help prepare its students for life in a society composed of many different cultural, racial, and ethnic strands. The extent to which the school equips its young people to work and to live within a country characterized by an assortment of races, cultures, and life-styles, each mutually celebrated, is an important indicator of its relevance to contemporary youth and its overall quality.[82]

The pivotal points of the evaluation are the characteristics of the school and its community, the general philosophy and objectives of the school, and the commitments of the school to education for a pluralistic society.

INDIVIDUALIZATION AND INSTRUCTIONAL OBJECTIVES: COMPLEMENTING OR CONFLICTING?

The authors believe that the two most marked characteristics of curriculum change in the high schools in the 1970s are, first, the focus on the individual student, and, second, the emphasis on goal setting or instructional objectives. As these characteristics operate in the same school they may complement each other quite well, with each student's program planned in terms of his needs, interests, and capacities and with his progress toward his goals carefully and individually checked to stimulate and assist his continuing performance. But in another school individualization may be interpreted only as individualized instruction to attain minimum performance objectives that are uniform for all students. Continuing improvement of the high school must be directed toward the first complementary relationship of individualization and instructional objectives, and away from the latter conflicting one.

We described in Chapter 2 the various options increasingly made possible for the individual student, and in Chapter 4 we will further

---

[82] National Study of School Evaluation, *Evaluation Guidelines for Multicultural/ Multiracial Education* (Arlington, Va.: The Study, 1973), p. 1.

Miami Springs, Florida, Senior High School is dedicated to the individualizing of instruction. A program of "continuous progress" instruction is explained to some of those beginning participation.

examine organizational options such as alternative schools and flexible schedules. In this chapter have been described many curriculum options for new elective courses, new programs in the established areas, and new objectives for existing programs. As noted in Chapter 2, the required units of credit for high school graduation are even coming into question: The New Jersey State Board of Education has discarded the Carnegie unit system of accounting for high school credit, substituting alternatives of a "uniform credit" plan or individualized programs with "specified measurable instructional objectives" for a set number of courses to be completed. In Maryland a state advisory committee has recommended as one route to high school graduation a personalized program for each student, with approval of parents and the school.

If graduation requirements are made more flexible by substitution of performance criteria, it does not necessarily follow that individual differences are better served. The question is whether performance is still required in the same subjects for all students, and whether a minimum level of performance is specified for all. If so, we may have examinations as the actual graduation requirements. If on the other hand there are alternate requirements among learning opportunities, with performance keyed to the individual's choices and goals, individualization may be really achieved.

Minicourses

Probably the most widespread techniques for individualizing the curriculum are elective courses, especially the now popular short courses or minicourses, and various sytems of individualized instruction. The minicourses may be simply units within the required course, with little option for students, or they may represent many different interests. Illustrating the latter, optional plan, Hillcrest High School in Jamaica, New York, as one of New York State's newest high schools, does not require students to take first year English, but rather the student may choose from as many as fifty different courses in the four forty-five-day terms of the school year; this arrangement is available in every area.[83] At some schools minicourses have been designed by students as "free form" days or weeks. For example, New Trier High School, Winnetka, Illinois, in a three-day "Experiment in Free Form Education" in 1972 offered 400 minicourses "from dog training to French impressionistic art."[84] Development of a successful minicourse program in English and social studies at Northwest Ashe High School, Warrensville, North Carolina, brought about much curriculum change in other areas, with "micro-mini" courses for all students in home economics, micro-math courses for students in vocational education classes, and individualized mathematics instruction for freshmen, using upperclassmen to aid instructors and students.

Another variant of minicourses is the "mini-term" program at Mariner High School, Mukilteo, Washington, where students enroll in two fifteen-week terms and elect one of the two six-week terms. In a recent year in addition to numerous short-term offerings of regular subjects, the following enrichment courses were offered during the mini-terms:

Boys' and Girls' Sports Programs
International Cultures
Wowie (World of Work in Education)
Greek and Roman Drama
Modern War (Causes and Effects)
Home Design
Fine Arts Appreciation
Girls' Auto Mechanics
Marine Field Biology
Minority Cultures
Film Analysis
Future Teachers of America Elementary Observation Program
Natural History of the Cascades
Pre-School Program for Three- to Five-Year-Olds
Stitchery
Personal Typing
Boys' Home Economics
Radio
Photography
Anthropology
Introduction to Computers

[83] See Daniel A. Salman, "New Options for Urban Secondary Education," *Bulletin of the National Association of Secondary School Principals*, 57:34–42 (February 1973).

[84] See "Flirting with Free Forming," *Nation's Schools*, 90:25–28 (July 1972).

As a part of the 1973 Sisseton, South Dakota, High School interim and mini course project, students were given opportunity to participate in survival training. Each was allowed a shelter cloth, bed roll, water, a small amount of beef jerky, and two matches. They were isolated in groups of two for a period of thirty-six hours and could not contact the other pairs. The experience was offered to both boys and girls.

Alternative schools (see Chapter 4) offer students not only the option of attending them, but many choices in their programs. The program of the Cambridge, Massachusetts, School, for example, has emphasized humanities on a nontracked, elective basis, with students taking most of their science, some mathematics and language, and all their shop and gym classes at the two regular high schools. Electives in social studies and English are described in one report as follows:

> Social studies electives have included such topics as Cambridge neighborhood studies, women's liberation, Vietnamese culture, law and student rights, native American history and culture, and child development (including work as teacher's aides in one of several local nursery schools). English electives have ranged from mythology to "Monsters in Literature" to "Great Books" to media and journalism to creative writing.

This description also notes that "many trips leave the school—to the wilderness for solocamping, to Cape Cod for a week as part of an environmental studies program, to a Vermont farm to help bring in the harvest, to a nearby state prison, to traditional schools, and other alternative schools in Philadelphia, Boston, and Vermont."[85] The options in many other alternative schools are equally wide, although varying with the purposes of the school and the resources of its community.

Individualized Instruction

As noted earlier, individualizing instruction is the other most widespread technique for focusing schooling on the individual. But whether individualized instruction truly serves individual needs, interests, and capacities depends very much on the type of individualized instruction used. Edling has made a useful classification of types as follows:[86]

MEDIA	OBJECTIVES	
	School-determined	Learner-selected
School-determined	Type A Individually diagnosed and prescribed	Type B Personalized
Learner-selected	Type C Self-directed	Type D Independent study

As we see it, Type A is the form of individualized instruction that is most prevalent; it is programed instruction with only the learner's beginning point and rate of progress varying from those of other learners. Thus it is somewhat characteristic of performance-based curriculum plans having identical objectives and performance standards for all learners. Such plans are relatively common in all curriculum areas and sequences in which skills predominate—for example, reading, typing, mechanical drawing.

Instructional systems (see pages 181–184) now available in many curriculum areas tend to utilize Type A individualized instruction almost exclusively. Obviously it is impossible for the producer of learning packages (see Chapter 6) for a wide national market to anticipate each learner's own objectives, although alternative sequences provided in some materials do permit variations for the learner's selection. And if specific performance criteria are anticipated, the producer of learning systems must provide devices for diagnosis or preassessment. These devices can be self-selected. In Type B the learner chooses his objectives, and in Type C he chooses the media, but observation indicates that teachers are rarely

[85] Robert C. Riordan, *Alternative Schools in Action* (Bloomington, Ind.: Phi Delta Kappa Educational Foundation, 1972), p. 15. See this "fastback" for description of the Cambridge Pilot School and the Metro High School, Chicago.

[86] Jack V. Edling, *Individualized Instruction*, No. 16 in the Series of PREP Reports (Washington, D.C.: U.S. Government Printing Office, 1972), p. 2.

willing to allow Types B and C activities, even if the package permits it. As for Type D, independent study (see Chapter 4) is uniquely a student-selected objectives and media program, and performance objectives and criteria must be individually developed, if used at all.

In concluding the present discussion of individualization and performance objectives (also see Chapters 5 and 6), it should be emphasized that neither notion is wholly innovative. High schools have long sought to serve the individual differences of their students, but only within the relatively recent past have so many options become available to students and so many instructional organizations and techniques emphasized individual rather than group instruction. High schools have also long sought to modify the behavior or performance of their students, but only relatively recently have instructional systems become so specific in their objectives and measures of performance as to make possible some reasonable assurance that some types of performance can be anticipated and demonstrated. Such systems can be developed locally,[87] although there is a growing body of commercially produced materials—learning systems, minisystems, learning packages, learning kits, instructional programs, as they are variously called—which are organized on or adapted to, an instructional design using behavioral objectives, preassessment, learning activities, postassessment, and performance criteria or similar sequences of a systems approach to instruction.

Thus the schools have today a much better chance of attaining their long-time goals of individualization and behavioral change. If the flexibility required for individualization can be retained in the alternatives written into objectives-based curriculum plans, these long-time goals can finally be achieved.

additional suggestions for further study

1. American Association of School Administrators, *Curriculum Handbook for School Executives*, Arlington, Va.: The Association, 1973. Authors representing professional associations of sixteen curriculum areas contributed chapters identifying emerging concepts in curriculum content, in the organization and application of knowledge, and

[87] See as examples of specific guidelines for preparing curriculum materials for individualized instruction utilizing performance-type objectives, Sidney J. Drumheller, *Handbook of Curriculum Design for Individualized Instruction: A Systems Approach* (Englewood Cliffs, N.J.: Educational Technology Publications, 1971), and Philip G. Kapfer and Glen F. Ovard, *Preparing and Using Individualized Learning Packages for Ungraded, Continuous Progress Education* (Englewood Cliffs, N.J.: Educational Technology Publications, 1971).

emerging methods of instruction. The handbook provides an overview of trends in curriculum developments.

2. Brown, B. Frank, *New Directions for the Comprehensive High School*. West Nyack, N.Y.: Parker, 1972. Disagreeing with the Conant recommendations (1959) and holding that there is today more emphasis on comprehensiveness in the British comprehensive high school than their American counterparts, Brown espouses his own formulas for improvement, including nongradedness, independent study, grouping, better vocational education, and year-round schools.

3. Cole, Henry P., *Process Education: The New Direction for Elementary–Secondary Schools*. Englewood Cliffs, N.J.: Educational Technology Publications, 1972. Definitive presentation of the theory of process education. Includes attention to steps and roles in implementing a process design.

4. Helgeson, Stanley L., Patricia E. Blosser, and Robert W. Howe, *Environmental Education Programs and Materials*. PREP Report No. 33. Washington, D.C.: U.S. Government Printing Office, 1972. Reviews research and other publications on environmental education, presents case studies of school programs, and has extensive descriptions of selected instructional programs, projects, and materials.

5. Inlow, Gail M., *The Emergent in Curriculum*, 2d ed. New York: Wiley, 1972. Social change, influences of radical educational reform, sensitivity, a new breed of students, and educational accountability are described as curriculum inputs. Controversial curriculum components are included in the discussion as well as the status of traditional subject-matter fields.

6. Saxe, Richard W. (Ed.), *Opening The Schools: Alternative Ways of Learning*. Berkeley, Calif.: McCutchan, 1972. Presents in Part Three, "Public School Alternatives," seventeen descriptions, by as many authors, of alternatives, defined as "activities to accomplish one or another objective of the curriculum and which do not take place within the regular classroom" (p. v).

7. Seyura, Flora and others, *Sex and Sex Education: A Bibliography*. New York: Bowker, 1973. Compilation of some 2300 works in this area as a comprehensive guide for parents, teachers, and others.

8. Special Task Force to the Secretary of Health, Education, and Welfare, *Work in America*. Cambridge, Mass.: MIT Press, 1973. A basic analysis of work conditions and problems in the United States that should be considered in any redesign of the high school's vocational education program.

9. Travers, Kenneth J., John W. LeDuc, and Garth E. Runion, *Teaching Resources for Low-Achieving Mathematics Classes*. PREP Report No. 30. Washington, D.C.: U.S. Government Printing Office, 1971. Includes summarization of research on characteristics of low achievers in mathematics, and reviews curriculum and instructional aids. Extensive bibliography of resources for teachers and their students.

10. Trump, J. Lloyd, and Delmas F. Miller, *Secondary School Curriculum Improvement*, 2d ed. Rockleigh, N.J.: Allyn and Bacon, 1973. The second edition of this popular text presents developments in high school curriculum, instruction and organization, and devotes four useful chapters (28–31) to procedures for improvement.

4

The Organization:
Toward Openness

Despite the difficulties of throwing off the weight of tradition, new concepts of time and attendance are appearing in high schools in all parts of the country: urban, suburban, and rural. New arrangements for opening the organization include year-round programs, four-day weeks, exit-entry plans, evening high schools, flexible schedules, open campus plans, alternative schools, and others. These are being interrelated with new curriculum content, humanistic ideals, development of students' self-responsibility, intercultural understandings, development of modern learning theories and methods of inquiry, attention to new uses of resources, and involvement with the world beyond the classroom.

New options in organizational arrangements are providing more opportunities for teachers and students to spend time when, where, and how they perceive it is needed. Options for providing flexibility are not mere manipulations designed to provide variety and relieve boredom but are far-reaching changes that recognize the uniqueness of individuals. Thoughtful educators are taking the position that if each student is to learn successfully and at his optimum rate and in an optimum manner, schools must eliminate some of the more rigid time and attendance conditions that can hinder individual progress.

The success of new organizational arrangements depends on the degree to which the secondary school becomes more personalized, meets the needs of individual students, and facilitates and encourages each student's progress. Effects on the learner as perceived by the learner are the most valuable type of data with which to assess the impact of any of the new organizational arrangements discussed in this chapter. These arrangements may be said to be successful to the degree that the learner believes that:

1. He can succeed and his progress is largely dependent on his own efforts.
2. His preferences and individual performance can influence selections for his program of studies.
3. He has choice in selecting instructional methods, materials, and other resources to suit his individual learning style.
4. He perceives the school staff and his peers primarily as human resources to further learning rather than as persons in dictatorial or competitive roles.
5. The student engages in work and learning activities when unsupervised and continues his learnings beyond the school premises.

But making organizational changes to meet perceptions such as these is not easy. Possibly one of the most difficult changes to make in a secondary school is a change in the conventional school schedule. Long years of custom and tradition and the pressures of the Carnegie unit have forced schools into the time-honored mold of fixed scheduling. The 8:30 to 3:00, September to June, pattern has been such an accepted part of Americana that schools are finding it necessary to involve their communities in planning before departing from the standard schedule. By so doing they will avoid the need for defensive tactics later, when citizens question why high school students are off campus during school time or are in the schoolhouse in evenings and summers. Careful planning and preparation are essential not only with regard to community attitudes but also state attendance laws, graduation requirements, and a host of other contingencies.

NEW CONCEPTS OF TIME AND ATTENDANCE

Innovations in the use of clock time and calendar time are appearing in a number of different forms. Descriptions follow of new practices that express changing views of school requirements for attendance. The continuum concept, discussed and illustrated in Chapter 2, underlies a number of the innovations presented here.

High School Graduation Requirements

Requirements for graduation imposed on high schools by state regulations are being widely amended and modified. In the past, state departments of education frequently required specific courses, a fixed number of calendar years of attendance, and use of the Carnegie unit system of measuring graduation credits. Recent changes made by several states give more latitude to local school boards, provide more flexibility in number of hours, days, or years to be spent in high school, and allow credit for educational experiences far different from the traditional six-period day in school with credit awarded for time spent in the classroom.

Newer regulations are based on student goals and accomplishments. In Oregon, the state board has adopted new requirements that are goal and competency oriented. Florida offers a performance program which allows a student to graduate without regard to credits or length of time in school upon fulfilling objectives previously outlined by teachers with participation by administrators, students, and the community. Florida students can also graduate early after completing ten credits if they are admitted to an accredited college. The State Department of Education of Missouri has revised its regulations to permit local school boards to make more of the decisions on requirements. Twenty credits are needed for graduation, earned in grades 9 through 12, with no specific courses named by the state, except that six credits must be earned from among the subject fields of communication skills, mathematics, social studies, and science plus one credit each in fine arts, practical arts, and physical education. As many as two achievement credits may be granted to students on the basis of advanced work and test scores. Credit for off-campus instructional programs may also be granted.

At the local level, districts in other states are making changes in graduation requirements. Specific course requirements have been altered by Sparks High School near Reno, Nevada, where the English department has removed the sequential requirement of freshmen, sophomore, and junior English for graduation. All students may now choose any course from a lengthy list of English courses offered each school year. Each course description is identified by a phase number which indicates the difficulty and complexity of the skills perceived. Students may select courses from any phase as they perceive their own abilities. Three credit hours are still required for graduation but these may be selected from a wide variety of courses.

The San Mateo Union High School District of California has removed graduation requirements that are spelled out in terms of class attendance and completion of certain courses. New requirements, although not incompatible with previous course instruction, emphasize demonstrated performance in specific expectancies instead. A similar plan is in effect at Dominican High School of Omaha, Nebraska. Students are no longer required to take a specific number of courses in English and mathematics to receive a diploma but must achieve a minimal level of performance in the basic skills in these subject areas. When the student has achieved this level, he may then select advanced course work in either or both subjects or devote his attention elsewhere.

School Attendance

Several factors are influencing the development of new interpretations of school attendance requirements. As noted in Chapter 1, compulsory attendance laws are being questioned from more than one point of view. In the large cities, attendance laws are virtually unenforceable and the existence of such laws puts an unnecessary repressive strain on the institution. Suspension or expulsion is a threat that does not frighten thousands of students who see themselves as captives of the school. Forced attendance, it can be observed, does not necessarily produce learning. The problem is not confined to large city schools.

Although analysts of the compulsory attendance situation concede that compulsory attendance laws will very likely stay on the books, such laws may become irrelevant without being repealed. Schools, by incorporating greater flexibility in attendance requirements, may be able to achieve "compulsory education" by diminishing the importance of "compulsory attendance." For example, various types of voucher systems have been proposed which would provide the student with the financial equivalent of his education in the public school so that he could make a free choice of educational institutions, thus expanding options and stimulating diversity. Vouchers could be exchanged for a vast range of educational services such as tutorials, apprenticeships, concerts, cable television, counseling services, and others. However, current experimentation with vouchers has been at the elementary and junior high school levels, with arrangements for children and parents to choose a particular style of school from among the schools of a district.

To overcome negative effects of compulsory school attendance, several kinds of adaptations are being made by high schools. A unique example of combining several organizational elements into a restructured educational program is that of Union High School of Grant County, West Virginia, a small rural high school. To release students from the constrictions of traditional attendance requirements, Union High School has reconstructed the school year into four quarters, the school day into modules, and the school week into four days of academic studies and one day in a work-activity. A work-activity is not defined as a work-study program or a make-work program, nor is it an activity to assist economically deprived children to earn money in order to afford to come to school. A work-activity is a personal and appropriate experience specifically chosen or designed to assist the individual to reach his goals. The high school has developed a placement office and a job bank to support the program. The job bank holds descriptions of various work-activity opportunities, and a comprehensive file on each student which details his interests, abilities, and other relevant information. Credit is received for the work-activity and there may or may not be pay.

The scope and variety of work activities are almost unlimited and are created through the imaginativeness and inventiveness of the students, the school staff, and the community. Relating to various interests of students are work activities in which a student may spend his day of work each week in a veterinarian's office, in a primary classroom as a teacher aide, preparing a nutritional meal for a home-bound invalid, assisting in a gasoline station or automotive shop, observing or performing duties in the various offices of the county courthouse, working with the county agricultural agent, assisting a social worker in a community betterment program, working in a retail sales establishment, or spending one day a week as a helper in a hospital, doctor's office, or dentist's office.

Students may enter, leave, and re-enter Union High's program as personal needs arise. There are no punitive consequences for leaves of absence. The flexibility of the year, week, and day permits continuing adaptations to the needs of students.

The Year-Round School

Increasing attention is being given to possibilities for using calendar time more effectively in various interpretations of the year-round school. Again, these involve organizational changes that have numerous ramifications. Changing from the traditional September-to-June school year (plus a remedial or enrichment summer program) to a genuine year-round operation is not an innovation to be lightly assumed. The roots of the traditional school year go very deep. Children were needed in our formerly agrarian society to assist with the crops, and school was not considered to be feasible in the summer anyway, as classwork was difficult when temperatures were high. This pattern has prevailed not only in America but in other countries. The fact that relatively few young people are needed on the farms in modern society and that technology has produced readily available air conditioning has removed the two most commonly cited reasons for the seasonal school year. Opposition to change frequently comes from school administrators who are unconvinced of the need for or the benefit from scheduling change. Many parents resist the thought of taking away children's summer vacation months, a custom which seems as American as apple pie. Also, in most states the present state aid formula which reimburses districts only for 180 days of schooling, excluding the summer months, has severely limited extensive development of the year-round concept.

Nevertheless, interest and experimentation are constantly increasing. In 1970 the Education Commission of States formally adopted a resolution which recommended that "the Education Commission of the States have as a major program element the promotion of the extended school year concept through identification of barriers to implementation; legal, financial and instructional implications and methods of implementing these concepts; and further to keep states informed concerning the latest developments in these areas."[1] Support from another source is the National Council on Year-Round Education, headquartered at the Virginia Polytechnic Institute. From these organizations, publicity, stimulation of research, and dissemination of ideas and promising practices are emanating.

Several states are studying year-round proposals and experimenting with plans, including Kentucky, Georgia, Delaware, Illinois, Missouri, Michigan, Florida, New York, Wyoming, Washington, and Pennsylvania. The year-round program, if established for the purpose of saving money by rotating students in and out of a traditional program over a staggered year's schedule, may bring disappointing results. Fundamental to the success of year-round education is a rationale for improving the quality of learning. Advocates of year-round systems are not in favor of requiring attendance for twelve months of school, but rather are proposing that the program be available all year. Students could remain in the nine month cycles, or could choose to go for longer periods of time if they wished, could complete high school requirements in less time than usual, or could enter and exit at varying times to suit individual, family, or community-life patterns.

Advocates of early graduation—that is, acceleration that permits students to complete the conventional school span of years in less time and at an earlier age than usual—recommend this procedure only for those who would benefit because of greater opportunities offered for discovering and/or developing potentialities. Early graduation programs are generally arranged only for students who have a definite plan to follow on departing from high school: entry into higher education, into a job as a beginning step on a career ladder, or work at an interim activity preceding further education. Indeed, the exit–entry pattern of schooling and work could continue throughout life.

A number of reasons can be given in support of the year-round concept. Many city officials and other citizens have learned to dread the summer months when youths are on the streets with little to do and are

[1] See "Exploring the School Year" issue of *Compact*, 4:3–49 (December 1970).

easily attracted toward activities that contribute to delinquency. Vandalism of school buildings presently peaks in the summer time. Year-round operation of schools could enhance the professionalization of teachers and permit ambitious, highly motivated teachers to be employed twelve months of the year at commensurately higher salaries. Flexibility in teaching contracts could permit variable teaching loads of less than a year for teachers whose aspirations are modest.

The humaneness factor in keeping schools open all year recognizes that life styles are changing. Construction work, carpentry, and other outdoor occupations prohibit family vacations in the summer. Industries are offering contracts with varying vacation periods. Winter vacations are becoming popular with the ease of travel to warm climates or winter sports areas. Therefore, many families that presently cannot take a vacation together would have opportunities to do so. Year-round opportunities provide more ways to reach the uniqueness of individuals by providing for different rates of learning or for patterns of learning that alternate in-school and out-of-school learnings. Under most year-round school plans a child can enter school at the beginning of the period nearest his school-entrance-qualifying birthday, thus enabling him to get a favorable start with his formal education. As he progresses, he would benefit by newly designed curriculum with shorter, more flexible subject content designed for the flexible time schedule of the year-round school. At the high school level he should find an interesting array of subject matter from which to choose, and if he selected an unsuitable subject the time wasted with it would not be as long and costly as in today's program. Opportunities for the high school student to intermingle work, community experiences, or travel with his school schedule would be greatly increased.

The economic factor is not to be overlooked. Although proponents of the year-round programs express caution in viewing the concept primarily as a money saver, and point out that quality year-round programs may cost more than traditional programs, still it is possible that there would be economic benefits. On a cost-effectiveness basis, it is most likely that more satisfying and effective learning for students can take place for the same or even less cost. Year-round options for student attendance or acceleration are estimated to reduce the school enrollment from two-thirds to four-fifths of the total school population in the school building at any one time. These plans might substantially reduce the need for new construction and reduce some of the pressure for additional taxes. Fewer buses, textbooks, reference materials, teaching machines, language labs, and laboratory equipment would be required at a given time to serve the total enrollment. Even a potential saving of only 1 or 2 percent in the operating budget cannot be disregarded by competent school administrators.

The following year-round education plans have been suggested or are being practiced by a number of school districts.

mandatory four-quarter plan. In this plan students are divided into four sections and the school is operated on a four-quarter basis. Each section of students is in school three of the four quarters of the year, and the sections are rotated in such a way that only three sections are in attendance each quarter, thus limiting attendance at any one time to 75 percent of the total enrollment. Major reasons for this plan are to cut operating expenses and avoid or limit new construction.

optional four-quarter plan. Several school systems of Georgia and the Jefferson County Schools of Kentucky are operating an optional four-quarter plan at the secondary level. The stated purpose of the program is to increase the quality of education, not to save money. In each case, the curriculum has been revised to provide a wider range of optional courses and to occupy the student's time during the summer. In Atlanta, beginning in the fall of 1968, a four-quarter school program was implemented in twenty-six high schools. The program was designed to be as flexible as possible and the redesigned curriculum presented challenging educational opportunities through which each student could experience success without becoming bored or discouraged. The equivalent of a regular load for three quarters is expected of each student. However, he has a choice as to which three quarters he will attend and whether he will take a full or partial load each quarter. The number of pupils working part time and scheduling work experience as part of the school day increased significantly within the first two years of the program. Significant increases are taking place in the percentage of students enrolling during the summer quarter.

45–15 plan. A variation of the four-quarter plan is the 45–15 system in which the student attends school for 45 days and is on vacation for 15 school days. All students are in school during all four quarters. Prince William County, Virginia, after experimenting with the 45–15 plan in elementary and junior high schools, put it in operation in all schools including the high schools. Prince William expects to offer an additional option to high school students in the form of a multiple entry and exit system; this would give students numerous options for attending classes, including the conventional school year.

eleven-month plan. Basically different from four-quarter designs, the eleven-month plan proposes to operate school for eleven months of the year instead of nine. In this way students could complete the traditional twelve years of work in ten. This plan was proposed by the National Conference of Lieutenant Governors in 1969 as a result of a five-year study in the state of New York. Experimentation with variations of the eleven-month plan is encouraged in New York State, but it has not been widely adopted at this time.

concept six. In Jefferson County, Colorado, a year-round plan is known as "Concept Six." The school calendar starts in January and continues through December with the school year divided into six equal-length segments. Students attend classes four terms and choose their vacations during the other two. A fifth term is available as an option for enrichment, remediation, or acceleration at no expense to the individual. Teachers work the normal 184-day work year but may choose to teach 215 days if enrollments permit. One-third of the students enrolled may be on vacation at one time. Various combinations of schooling and vacationing are available. The year-long courses have been broken down into multiple in-depth units of nine weeks, comprised of performance-based elements and, whenever possible, are nonsequential in nature. The intent is to make self-paced learning a reality for students and to promote maximum exploration and enrichment. Students at all grade levels may be rescheduled or regrouped every nine weeks and at other intervals if desirable. Single-section elective courses at the secondary level as well as large teaching teams with differentiated staffing are offered.

quinmester plan. Florida is one of the states that has enacted legislation to allow districts to develop year-round education programs. The intent of the legislation is to encourage innovations. K through 12 programs are included in the concept, as are community-college programs and those of universities. Florida is more interested in expanding the extended school year than in merely extending the regular school year.

The high schools of Dade County, Florida, are offering the quinmester plan and have divided the school year into five nine-week sessions of forty-five school days each. Each pupil may elect to attend any four quinmesters during the school year in order to fulfill the present state requirements of 180 instructional days. A student may also accelerate his program by attending all five quinmesters for a total of 225 instructional days. Educational advantages to the plan are said to be these: (1) It provides a richer curriculum by offering a variety of minicourses that can be related to one subject—for example, American literature—which can reach a diversity of interests and aptitudes. A student may choose any four offerings to earn a year's credit. (2) The quinmester plan encourages scholastic experimentation. The student may try a new subject at no great risk. If, after nine weeks of chemistry, for example, he decides not to pursue the subject further he may drop it in favor of something else. (3) It has the potential to reduce failure. The student need not fail a full-year course. If he is failing a nine-week course, he would lose only one-quarter of a year and his problem could be more easily remedied by shifting to a more suitable option the following quarter.

flexible all-year school plan. Perhaps the most unique year-round plan in operation is the flexible all-year approach. With no beginning or ending of the school year, and with both instruction and time individualized, the school operates in such a way that any student or teacher may take his vacation any time of the year for any length of time needed, then return to school without loss of continuity. High school students usually attend school on a regular basis except when attending college courses, participating in training programs, working, or some other important activity. The student may then return periodically to the high school without loss of continuity. A student cannot fail at the end of the year, as there is no end, nor is there any beginning to be sent back to and no need to repeat the year. States an advocate:

> The Flexible All-year School probably will emerge as the institution most capable of meeting the educational needs of the technologically advanced, rapidly changing society because it is designed to adapt to the needs of the individual and the changing society and because it is designed to make optimum use of time. In the long run such a school likely will be the most economically efficient as well.[2]

The Wilson Campus School of Mankato State College, Minnesota, is experimenting with a completely individualized, personalized in-and-out flexible all-year school plan in which students may come and go as their personal, community, or family life-style needs are met. A research-demonstration model of the flexible all-year school is being developed at Clarion State College, Pennsylvania, as a learning systems component of the Research-Learning Center.

Evening High School

New concepts of time are affecting not only new calendar arrangements but also time-of-day arrangements. Las Vegas, Nevada, offers a complete high school program beginning at 4:30 P.M. and continuing until 10:00 P.M. In a building facility which is used during the day for its normal capacity of 2500 students, another 500 students begin their school day in the late afternoon. The evening high school is not offered because the school is overcrowded, nor is it set up for discipline cases, nor primarily for working students. All of the students enrolled in the program voluntarily and the student body represents a cross secton of the school population. Many do work during the day and there are some who have had

---

[2] John McLain, "Developing Flexible All-Year Schools," *Educational Leadership*, 28:475 (February 1971).

problems in school. However, most of the students chose the evening high school because of the greater flexibility in the program and greater opportunities for students to determine and design programs of instruction.

Similarly, Pasadena, California, provides an evening high school with approximately 200 students enrolled in grades 9 through 12, from 4:30 to 9:30 P.M., Monday through Thursday. Because of the unique opportunity offered by creation of a new high school in the evening hours, students have been more than customarily involved in decisions about the organization and program of the school, including budget decisions, regulations for student behavior, scheduling of courses, and curricular content decisions. Although students found these responsibilities to be more arduous than they had expected, the evening high school continues to attract working students and other capable and motivated students from the regular high school.

Miami Springs Senior High School, Florida, has opened an evening high school on a pilot basis by offering several elective courses. As Miami Springs utilizes college-type scheduling with an open-campus plan whereby students come to classes at various times throughout the day, rather than being assigned to one specific session, the evening program offers still more opportunities for student selection of class time. University City, Missouri, offers high school credit for numerous courses in the evening classes of the School for Continuing Education. Previously the evening program had attracted only adults, but has now been opened to students of all ages who mingle in various courses.

Continuation High Schools

Continuation high schools are unlike the evening high schools described above or the alternative high schools described later in this chapter in that they are expressly organized for divergent students who would otherwise drop out of school. Both the evening high schools and the alternative high schools are designed to serve a cross section of students who either prefer to come to school at nonconventional times of day or who prefer to have much more personal involvement in designing their own learning experiences. California is unique among the fifty states in its widespread attempts to provide educational programs for would-be drop-outs under the age of eighteen. While many states legally provide for special schools or classes for truants or incorrigibles, actual implementation is a local option. The NEA's annual reports on state school legislation have revealed no state thus far that approaches the size and scope of continuation education in California. Students served by the continuation high schools include those who have had excessive truancy and behavioral problems; students with emotional problems which may have been caused by low academic achievement; girls who are pregnant (married or unmarried) and young mothers; students who are entering school late in a semester, possibly because they are returning from camp, juvenile or foster home placements; and a few who attend because they or their parents feel a need for smaller classes and increased opportunities for success.

For most students who attend continuation classes, the required time is three hours per day. A student who is regularly employed may fulfill a minimum requirement of four hours per week. In California, continuation schools may operate during regular school hours as independent units within another school or may operate in buildings separate from the schools. Some continuation schools are held after school hours or on Saturdays. The unique features of the program of continuation high school programs include an individualized approach, orientation toward guidance and counseling rather than subject matter and academic achievement, deliberate and conscious use of short-term goals and frequent rewards, autonomy of the school to plan flexible programs suitable to individual needs, and opportunities for meaningful relationships with adults including both staff and interested citizens. The word "continuation" is being dropped from the title in many cases.

Innovative programs for potential drop-outs have also appeared in other parts of the country in recent years. An example is an experimental high school in Tulsa, Oklahoma, housed in an annex of one of the elementary schools. Tulsa's experimental high school offers morning and afternoon sessions of three hours each for two different groups of students. Classes are small and informal, adaptable to individual student needs, and take advantage of many types of field learning opportunities and a variety of materials and teaching techniques.

A Four-day School Week

Initially developed to curb rising school costs, a four-day school week in Maine's School Administrative District Number 3 produced educational benefits as well, and continued in a strengthened plan after a one-year experimental program. The school district is composed of eleven communities in central Maine and serves approximately 1700 students, K through 12. In the fall of 1971, the state board of education gave cautious permission by placing limits on the number of four-day weeks for the first year. An evaluation plan was designed in cooperation with the state department of education. For the first year, Fridays were dropped from the school calendar from September through December. From January to March, every other Friday was dropped and from March until June, one of four Fridays was dropped. Thirty-five minutes were added to each school day. Fridays, while free days for students, were in-service days for teachers.

Special four-hour workshops geared to individualized instruction were conducted every Friday morning when students were not in school, so that teachers could study new teaching and learning methods to be implemented during the week.

Evaluation included both attitudinal and achievement measures. Achievement on a standardized testing battery indicated that gains clearly outweighed losses when considering the grade equivalent scores of all students tested. Parents, students, and faculty expressed satisfaction with the four-day week program and students expressed positive attitudes toward their school experience. Teachers felt that they had been able to implement more effective teaching changes. The in-service education program was found to be a particularly strong asset of the program. Teacher training sessions had far greater impact because they took place on Friday mornings rather than late afternoons on school days. The success of the experiment was endorsed by the Board of Directors of the Maine School Administrative District Number 3, who voted that the entire school year following the first experimental year should consist of four-day student weeks. Teachers and administrators would continue their workshop activities each Friday.

Another four-day week plan is being piloted at Shrewsbury High School in Massachusetts; however, here it is designed to solve an overcrowding problem. Students may choose from among three schedule

Mount View, Maine, High School students and faculty participate in a Friday workshop activity designed to improve education through total community involvement in the decision-making process. (Photo by Darrell Hubbs)

options, one of which is a four-day week in which each day is extended by two hours. The new plan has made it possible to add more than 100 electives to the schedule and to serve 1600 students in a facility designed for 1200. The Massachusetts State Board of Education has stated that it regards the plan as a test which may provide a desirable model for other schools in the state.

Four days to teach and one day to plan have been built into the high school schedule for teachers, while students are still scheduled for five consecutive days of classes at the Altmar-Parish-Williamstown (New York) Central School. By reducing an eight-period day to a seven-period day, the same amount of instructional time is provided in four days that was formerly allotted to five days. One subject is omitted each day which provides large blocks of planning time, organized by departments. In-service education is a regular part of the school's program.

MODIFYING THE TRADITIONAL ORGANIZATION

The traditional and still dominant instructional organization is the "class," typically consisting of from twenty-five to thirty learners and a teacher of the subject. Since the fifties, high schools have been seeking modifications of the traditional organization and variations are becoming more and more common. A formula widely known earlier as the "Trump Plan,"[3] in which large and small group instruction provided unscheduled time for students to pursue independent study and planning time for teachers to work as teams, gained considerable strength during the sixties. However, to the disappointment of many innovators, a substantial proportion of students in some high schools did not use their unscheduled time wisely and problems of students wandering around, skipping classes, creating discipline problems, plus thefts and vandalism, caused a tightening up in many schools. If the high school was one that experienced a student revolt during the activism period of the late sixties, it probably also hastily reverted to a traditional organization as an expedient rather than a developmental solution to a deeper problem.

Schools that have included wide involvement of teachers, students, parents, and administrators in planning modified organizations have continued to create effective innovations, and new practices seem to be increasing again after a temporary slump. These include a multitude of flexible scheduling arrangements and alternative organizational units.

[3] J. Lloyd Trump was director of the sponsoring organization: the National Association of Secondary School Principals Commission on Staff Utilization.

Flexible Scheduling

More openness is being introduced into the organization of traditional high schools by modification of schedules. Variations in scheduling range from moderate flexibility within the conventional school building and school day to "open campus" schedules that extend into the homes and community and disregard standard school hours.

Flexible scheduling is one of several interdependent practices and has little effectiveness except in combination with other closely related procedures. Both students and teachers must give attention to the development of new roles. Students must be involved in selection of their own goals and attain them by making productive choices from among a range of means and resources. Teachers must assume greater participation in curriculum planning, in the development of new instructional methods more consistent with individual student abilities, and develop adaptability for large-group, small-group, and individual instruction. The prime objective of flexible-modular scheduling is improvement in the quality of education; it has been defined as follows:

> Flexible scheduling is an operating framework characterized by classes of unequal length which meet at differing periods throughout the week and which are geared to the individual needs of students. Flexible scheduling may vary from merely rearranging time allotments and sequences of established courses to a complex modular approach in which schedules for each student are generated daily and picked up by the student each morning.[4]

Although there are innumerable variations of flexible schedules, some major categories can be identified:

1. *Block schedules.* One or more teaching teams have identical schedules which permit joint planning time. Opportunities for large- and small-group instruction, independent study, and wider use of resources are provided.
2. *Open-lab schedules.* A student is required to attend all his classes, but is free to choose an activity during nonclass time, which may include studying in a voluntary study hall, the library, a departmental study area, or in an open laboratory. He may use the time for conferring with a teacher or counselor, participation in a noncredit seminar, or in a part-time job.
3. *Rotating schedules.* Many alternatives can be designed into this type of schedule. An example is fitting a seven-period day in six periods with

---

[4] James E. Heathman and Alyce J. Nafziger, *Scheduling for Flexibility: A Manual for Administrators of Small Schools* (Las Cruces: ERIC Clearinghouse on Rural Education and Small Schools, 1971) p. 3.

constant rotation so that each class meets four times a week and each day has a different schedule. More courses can be offered while retaining the six-period day. Another type of rotation is to schedule variable time blocks so that each course has some longer and some shorter periods in a week's time.

4. *Flexible modular scheduling.* While appearing in slightly different format in various high schools, flexible modular scheduling has several basic characteristics. Modular scheduling is designed to break the rigidity of the traditional six-period or seven-period day. It is based on dividing the school day into periods of time called modules. A module might be twenty, twenty-six, or some other number of minutes. Class periods vary in length by utilizing more or fewer modules depending on optimum conditions for each situation. Opportunities are provided for large class activities, small group discussion and independent study. Usually, no class meets five days a week and often no two days are alike. A portion of the student's day is unscheduled and intended to be used for independent study, meetings with counselors and teachers, work in open labs, and so forth.

Although many schools prefer hand scheduling for moderately flexible schedules, others utilize computer services. In either case, secondary school administrators need special preparation and training for the complex task of scheduling if the important variables of individual differences, learning processes, and a wide range of methodologies and resources are to be brought together in a complex but effective program. A flexible modular schedule is difficult to generate manually and usually involves the use of a computer. A widely known computerized system of scheduling is the Stanford School Scheduling System (S–4 or SSSS). This system utilizes the computer to provide maximum freedom in choosing a schedule reflecting the abilities and interests of students and the special qualifications of teachers, students, rooms, and limits of time, thereby satisfying a high percentage of student schedule requests. Marshall High School in Portland, Oregon, and North Miami Senior High School, Florida, are among high schools using the Stanford School Scheduling System.

Parkland Senior High School of Winston-Salem, North Carolina, operates its program on a flexible modular schedule of 26-minute modules and three-day cycles. Athens High School in Ohio divides the school day into twenty-seven 15-minute modules and a five-day cycle. Andrew Lewis High School, of Salem, Virginia, utilizes 17-minute modules and a six-day cycle. In all three high schools the modular schedule allows for different types of large and small group instruction and provides a reasonable portion of the student's day to be unscheduled. It is emphasized in each school that this does not mean play time. A student who demonstrates an inability to utilize his unscheduled time constructively soon finds that he has lost the privilege and has been assigned to a supervised area. The description of Andrew Lewis High School that follows is not unlike the program of the others.

The Andrew Lewis schedule is computer-built. The scheduling utilized is the GASP Program (Generalized Academic Scheduling Program). Features of the instructional program include varied class length, frequency, and size; team teaching; a six-day cycle; and no study halls for most students. Unscheduled time is called GAIN time, an acronym for Going Ahead INdependently, which can be spent in a variety of locations and activities. Study halls are provided only for those who fail to cope with the freedom of unscheduled time. Three general phases of instruction are lecture-demonstration, lab, and interaction. Many courses include all of these phases. The lecture-demonstration phase may reach twelve to one hundred sixty students, meet one to three times per cycle, and be 34 or 51 minutes long. It is the chief vehicle for the presentation of course content and is intended to inform and stimulate interest. Students are expected to listen, observe, and take notes.

Laboratory groups usually include twelve to forty-five students, may meet one to five times per cycle, and be 51 to 102 minutes long. Laboratory work is included in almost every course at Andrew Lewis. All labs are open; that is, students other than those scheduled into a lab may attend labs for independent study purposes if work stations are available. Structured labs are scheduled for students in a specific course of study such as Chemistry A or Chemistry B. Mixed or departmental labs may include students from several courses. For example, students from several English courses may all be scheduled into the English lab at the same time. Here the focus is on independent study and individualized instruction and the teacher in charge acts as a tutor and resource person rather than as a classroom teacher in the traditional sense. Unscheduled labs are meant for students during their GAIN time.

An interaction phase includes six to eighteen students, one to three meetings per cycle, and each meeting is 51 to 68 minutes long. As in most schools which employ the large–small group concept, interaction in the small group is the focal point of the instructional program. Interaction is closely tied to both lab and lecture-demonstration and provides a forum in which content and concepts can be explored in depth. This phase of instruction is chiefly student-oriented and several well-designed small-group techniques are utilized.

The program at Andrew Lewis has been developing over several years with constant attention to improving deficiencies that occasionally appear. Five times as many students used the library in 1973 as in 1968. More students than before are coming to the guidance office to discuss personal or academic problems or to browse through the literature on display. Two other high schools of Roanoke County follow a similar program.

Independent Study

Although not a new idea, independent study is worthy of discussion as an organizational component because of its application in a variety of settings. Frequently used as an option in otherwise traditional schools, independent study also is an important part of flexible-modular scheduling programs and is finding interpretations in the newer alternative schools. Uses of the term "independent study" as a convenient label for study time, unassigned time, or conventional homework are to be distinguished from independent study in the sense it is used here: to achieve the broad goal of developing the self-directed learner. Independent study is defined here as "independent" of the class and of uniform class assignments, but is under the supervision of the school's faculty.

Independent study is based on the premise that real learning can take place only when the desire to learn comes from within the individual. As this desire does not spring forth full-blown in all students, it is the teacher's responsibility, beginning in the early years in school and with increasing attention in the secondary years, to help students develop the skills needed for pursuing a study independently. It is important for students to develop the will to assume more and more self-responsibility for learning in recognition of the reality that almost all learning after high school, whether in college or on a job, is a form of independent study requiring self-direction and self-discipline from each individual.

Independent study in high school must be student-motivated rather than teacher-assigned and is individualized but not identical with individualized instruction or individual study, either of which could include pieces of work without the depth and cohesive quality of an independent study program. Independent study emphasizes that the student has moved from dependence on teacher-selected objectives and criteria for evaluation toward self-directed education in which the student determines his objectives in relation to his particular needs and interests and is able to evaluate whether or not the objectives are being achieved.[5]

High schools frequently issue a written statement to their students, advising them of the opportunities available for independent study and the student's responsibilities for it. An example is Whitmer High School, Toledo, Ohio, where it is possible for a student to do the majority of his work on independent study if certain conditions are met. Students must take the initiative and apply for permission to engage in independent study. If accepted, they come to school as usual and work in labs, library,

---

[5] William M. Alexander, Vynce A. Hynes, and Associates, *Independent Study in Secondary Schools* (New York: Holt, Rinehart and Winston, 1967), pp. 83–87. For a follow-up report see also William M. Alexander and William I. Burke, "Independent Study in Secondary Schools," *Interchange*, 3:101–113 (Numbers 2–3, 1972).

or other work areas for the minimum attendance requirement but with alternate times of day available. They must be present in class for physical education, vocational education, and instrumental and vocal music. Otherwise, all subjects may be studied in full-time independent study. An Independent Study Team of faculty members guides the program, constantly working with the students to adjust and improve it. The classroom teacher's role is that of advisor and resource person. During the first week of a new term, the student, classroom teacher, and team member meet to discuss the student's proposed course of study including objectives, subject material, and arrangements for testing.

Similarly, in the Independent Study program of the Kent County Public Schools, Chestertown, Maryland, a student must request independent study of his own volition; in no case is he under compulsion to undertake it. The independent study period is flexible and may run for a week or as long as an entire year. Teacher and student work out an agreement in advance including purpose, topic, duration, class exemptions, provisions for consultations with the teacher, and plans for evaluation of the work. The student is encouraged to develop the ability to self-evaluate his finished product, study methods, motivation, and sources of information. Evaluation of the product may be in the form of appraisal of a formal research paper, a written evaluation by student and/or teacher, an interview with one or more persons knowledgeable on the topic, or by some other method.

Open Campus

A number of high schools are instituting open campus plans in which students may leave the school premises when not scheduled for classes. Frequently, it is regarded as a privilege to be reserved for seniors, but other forms of open campus or open scheduling are also appearing.

In Idaho, the Coeur d'Alene Senior High School, which enrolls only eleventh and twelfth graders, has a semi-open campus in which the students arrive at eight or nine o'clock, complete four, five, or six classes consecutively as they desire, then are free to go home or go to work as they and their parents may request; or they may stay for a study hour until the close of the school day. The decision on each student's plan is made at enrollment time.

In an open scheduling plan adopted by Dominican High School, Omaha, Nebraska, students are not assigned specific hours during which to report for work, except for classes necessarily involving groups such as physical education and chorus. The frequency with which a student confers with his teacher in any given class depends on his needs and the facility he has in accomplishing his work. Faculty members are available for conferences, direction, and evaluation throughout the school day and on certain evenings each week. The purpose of the open scheduling plan is to help each student assume personal responsibility for his own use of time. Faculty advisors assist students in planning their use of time and evaluate schedules when needed.

Advantages of an open campus plan include increased accommodation for students and better use of teacher time. Lawrence High School in Falmouth, Massachusetts, found that 1200 students could be comfortably housed in a school originally designed for 950 students with its open-campus organization. Jones High School, Beeville, Texas, increased its capacity from 970 to 1200 students by combining open campus with an extended school day. When teachers are freed from study hall assignments and hall duty, more time can be built in to plan and prepare lessons, have individual conferences with students, and engage in competency-development activities.

The James Madison Memorial Senior High School of Madison, Wisconsin, has moved within a few years from a school which, although scheduled modularly, was essentially traditional in curriculum, student activities, and control, to an open-campus plan supported by several other innovations. An advisor–advisee program is especially important. Every professional staff member, as the advisor to a number of student advisees, meets with them regularly to monitor progress, discuss the use of unstructured time, assist with problems and concerns, and confer regarding educational decisions. The open campus plan is supported by continuous progress instruction, options in types of class schedules, grade reporting, and a variety of learning activities and resources.

Sisseton (South Dakota) High School, which has a large enrollment of Sante Sioux Indians, offers an open-campus plan to seniors as one of several innovations which include the teaching of the Dakota language and courses in American Indian studies.

School-within-a-School Organization

Growing concern for the need to personalize the education of high school students has stimulated various new interpretations of the school-within-a-school. An example is the Mini-School within Banning High School of Los Angeles. One hundred tenth-graders whose junior high records indicate some academic insecurities are selected for the program. A four-hour core program includes English, science, math, driver education, guidance, and health. Planned activities include daily-demand scheduling in a flexible pattern, independent study, field trips, listening to outside speakers, and other provisions for attention to individual interests.

An experimental school-within-a-school enrolling 150 students in grades 9 through 12 is housed in and is part of Oak Park and River Forest High School of Oak Park, Illinois. The program is organized around an open classroom concept in which students assume responsibilities for deciding what credits are needed, what must be done to fulfill these credits, and seeking resource help as needed. Faculty members are there to advise and to teach but it is the student's responsibility to seek assistance from the teachers. In most cases, students contract for a plan of study which usually includes independent study, class study, or a combination of the two. Community resources are available to support both experimental and traditional courses. Students may choose from pass–fail, letter grades, or credit–no credit. The latter is the most frequent choice. The majority of students in the program go on to college.

A unique school-within-a-school organizational arrangement is Horton Watkins High School of Ladue, Missouri. Horton Watkins offers two intermingled programs within its 1600-student facility. A program called "Innovation" is housed with the traditional program of the school. Introduced in the fall of 1967, Innovation enrolled 400 students during its first year and within five years expanded to include all 1600 students for English and 1100 others who were taking at least one course in Innovation. Students all understand the concept represented by the term Innovation and when a student says, "I take science in Innovation," the others know what he is talking about.

Five academic areas are included in Innovation: English, social studies, math, science, and foreign languages. In each case, the five class periods per week allotted to these subjects are spent in large-group instruction, seminar discussions, and individual study periods. Experimental courses are also available in art, home economics, and power mechanics. Students may combine Innovation courses and regular school courses in their overall schedules. For Innovation courses, teachers have prepared "packages" that outline the course in two-week segments and provide individual activities to complete the unit. In social studies, for example, the traditional tenth-grade program consists of a one-semester Survey of Western Civilization and one semester Survey of Four Countries to make up a year's course in World History. This course uses closed circuit television and team teaching. In the junior year, students remaining in the traditional program take American History and may elect American Principles as seniors. In the Innovation program, social studies is arranged in quarter topics and at each grade level a student may select from among seven or eight topics, each of which uses the inductive approach with a stress on critical thinking. Independent study, scheduled into the Innovation program, gives the student wide latitude for choice from among topics.

The large high schools, concerned about the feeling of anonymity of many students, have frequently devised ways to organize smaller units within the school. For some years the Evanston, Illinois, Township High School has been organized as four semi-independent schools each with its own identity and student body of approximately 1200. Newton (Massachusetts) High School employs a house plan in which the school is divided into seven houses, each with a student population of 380 to 450 students. In organizational and other ways, schools are attempting to give more individual attention to each student.

ALTERNATIVE HIGH SCHOOLS

Within five years after Philadelphia opened its Parkway Program in 1969 with a new kind of high school known as the School without Walls, an estimated sixty public school districts began developing and operating about 200 alternative schools, mostly high schools. The public alternative schools followed the lead of privately organized "free" schools which were springing up by the score in the late 1960s.

Private and Public

The free schools outside of the public system range across a wide spectrum in terms of educational philosophy and location, from rural commune to ghetto storefront. A common assumption of all, however, is that public schools are not serving some children well. The goal of free schools is to foster self-respect and a sense of community through processes of shared decision making, in which students can assume a major role in determining the nature and direction of their own education. Many of the private free schools operate in settings closely tied to the community, utilizing community resources and working on community problems. The extent of private free schools has ranged in estimates from 200 to 1600 with a considered count in 1972 of 346 free schools, all levels, and an average school size of thirty-three students.[6] An example is Logos, a free school for students of high school age, which operates in a renovated warehouse in midtown St. Louis. "Logos is designed to fill the needs of students that were bypassed or ignored by the public schools," says a Logos brochure. Emphasis is on helping the severely alienated student to get a fresh outlook on life and begin to work toward constructive goals. Math, verbal, and general learning skills are taught, frequently on a tutorial basis. Stu-

---

[6] Allen Graubard, "The Free School Movement," *Harvard Educational Review,* 42:351–373 (August 1972).

dents use the city as a classroom and take courses leading to community involvement. Personal and vocational counseling help each student receive a personalized high school education and go on to college or a job after graduation.

Numerous free schools of the United States and Canada listed in past issues of the *New Schools Exchange* and the *New Schools Directory* (Santa Barbara, California) have come and gone within a few years time. Financing was precarious in many instances. In others, lofty goals were difficult to attain. Recent observers speculate that the "free school" movement is declining, and will continue to drop as public schools and conventional private schools increase diversification of programs and learning options.

The alternative school as an adjunct to the conventional high school is usually distinguishable from the school-within-a-school program in several ways. Common characteristics of public alternative schools are these:

1. The program or curriculum is signficantly different from the conventional or regular program.
2. The alternative school provides the students and their parents with a choice. If there is no free choice, the program would be little more than a grouping device.
3. Parents, students, and teachers are involved in the planning, development, operation, and evaluation of the alternative.
4. It is a total program, not just a short class or a part of the school day.
5. The location can be identified geographically from the regular school program, whether in a separate building, a wing of a school, a community facility, or a few designated classrooms.[7]

The separate geographical identification is an important feature of the public alternative high schools now operating. They are housed in storefronts, community facilities, refurbished homes, offices, and wings of existing school buildings. In some districts (e.g., Berkeley, Seattle, Minneapolis, and Philadelphia) there are multiple alternatives. The interest in educational alternatives suggests that the trend toward diversification in school offerings to reach individual learning styles and needs is gathering momentum.

Some cautions have been expressed by Fantini for public school systems considering the addition of an alternative school: no student, teacher, or parent should be assigned against his wish to an alternative school; the staff should avoid extravagant claims of the alternative's success or superiority as such statements tend to create a negative attitude in

---

[7] From *Changing Schools, An Occasional Newsletter on Alternative Schools,* Number 001, Educational Alternatives Project, Indiana University, Bloomington (undated), p. 16.

others; alternative schools must provide equal access to all students, not promote exclusivity for a group; finances must be kept within the normal school budget; the alternative school must be accountable for a comprehensive set of educational objectives, those for which the public school is accountable, and not merely selected ones.[8]

The Wayne County Intermediate School District, Detroit, sponsors a project known as Planning for Alternatives in Education, which has issued a list of optional educational programs in Michigan that meet the following criteria:

—they are voluntary, programs of choice, for most, if not all, of the students and teachers
—they involve teachers, students, and parents to some degree in planning, operating, and evaluating the program
—they are locally developed and share comprehensive educational objectives with other schools in the district
—they operate near per pupil costs customary for the district
—they seek diverse enrollments, students representative of the range in the district
—they are small in size, usually informal in style
—they stress basic communication and mathematical skills and nourish talents and interests
—they are options in core subject areas, not just enrichment or elective courses
—they have built-in accountability—if students do not choose them, they do not survive
—they meet requirements normal in the district or area
—often test out new management or administrative arrangements, different marking systems, cross-graded groups, multidisciplinary approaches.[9]

Efforts to provide students with alternative learning options within the public schools must recognize that there is no single panacea or strategy which can provide the answer to the many questions and challenges before education today. A wide diversity of ideas and programs can keep options open and serve as dynamic checks against each other. The tasks before education today are too important to relinquish the advantages that variety in programs offers. For example, some people like drill, discipline, and rigid structure; others prefer involvement in planning, self-direction, and discovery methods. The concept of educational alternatives is consistent with the democratic principle of freedom of individ-

[8] Mario Fantini, "Alternatives within Public Schools," *Phi Delta Kappan*, 54: 444–445 (March 1973).
[9] *Planning for Alternatives in Education* (newsletter), Wayne County Intermediate School District, Detroit, March 1973.

ual choice, the pluralistic nature of American culture, with the need for institutional self-renewal of public education, the need for financial conservation, and the need for community involvement in public education.

Alternative high schools span a broad spectrum of styles. Schools without walls and open schools stress self-directed learning and community-based experiences. Cultural and multicultural schools emphasize racial and ethnic studies. Community schools focus on student decision making. Learning centers accent special interest and skills in areas like ecology, futuristics, or the performing arts. Some examples follow.

Schools without Walls

The Parkway Program, Philadelphia's School without Walls, is organized into several units or "communities" each of which is limited to 180 students who have volunteered for the program. One of the most outstanding aspects of the Parkway Program is that it has no school building. Central headquarters are provided for each unit where teachers have office space and students have lockers, but all classes operate in community facilities. The finding of space is an activity shared by all members of the program, including students, and is considered an educational activity in itself. Learning options are offered in hospitals, museums, social agencies, and local businesses. For example, art students may be studying at the art museum, biology students at the zoo, and business and vocational students at newspaper offices, garages, and so on. Academic classes meet in churches, business conference rooms, vacant offices, and public lobbies. Often courses are traditional in content and learning objectives, but the diversity of locations and experiences has a strong appeal for students. Numerous other replications of Philadelphia's program are in operation in other cities, including Chicago, Boston, New Orleans, Cleveland, and Madison. The Gateway High School of New Orleans is housed in a community center and enrolls 145 students. Metro High School is an alternative high school without walls operating within the Chicago Public School System. A research program conducted by the Center for New Schools of Chicago is engaged in an analysis of fifteen interrelated topics for the purpose of gaining a detailed understanding of the processes and outcomes involved in attempts to establish alternative social institutions.

Open Schools

Open schools take the nongraded approach and allow students of different ages to work together in programs that accent informality, independence, and creativity; they are usually organized for elementary schools. The St. Paul (Minnesota) Open School is unique in that it enrolls students of ages five to eighteen. Most of the teachers are certified, but they

Parkway students learn basic electricity using the facilities and staff of the Philadelphia Gas Works, voluntary additions to the curriculum of the "school without walls."

are assisted by poets, artists, and other talented community volunteers. The St. Paul Open School is a research and demonstration project of the public school system. Key elements include major resource areas which provide an array of learning activities, integrated learnings, student-selection of courses and activities, utilization of resource people and of the community as a classroom, emphasis on cross-age grouping, heterogeneous student body, and shared decision making.

The teacher's role, in the St. Paul Open School, has changed from an information giver to a facilitator who arranges exciting learning experiences, clears obstacles which may hinder learning, suggests new possibilities, helps students with personal goals and purpose, and becomes a guide to resources. "Life skills" or competencies needed to be a successful person are important goals of the school. These include being articulate, knowing how to find information, and how to solve problems. Other life skills are critical thinking, reading skills, computation skills, physical fitness, and good health habits, as well as becoming able to cope with daily tasks and challenges. How one feels is considered to be important as well as what one knows. Positive self-concept, values, attitudes, a can-do spirit, acceptance of others, enthusiasm, responsibility, and initiative are also areas of emphasis in the learning activities of the Open School.

Community Schools

In community schools students and parents share policy making with professional educators. The extent of student power varies considerably from school to school, however. A community high school in Great Neck, New York, is known as the Village School. Teen-agers design their own programs and courses with assistance from teachers if called upon. Youngsters also select their instructors, evaluate their own progress, and suggest grades. The school serves approximately sixty-four students with four full-time faculty members and a number of part-time volunteers. The students are selected at random from those who apply and have the written permission of their parents. Courses cover a wide range of topics; the school extends beyond the confines of the building and is involved with nearby universities, the Great Neck Adult Education Program, a local senior citizens center, museums, and the two regular high schools of Great Neck. Independent studies and projects are featured in the program.

A program similar to the Village School, except that it is housed in a wing of the senior high school, is an alternative high school known as the Webster Community Campus of Webster Groves, Missouri. Each student may choose his own areas for investigation, and work outward from his basic interest or interests toward relevant skills, knowledge, philosophy, and application. The high school quarters serve as the main learning center but the student may earn credits in various community settings, at nearby Webster College or in the regular high school. Cubberly High School of Palo Alto, California, also housed within a regular high school, enrolls students who were not satisfied with their opportunities within the regular high school structure. Using their teachers as resources, these students define their goals and select activities.

Cultural and Multicultural Schools

Berkeley, California, has created an extraordinary set of several alternative schools, some of which are designed with a racial or multicultural emphasis. Berkeley's desegregated public schools serve 16,000 elementary and secondary students who are 45 percent black, 44 percent white, and 11 percent Chicano and Asian. The alternative schools enroll approximately one-quarter of the city's entire school population. Each alternative school is different from the others. All, however, state that they expect to deliver basic academic skills and work toward the elimination of institutional racism. Agora Alternative High School is designed to teach an appreciation of racial differences and keeps its staff and enrollment balanced at one-quarter each: white, black, Chicano, and Asian, and promises a structured multicultural experience for its 120 students. Black Perspective, open to all races, emphasizes attention to minority problems as does an Asian-emphasis alternative school, New Ark.

An experimental high school in Minneapolis is Marshall-University High School, an alternative high school offering multiple alternatives to a heterogeneous student population specifically dedicated to bringing different types of people together in an atmosphere of respect and trust. Its features include a program of wilderness and urban survival training, independent study, small-group counseling, and single-discipline choices.

Street Academies

Some of the earliest departures from convention in school program and facilities were the storefront schools or "street academies" that appeared in Chicago and New York in the mid-sixties. Before the term "alternative school" became widely used, these private schools, sponsored by foundations and corporations, were created to serve semiliterate, unemployed young people who had dropped out of school and seemed to have nothing to do but congregate on the inner-city streets. Sixteen street academies known as the Harlem Preparatory Schools were opened throughout Harlem, the Lower East Side, the South Bronx, and Brooklyn.

High school drop-outs, aged fifteen to twenty-five, many of whom had police records, were attracted to studies much different from the usual offerings. The schools gained the commitment and held the interest of most of their students and produced academic gains that were in some cases spectacular. After one year of operation, a substantial number of graduates, who previously had been headed nowhere, went on to college.

At the heart of the storefront program were street workers, young men and women, both black and white, who lived in the neighborhood and who were available literally all the time. The schools' facilities were simple. In one room there might be homemade equipment for scientific experiments; in another, a cluttered art studio; in another, a space whose only wall decorations were students' essays and poems. The storefront workers hoped that by bringing habitual truants and likely drop-outs from the street into the caring environment of the street academy, they would after a period of transition, move ahead in school and thence on the road toward a career.

The private street academies successfully provided a model that has been adopted by the public schools of New York City. As the private "start-up" funds phased out, the board of education began establishing alternate schools, known as minischools, affiliated with high schools throughout the city. Fifty to 100 students who were barely hanging on in the huge traditional high schools have been invited to enroll in each of the pilot minischools. A change of environment from the big school to makeshift quarters seems to reduce much of the tension that earlier prevented the students from succeeding. Teachers, whom the students have a part in selecting, tend to be young and deeply interested in rescuing students who might otherwise be lost. Wingate, one of the mini-schools, wrestles with problems of making math relevant to students who see abstractions as meaningless, while at the same time offering other students a Saturday morning computer technology course for credit. Students may earn credit for independent study, community service, work at agencies and institutions and even for time spent in detention, whether in a drug program or in jail. A carefully structured group counseling program is central to the school's success in dealing with students as people. The physical facilities are formed with brightly colored dividers in a previously vacant warehouse.

The alternative schools, as with other modifications of the organization and applications of new concepts of time and attendance, are expressions of the determination of educators to serve the diversity of students. The alternative schools seem to extrapolate and put together in new ways threads of ideas from contract methods, voucher education, cross-cultural programs, community schools, drop-out centers, and the schools-without-walls concept, and create significant alternative learning options that may find variations in every school district in America.

additional suggestions for further study

1. Bremer, John, and Michael von Moschzisker, *The School without Walls*. New York: Holt, Rinehart and Winston, 1971. Philadelphia's Parkway Program is described in detail with appraisal of its various aspects.
2. *Changing Schools*, a newsletter on alternative schools, published by the Educational Alternatives Project, Indiana University, Bloomington, is an excellent source of information on alternative public schools.
3. Florida State Department of Education, *Flexible Scheduling: A Vehicle for Change*. Tallahassee: The Department, 1972. Explicit descriptions are given of several types of flexible scheduling with diagrams for implementation and commentary on potentialities of each type.
4. Hillson, Maurie, and Joseph Bongo, *Continuous-Progress Education*. Chicago: Science Research, 1973. Useful to any educator, the book offers practical orientation to continuous progress, including such areas as recording, reporting, and community relations.
5. Hillson, Maurie, and Ronald T. Hyman (Eds.), *Change and Innovation in Elementary and Secondary Organization*. New York: Holt, Rinehart and Winston, 1971. Trends that can be noted in secondary school process and organization are identified by numerous writers who emphasize personalization of instruction, creation of new programs, collaborative or team efforts in education, and relevance in content and process.

6. Illich, Ivan, and others. *After Deschooling, What?* New York: Harper & Row, 1973. Illich reflects on the consequences of deschooling as do a number of critics who discuss the pros and cons of the idea.

7. Reimer, Everitt, *School Is Dead.* New York: Doubleday, 1971. A proposal to support Ivan Illich's *Deschooling Society* (New York, Harper & Row, 1971) is described. Reimer suggests a network system in which learning resources of all kinds, including people and media, would be readily available, thus replacing schools as they now exist.

8. Riordan, Robert C., *Alternative Schools in Action.* Bloomington, Indiana: Phi Delta Kappa Educational Foundation, 1972. Two public alternative high schools are discussed in detail with analytical comments in this "fastback" booklet.

9. Saxe, Richard W., *Opening the Schools: Alternative Ways of Learning.* Berkeley, Calif.: McCutchan, 1972. This collection of readings identifies responses of the schools to new challenges to education. The underlying assumption of the book is that it is better to reform educational institutions than to destroy them.

The Staff: New Roles and Partnerships

New roles for the staff are created by all of the innovations described in this book. Options for students, new curriculum patterns and components, organizational innovations, changes in media and facilities, all affect the teacher's role, and indeed cannot be effective unless teachers have the competencies to use these innovations well. Especially is the teacher's role affected by the current trends toward individualizing and humanizing instruction, trends that in practice may be conflicting if individualizing mechanizes teaching through technology and self-teaching instructional packages. Changes in the teacher's roles are also, perhaps belatedly, affecting teacher education and staff development plans. Overriding all of these changes is a movement toward greater accountability of schools and their personnel for results.

CHANGING ROLES OF TEACHERS

Teachers in secondary schools have generally had only one formal role in education: teaching classes, usually of some twenty-five to thirty students, with variations in particular fields such as vocational education and physical education. The task of the teacher in the class has been to stimulate, direct, and evaluate learning, typically of somewhat prescribed content. Recitation, some discussion perhaps, and teacher talk predominated. This remains a very common interpretation of the teaching role, and indeed it is still to be widely observed in practice. Many developments of the past generation, however, have brought this limited view of teaching under severe criticism; changing roles have been widely called for and new practices are to be found in an increasing number of high schools. The developments include: new kinds of learning theory and research; staff utilization studies involving instruction of students in large groups and small groups,[1] and through independent study arrangements; plans for helping students who do not learn effectively in usual teaching situations; efforts to advance specialization in teaching through team teaching and differentiated staffing patterns; increased availability of many media (see Chapter 6); and renewed interest in the individual student and his success and continuation in school. From these developments come four new emphases which are changing the teacher's role from the stereotype of one teacher-per class-per subject-per period solely responsible for stimulating, directing, and evaluating student learning in his subject(s) and classes: (1) the teacher as specialist in many specific teaching roles; (2) the teacher as a team member; (3) the teacher as a differentiated staff specialist; and (4) the teacher as a guide in individualized instruction.

The Teacher as Specialist in Many Specific Teaching Roles

With increased knowledge of learning styles and processes, teaching analysts identify many specific teaching activities that may be grouped and defined in the following roles to be discharged by the effective teacher, or perhaps by the teaching team or staff:

counselor-teacher: helping the student identify his goals and needs, and assisting in the planning of his curriculum, learning activities, and other school-related matters.

curriculum developer: working with the faculty, teaching team or staff or department, and other groups concerned to develop curriculum plans, and making detailed plans for his own instructional program.

diagnostician: analyzing the conditions affecting student learning; identifying the status of students' learning difficulties and progress; diagnosing students' needs for individual assistance and direction.

---

[1] See Institute for Development of Educational Activities, Inc., *Learning in the Small Group* (Dayton, Ohio: The Institute, 1971), pp. 17–30, for a description of twelve different types of small groups teachers may use for instructional purposes.

evaluator: observing changes in student performance; keeping analytic records, using appropriate evaluative instruments; building students' self-evaluation skills; working with other staff members to evaluate instruction and the program.

facilitator: helping students (and colleagues) through identifying and/or procuring needed resources for learning.

guide: working with individual students in selecting and using the learning opportunities right for each student.

manager: organizing the groupings and the resources for student learning, and monitoring and adapting their use.

strategist: planning and designing the best route for each student, and the stimuli and reinforcement necessary to keep the student on the right route, with adjustments as indicated.

Even in the still common situations where the high school teacher instructs a different class of some twenty-five students each period and is solely responsible for the instruction of each class, these roles are needed. In other situations where there is shared responsibility, the roles may be in part distributed, or the individual teacher may have different groups from time to time but still be expected to perform these roles for the students in each group. Thus regardless of organization, the teacher needs competence in each of the foregoing roles and probably others demanded in particular situations, such as disciplinarian, media technician, parent consultant, record-keeper, resource leader in the discipline.

The Teacher as a Team Member

Despite at least two decades of much exhortation for and descriptions of team teaching in the literature of education, reliable data as to the extent of team teaching in practice are not available. It is clear that many so-called team teaching arrangements do not meet such standard definitions of essential elements as the following:

1. Formalized arrangements (official status, administrative support for continuity, assigned team membership, specified time arrangements, stated aims and objectives);
2. Minimum of two professional teachers, with or without aides;
3. Joint _planning, teaching_ and _evaluating_;
4. Built-in systematic evaluation of the team teaching plan.[2]

[2] William M. Alexander, J. Galen Saylor, and Emmett L. Williams, _The High School: Today and Tomorrow_ (New York: Holt, Rinehart and Winston, 1971), p. 372.

Probably the elements lacking in most team teaching plans are the latter two: frequently, planning and evaluating are jointly done, but teaching is by "turn" rather than by team; and relatively few built-in evaluation plans get reported. Nevertheless, many high schools do utilize teaming, especially of the intradisciplinary or single subject type. In this plan, two or more teachers from a single subject area form a team for one or more scheduled classes on a continuing basis. Most plans include three to five teachers.

Team leadership may be designated on a hierarchical basis or may rotate on a chairmanship-type basis. Typically, an active team of three or more professional staff members have the part-time services of a teacher aide. The teachers have a common planning time daily. Student teachers are frequently included in the team structure as junior but participating members.

This plan permits easy grouping and regrouping of students, and also allows teachers to specialize in depth in one or more areas within the subject discipline. In an English team, for example, consisting of three English teachers and ninety or so students, one teacher would serve as resource specialist for language study, another would lead in the literature study, and the third would specialize in composition. Each teacher might be primarily responsible for instructing one-third of the student membership, but might work with other students in the team as special needs arose, or as special units of instruction were planned.

Another somewhat common type of team teaching that may be used in either interdisciplinary or single-subject plans was developed through the staff utilization studies of the 1950s and 1960s directed by J. Lloyd Trump for the National Association of Secondary School Principals and affiliated organizations, and is commonly called the "Trump Plan." This plan involves the use of large-group presentations, small-group discussion and other activities, and individual study, and is facilitated by a modular-type schedule (see Chapter 4). Team members may share in the large-group presentations; each leads one or more of the small groups and each is responsible for guiding the individual study of a portion of the students in the team. Thus, an individual teacher is responsible for sharing in the planning of the organization and the learning opportunities provided, in the teaching of large groups, small groups, and individuals, and in evaluating the progress of students and the teaming operation as a whole.

Two other types of teaming are less frequent, but perhaps more promising. One is the interdisciplinary, or core, pattern in which teachers of different subjects work together in a team relationship to teach correlated materials, as in English and history, mathematics and science, or a foreign language and history. Common sections in the subjects with back-to-back scheduling (as shown in the following diagram) facilitate this pattern, which was quite common in the 1930s era of the core cur-

(Back-to-back Scheduling)

Teacher	Period 1	Period 2
Smith (Room 110)	English 10 Section A	English 10 Section B
Jones (Room 111)	History 10 Section B	History 10 Section A

(Sections A and B each consists of thirty grade 10 students)

riculum and has more recently been revived in teaching such interdisciplinary or perhaps extradisciplinary areas (see Chapter 3) as drug education, environmental education, family life and sex education, and humanities. Such a plan is illustrated by the following description of a humanities program at Del Norte High School, Albuquerque, New Mexico:

To meet the needs set forth in the curricular objectives, the traditionally required courses at the junior and senior levels were combined as follows:

Grade	Required Subjects	New Designation
11	U.S. History English III	Junior Humanities
12	World History English IV	Senior Humanities

Students are assigned to teams composed of four teachers (two English and two history) for four modules daily (modules are of 25-minute duration). The teams, assisted by the music and art teachers who serve as consultants and develop special programs for and with students, evolve their own schedule, organizing large-group presentations, small-group activities, and individual conferences. The student–teacher ratio is approximately 30 to one, and there are three tracks: college preparatory, technical-vocational, and developmental. Teams are permitted wide latitude in arranging course content, program, and schedules. It should also be emphasized that student advisory groups in each team are included in the planning and development and often in the conduct of the class.[3]

---

[3] Richard R. Adler, *Humanities Programs Today* (New York: Citation Press, 1970), p. 102.

Another possible type of team teaching would be based on such teaching functions or roles as described earlier in this chapter. That is, one member of the team could be the diagnostician and evaluator, another the curriculum developer and manager, and so forth. Actually these roles are frequently and informally distributed in teaching teams of other types; we know of no examples in which the teaming is wholly on the basis of such roles, but would see as desirable some specialization in certain roles with others such as "guiding" being common to all team members.

The Teacher as a Differentiated Staff Member

The teaching team involves some differentiation of tasks, but "differentiated staffing" has come to have a more particular meaning: differentiation of training, responsibility, and pay. Thus if the teaching team involves the hierarchical arrangement in which the team leader has special responsibilities and receives special pay, it is differentiated staffing; but if the team chairmanship is rotating and unpaid, it is not. Differentiated staffing plans generally include some type of team teaching, but this is not required by the usual definition. Dwight Allen is credited in a special report on differentiated staffing, with this definition of three conditions "essential to a viable differentiated staff structure:"

1. A minimum of three differentiated staff teaching levels, each having a different salary range.
2. A maximum salary at the top teaching category that is at least double the maximum at the lowest.
3. Substantial direct teaching responsibility for all teachers at all salary levels, including those in the top brackets.

    Allen warns that simply "inventing" responsibility levels, writing job descriptions, and assigning teachers arbitrarily will not work. The DS concept, he insists, calls for innovation and reorganization of the basic structure of the schools, with the full participation of the teaching staff.[4]

The various patterns of staff differentiation attempted use of a variety of hierarchical staff designations such as teaching research specialist or associate, teaching curriculum specialist or associate, senior teacher, staff teacher, associate teacher, assistant teacher, educational technician, teacher's aide; or more simply, team or unit leader, master teacher, teacher, intern, teaching assistant, aide. The hierarchy is somewhat related to the traditional university ranks—professor, associate professor, assistant professor, instructor, assistant—although the differentiated staffing concept involves more distinction between responsibilities than is typically true of professional ranks.

    [4] *Education U.S.A.* Staff, *Differentiated Staffing in Schools*, Special Report (Washington, D.C.: National School Public Relations Association, 1971), pp. 5–6.

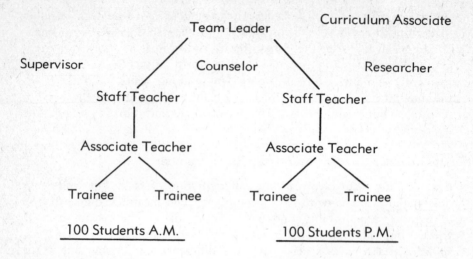

FIGURE 1   Differentiated staffing (John Adams High School, Portland, Oregon). From Al Dobbins, John Parker, and Patricia Wertheimer, "The John Adams Differentiated Staffing Model," Ch. 5 in *Strategies for Differentiated Staffing*, Fenwick W. English and Donald K. Sharpes (Eds.) (Berkeley, Calif.: McCutchan Publishing Corporation, 1972), p. 213.

An application of differentiated staffing in the John Adams High School, Portland, Oregon, is shown in the accompanying figure, as it existed in the spring, 1971. Teams at Adams were organized to teach the required "general education," an interdisciplinary course taught in lieu of the English-social studies-mathematics-basic science requirements. A description of the team operation follows:

> Most teams consist of a leader, two or three experienced teachers, and a number of trainees working toward certification. Team members have different academic backgrounds, thereby bringing to each team the perspective of several disciplines. Each team is responsible for approximately 200 students, grades nine through twelve. A typical team meets with half of its students for ninety minutes every morning, and with the other half in the afternoon. Working closely with such resource persons as a counselor and a social worker, each team is responsible for designing, developing, implementing, and evaluating its own problem-centered, interdisciplinary course of study.[5]

Two other persons, positioned in the horizontal segment of the staffing pattern, worked with the team: a supervisor to assist the trainees in planning and teaching and providing feedback on their effectiveness, and a

[5] Al Dobbins, John Parker, and Patricia Wertheimer, "The John Adams Differentiated Staffing Model," Ch. 5 in *Strategies for Differentiated Staffing*, Fenwick W. English and Donald K. Sharpes (Eds.) (Berkeley, Calif.: McCutchan, 1972), p. 212.

researcher to assist in getting information about student learning and attitudes.

Opposition to differentiated staffing as a form of the generally unpopular merit-pay concept has mitigated against its widespread adoption, at least as a pattern of pay differentials. Nevertheless, the basic principles of specialization in teaching functions with cooperative activity in the guidance of learning are recognized in other ways that amount to differentiated staffing. The growing use of many adults in instruction through the various innovations described in a later section does call for specialized training and qualifications and does require cooperative activity of the adults concerned. Note, too, that teachers, aides, interns, assistants, and clerks do get paid on different salary bases; the problem of differentiation of pay comes only as distinction is made between teachers with similar certification and paper qualifications who have long been paid on a uniform salary schedule with differences existing only as to experience and training in amounts written into the schedule. Some classification of teaching personnel is better accepted, and we can probably expect to have the classifications extended to include preparation for and assignment to some of the specialties the differentiated staffing patterns suggest. As classifications are created, special qualifications and training are specified and salaries set accordingly. We expect therefore continued need for extending specialization in teaching and in preparation and renewal of training for the various teaching roles. To use the right teacher for the right function in the learning situation is an obvious requirement of quality education.

The Teacher as a Guide in Individualized Instruction

The practice of teaching and the education of teachers are rapidly shifting from focus on classes to focus on learners. Whatever his specialty or level of teaching, the teacher of today and tomorrow must be first of all competent in forming one-to-one relationships with students. We turn next to these relationships.

In closing this section on changing roles of teachers, we would emphasize the fact that some teachers have long been effective in one-to-one relationships, in discharging most or all of the roles listed earlier, in working cooperatively in informal teaming patterns, and even in differentiating their functions from those of interns or such other personnel as available. But today it is expected that teachers in general be able to perform in these ways, and that the old informal arrangements for sharing, specializing, and individualizing will be supplanted by formal arrangements for these purposes. With more formal evaluation and accountability programs, competence in these roles will be required and its absence will be grounds for denying or terminating employment or requiring additional training.

STUDENT–TEACHER PARTNERSHIPS
FOR INDIVIDUALIZATION

The common denominator of the many approaches to individualizing instruction currently employed in schools is a one-to-one relationship of teacher and student. Regardless of how fully technology is used, effective individualized instruction at some point, and usually at many points, requires the teacher to work directly and individually with each student. The purpose of this section is to identify the various specific tasks and relationships involved.

The Teacher and Various Approaches
to Individualized Instruction

The term "individualized instruction" is currently used as a label for a great many practices, some old and some new, some good and some not so good, that in one way or another focus on the individual needs and motivations of students. Group instruction is even called "individualized" if there is some effort made to stimulate individual activity. But we believe the use of the term should be reserved for those phases of instruction which are primarily of a one-to-one relationship, however much other phases such as small and large group instruction may be used. Among various schemes[6] of classifying individualized instructional strategies, we find most useful here (and in Chapter 3) Edling's classification. Edling's PREP (Putting Research into Educational Practice) report classified procedures for individualization according to (1) whether the learning activities are directed (prescribed) by the teacher or selected by the student; (2) whether the learning area is a single classroom for a single discipline with a single teacher or a multiple area for more than one discipline and with more than one teacher; and (3) whether the time in the area is scheduled *for* the student and/or subject or is scheduled *by* the student within a large block of time.[7] Each type of individualization related to this classification makes somewhat different demands on the teacher, as we now note.

---

[6] See *Education U.S.A.* Staff, *Individualization in Schools*, Special Report (Washington, D.C.: National School Public Relations Association, 1971), pp. 3–4.

[7] See Jack V. Edling, *Individualized Instruction*, No. 16 in the Series of PREP Reports; DHEW Publication No. (OE) 72–9 (Washington, D.C.: U.S. Government Printing Office, 1972), pp. 18–25. In addition to its review of research and practice on individualization, this report includes a list of forty-eight schools surveyed, classified as elementary or secondary, urban, suburban or rural, and indicating the type of emphasis in each school. It also includes a bibliography of materials useful for individualizing instruction, and of other publications on the topic.

activities directed, multiple learning area, time scheduled. Although Edling cited only elementary schools using this type of individualization, it is also used in general shop, physical education, home economics, and other secondary fields, and could be used effectively in interdisciplinary team teaching situations. It requires a definite set of materials and activities available to or prepared by the teachers, and extensive checking of student progress, as well as preplanning of time distribution and assignment of students to learning stations and teachers.

activities directed, multiple learning area, time unscheduled. In this approach, students have larger blocks of time or alternate periods in which they may work in the learning area. Teacher planning must provide schemes whereby students can be guided to move on their own from one learning station (or center or corner) to another. Instructional systems (see section below) providing individual learning activities are frequently used.

activities directed, single learning area, time scheduled. Edling found this to be the most prevalent arrangement in secondary schools. Utilizing the traditionally scheduled, departmentalized classroom, the subject is taught through some series of learning activities preadopted or prepared by the teacher, whose role in the classroom becomes that of diagnostician, advisor, and evaluator as each student proceeds through the series within the time periods assigned.

activities directed, single learning area, time unscheduled. This modification of the preceding approach requires that the learning area be available to students for larger blocks of time, preferably throughout the school day and even afterwards. Such a program is approached through laboratories, libraries, and classrooms open to students at times other than during the class schedule and with a teacher present. For example, typing rooms are made available to students during their unscheduled time for working through their typing manuals. With use of variable purpose rooms and auxiliary staff, many more laboratories and other stations in the high school can be made available for this type of individualized instruction.

activities selected, multiple learning area, time scheduled. This approach, frequently described as the "open classroom" involves teachers serving as advisors to students as the latter select their learning activities and their scheduling of these, within the time scheduled for the area. Although Edling cited mostly elementary school practices, he did note that the K through 12 Punahou School in Honolulu used this approach within the traditional high school schedule by making available throughout the day a very extensive library and audiovisual center with television, dial access system, and an abundance of learning materials, all open to students for their individualized projects. The teacher's responsibility in this type of situation involves extensive knowledge of the resources and time and competence to advise students on the selection and pursuit of their project interests.

activities selected, multiple learning area, time unscheduled. This is the approach of independent study, providing the greatest amount of student choice, and requiring a very rich resource center and very versatile teachers. Edling's description of an application of the approach at John Murray Junior High School, Pendleton, Oregon, suggests its requirements and the possibilities:

> This program was originally designed for students who were achieving considerably below expected levels of performance and for whom the regular program had failed. It was discovered, though, that the program needed not only underachievers but also children of all achievement levels to make it work and be acceptable. The school year started with group activities in subjects and activities that were thought to be of general interest. No attempt was made to evaluate achievement. The goal was to reduce fear and academic expectations so teachers could get to know each individual as a person. There is no fixed subject matter content. A block of time is provided for the program, and the student uses it as he sees fit. Many different kinds of materials are available in the learning areas, including games and a variety of audiovisual media. The teacher's main responsibility is to acquire materials desired by students and to maintain the learning areas.
>
> While the experience has been rather traumatic for teachers, the results have been surprising. Several students rated as underachievers were found to be functioning at appropriate grade levels at the end of one year. The dire predictions of the traditionalists were unconfirmed. While students were freed from usual constraints, their new-found identity with teachers created an entirely different learning atmosphere.[8]

activities selected, single learning area, time scheduled. Edling found this arrangement second in frequency in secondary schools. Its basic requirements are multiple resources in the learning area or available to it, and a teacher competent to guide students in their choice and use of activities, materials, and media.

activities selected, single learning area, time unscheduled. As in the other approaches using unscheduled time, the teacher or his counterpart and the

[8] Edling, pp. 23–24.

learning area must be available to students for large blocks of time or throughout and even after the school day. One means used in secondary schools is a modular schedule in which the teacher is available in the learning area for student consultation during many modules.

Partnerships through Informal Education

"Informal education" and "open classroom" became in the early 1970s labels for almost any educational practices which departed from the standard models of schedule, classes, and credits;[9] they tended to replace or at least to encompass earlier drives for flexibility. Influenced undoubtedly by visits to the British infant and primary schools, by Charles Silberman's *Crisis in the Classroom*, and by the many trends toward greater focus on the student already reviewed in this book, critics in and out of education were demanding and getting considerable relaxation of the formalism especially characteristic of the secondary school. Silberman had noted "a growing ferment" in high schools around the country, a ferment we believed his book accelerated, and he classified the changes going on in these categories:

> Modest changes in school regulations designed to create a freer and more humane atmosphere outside the classroom;
> Somewhat bolder attempts to humanize the schools as a whole—for example, by cutting the number of required classes, leaving students with a third or more of their time unscheduled, to be used for independent study, for taking more elective courses, for fulfilling some course requirements outside the classroom, or for relaxation and leisure;
> Radical experiments involving changes of the most fundamental sort —reordering the curriculum and indeed the entire teaching–learning process, and in some instances broadening the very concept of what constitutes a school.[10]

Silberman's own preference for changes of the third sort was clear, for he noted that for students to develop "the knowledge and skills they need to make sense out of their experience—their experience with themselves, with others, and with the world—not just during adolescence, but for the rest of their lives," it is "not just the curriculum that will have to change, but the entire way in which high schools are organized and run."[11]

---

[9] See *Education U.S.A.* Staff, *Informal Education: Open Classroom Provides Climate, Controversy* (Washington, D.C.: National School Public Relations Association, 1972) for many examples of these practices.

[10] Charles E. Silberman, *Crisis in the Classroom* (New York: Random House, 1970), p. 337.

[11] Silberman, p. 336.

Silberman's second and third types of innovations constitute the substance of the present book, and it would be fallacious to separate them into formal and informal education. In fact, we do not find the latter term very definitive and suspect it will soon be replaced by some other. However, "informal" does describe quite directly the teacher–student relationship required in the partnership-for-learning approach to effective secondary education.[12] Some educators have called the same relationship "personalizing" instruction. It is in the informal, friendly, flexible, personal, open interaction of teacher and student that innovation is nurtured, and individual learning increased. The extent that freer use of time, greater options in curriculum, choices of learning activities, characterize informal education and improve learning, is directly dependent, we believe, on the ease with which all adults involved, especially teachers, adapt themselves to such relationships with students.

Instructional Systems and the Teacher

Various instructional systems are now commercially available and many others are at various stages of development in local school districts. These systems in general relate learning activities to objectives, provide considerable opportunity for self-pacing and self-evaluation, and include a variety of materials and media (see Chapter 6). Here, to indicate the role of teachers in the use of such systems, we briefly describe two that are available for secondary schools, and also an organizational system really designed for local development of a school's own instructional system.

Project PLAN (Program for Learning in Accordance with Needs), developed jointly by the American Institute for Research and Westinghouse Learning Corporation, for instruction in language arts, mathematics, science, and social studies, grades 1 through 12, is an ungraded, computer-supported program relating objectives, content, rate, and instructional materials to the individual student. It utilizes currently available instructional materials in its learning units (TLU's). A review of PLAN in the *Education U.S.A.* Special Report on *Individualization in Schools* describes the teacher's role in relation to PLAN in these terms:

> Contrary to what is often heard, PLAN considerably expands the role of the teacher. He becomes a tutor, a counselor, reinforcer, organizer, strategist and resource person. Under the teacher's guidance, each student selects an individualized, student-managed program of studies based on diagnostic testing, academic records and interviews with the child to determine his long-range goals and interests.

[12] See Aase Eriksen and Frederick M. Fiske, "Teacher Adaptation to an Informal School," *NASSP Bulletin*, 57:1–9, for an account of teachers' experiences in an alternative public high school, the West Philadelphia Community Free School.

The teacher uses the computer to monitor tests and other data for each pupil on a daily, continuing basis. Instantaneous retrieval of the data by the computer makes it possible for the teacher to pick up a printout for her class at the start of each school day. The printouts contain test scores, analysis of teacher actions and other guidance information.

The information is further supplemented by weekly processing of a pupil status card indicating achievement with a specific teaching–learning unit. This and other data are used by the teacher in planning and modifying individual programs for each child.[13]

PLATO (Programmed Logic for Automated Teaching Operations), begun by the Computer-Based Education Research Laboratory in 1960 at the University of Illinois is a computer-assisted instructional system used in a variety of subjects (1300 programs in thirty-five subject areas in 1971) for serving students of almost any age. The role of the teacher is indicated in this description of PLATO's operation:

> PLATO allows each student to work at his own pace in an individualized way. Under the system, teacher, computer, and students are all members of an interactive team. The teacher designs the instructional material, using a simplified special computer language called "Tutor"; the computer presents the material to the students, at the same time monitoring and evaluating their performance; and students interact with the computer providing information on lesson effectiveness. Each student works at his own pace on material which can provide special information and help when problems arise. PLATO frees the teacher for special work with students which conventional teaching does not usually permit.[14]

IGE (Individually Guided Education), unlike PLAN and PLATO, is really a planning and organization system rather than a system of instruction. It is not tied to computer or to any series of teaching–learning units or packages, although one of its sponsors, /I/D/E/A/ (the Institute for Development of Educational Activities, a division of the Kettering Foundation), has also sponsored the development by teachers of UNIPAC's (sets of self-instructing materials), and made them available to participating teachers. IGE, which has been developed jointly by the Wisconsin Research and Development Center for Cognitive Learning and /I/D/E/A/, was originally regarded by its sponsors as a comprehensive design of elementary education aiming to replace conventional organizational schemes and teaching practices with a planning and teaching pattern moving from goals and objectives to individualized programs and instruction. The teacher has a major, persistent role as a planner and

---

[13] *Individualization in Schools*, p. 23.
[14] *Individualization in Schools*, p. 51.

Meeting of full time independent study team at Whitmer High School, Toledo, Ohio.

implementer. The system involves the division of a school into units (each with a unit leader, teachers, auxiliary personnel, and students) with each member of the unit having fixed responsibilities. For example, a 1972 description of the IGE system designated these "Outcomes" as responsibilities of the teacher:

> Individual teacher's decisions are consistent with the unit's operations.
>
> The following are considered when students are matched to learning activities: peer relationships, achievement, learning styles, interest in subject areas, self-concept.
>
> Unit teachers insure that each student has personal rapport established with at least one teacher.
>
> Adequate opportunity is provided (through discussion and written communication) to insure that each teacher is fully aware of perceptions and suggestions of other unit members relating to the students with whom each has developed special rapport.
>
> Each student is involved in self-assessment procedures and analyses of the assessments.
>
> Each student participates in the selection of learning activities to pursue learning objectives.
>
> Each student can state learning objectives for the learning activities in which he is engaged.[15]

/I/D/E/A/ is expanding IGE to include middle schools, junior high schools, and high schools. Leagues of schools are organized for participation in the program, with /I/D/E/A/ providing training services and

[15] *Education U.S.A.* Staff, *Individually Guided Education and the Multiunit School. Education U.S.A.* Special Report (Washington, D.C.: National School Public Relations Association, 1972), p. 13.

materials to the leagues and member schools. Thus the intent and the program focus on helping schools establish patterns of operation which are conducive to more effective teacher–student relationships in the learning process. Teachers have much more to do with the operation of the IGE program itself than in instructional systems which are tied to particular instructional programs, and materials. In IGE teachers have considerably more leeway to develop their own systems. At the same time IGE is probably more demanding of teachers' time and their creative processes, although such programs as PLAN and PLATO also require that students and their records be extensively studied and much counseling be given.

Comparison of the two computer-related systems previously described with the IGE organization system illustrates the dilemma of the respective roles of technology and human teachers in the learning process. Probably the ideal operation, yet to be fully modeled and implemented, will have all of the organizational and human interactions involved in IGE and all of the technological resources involved in PLAN and PLATO. Then the partnership might be an optimum one of student, teacher, and machine. Meanwhile staffing innovations in the high schools must create more partnership roles by which teachers can help individual students to become fully self-directing learners.

NEW MEMBERS OF THE STAFF

The traditional staffing pattern of the high school consisted of a principal, possibly a corps of assistant principals, deans, and counselors, and a faculty of teachers representing the various subject areas offered by the school. Today the services of these personnel, now frequently reorganized into teams, little schools, and other arrangements, in many schools are greatly augmented by various other personnel, both paid and volunteer.

Preservice Interns and Teachers

In addition to the usual experience in student teaching, teachers in training are now frequently aided by their college and cooperating schools to have additional training on the job through services as aides[16] or tutors, sometimes for pay or for credit, prior to their student teaching experience,

[16] See John C. Reynolds, Jr., "University-Based Teacher Aides," *Educational Leadership*, 30:423–424 (February 1973), for a description of an illustrative program using teaching education students as aides. Sophomore and junior students in secondary education at the University of Georgia may take a field course involving several hours per week service as aides, with supervision by a teacher aide coordinator from the university.

and as interns following or even in lieu of the student teaching program. Internships, jointly planned and supervised by the school and college, follow other phases of the preservice teacher education program, usually including student teaching. The intern has a lightened load for a quarter, semester, or year, and time to study and prepare as well as to work with supervisory personnel from school and college who help him plan and evaluate his teaching. He becomes a member of the school faculty and can be a valuable resource as another adult to work with students.

For example, the Associate Teacher Program (Intern) at Staples, Minnesota, provides college students in their senior year of teacher-preparation with a year-long program of practical teaching experience following a visitation and participation program during the sophomore and junior years. An announcement of the program states that "a suggested schedule for the interns' school year is 75 percent in classroom-oriented activities and 25 percent in completion of college requirements for certification" and lists the following responsibilities of interns in the pilot school:

1. Plan with teachers in all educational programs.
2. Assist the teacher in all areas of classroom activity.
3. Participate in the program and pupil evaluation with the teacher.
4. Assume supervisory responsibility in the limited absence of the regular teacher.
5. Assume other general supervisory duties.
6. Plan projects and help children carry them out.
7. Work with small groups while the teacher works with larger groups.
8. Assume full classroom responsibility as increasing competency is noted by his supervisors.

The potential value to both the intern and the school staff and students is apparent. To be successful, such internships require close cooperation of school and college, and the college supervisor also becomes a resource for the school (and school personnel for the college). Such programs are illustrative of the school–university alliances described in a later section as essential to improved teacher education. But our present point is that well-trained student teachers and interns are also valued new members of the school staff.

Aides and Assistants

The Elementary and Secondary Education Act of 1965 gave a pronounced impetus to the already growing use of subprofessional personnel in the schools, and later cutbacks in federal funding did not result in their elimination in all school districts affected. The recognized value of additional subprofessional adults helping in many school routines has proved a great boon to education in many communities. In 1973 it was reported that paraprofessionals had become the largest growing body of employees in United States schools, and that they helped to increase student achievement, freed teachers to teach, and "unfroze" traditional school organization.[17]

The growing family of paraprofessional or auxiliary personnel includes teacher aides, composition aides, cafeteria aides, library aides, counselor aides, nurse's aides, social worker's aides, media aides, office aides, instructional secretaries, playground-hall supervisors, laboratory assistants, technical assistants, and community workers.[18] School aides are trained by school districts, by various community junior colleges, and in other continuation and adult education programs. School districts also provide staff development programs to train the professional personnel in using aides and assistants effectively. Personnel allocation systems in some districts allow school units to choose whether to employ aides or additional teachers on a basis such as two and a half aides or one teacher.

Parents

Although parents of elementary school-age children are more widely involved in the programs of their schools, some high schools also make determined and successful efforts to bring the parent to school as a partner in the educational process. An appeal to parents to participate in a "Parent–School Partnership" in the Newark, California, Unified School District stated:

> Parents help to develop curricula, serve as aides, plan activities, help with the governance of the school, and participate in a variety of ways. Whenever a partnership is formed between home and school, everyone benefits. We need your talents, your abilities, your help, and your support.

The following activities were listed as possible means of involvement:

The School District Resource and Talent Bank
The Community Advisory Program
The Golden Pass Program for Senior Citizens
The Tutorial Program
Daytime Renewal Classes
The Volunteer School Aide Program
The Parent–Teacher Association

[17] *Education U.S.A.* Staff, *Paraprofessionals in Schools, Education U.S.A.* Special Report (Washington, D.C.: National School Public Relations Association, 1973).

[18] See Howard G. Getz, *Paraprofessionals in the English Department*, NCTE/ERIC Studies in the Teaching of English (Urbana, Ill.: National Council of Teachers of English, April 1972) for a survey and analysis of the use of paraprofessionals for various purposes in the teaching of English.

The Music Action Committee
The Booster Clubs
The Parent Surveillance Programs

Parents were asked to participate with their children in a registration and information program at the beginning of the 1972–1973 school year, and specific activities requiring parental presence were listed.

Such parental involvement programs have these potential advantages high schools may increasingly seek: (1) mutual understanding of the student and his school program and home background; (2) creation of an opportunity for parental feedback on the school program; (3) parental services to the school.

Volunteers

The burgeoning movement toward use of adult volunteers in schools accommodates parents and all others interested and able to provide services to the schools. An April, 1973, report estimated that more than two million citizens were donating their services to 3000 programs in all fifty states.[19] Contributing to the growth of the volunteer movement is the widespread service of college students as volunteers, with about 80 percent of the nation's colleges having volunteer programs involving 400,000 students.

Volunteers are used in every aspect of the school program; for example, a newspaper advertisement by the Alachua County, Florida, school board in the spring, 1973, called for volunteers for both elementary and secondary levels in these areas:

Arts/Crafts
Library/Media
Tutorial
  English
  Languages
  Mathematics
  Reading
  Science
Clinic
Clerical

The National Reading Center has used a national television spot announcement narrated by Lucille Ball to recruit volunteer reading tutors. The Center began in 1972 a series of tutor training workshops in twenty states, and planned to expand the program to all states.

[19] "School Volunteer Programs Gain Wide Acceptance," Education U.S.A., April 9, 1973, p. 174.

A 1972 publication, *School Volunteers: What They Do—How They Do It* described the then fifteen-year-old New York City School Volunteer Program, which had these basic aims:

1. Relieve teachers of nonprofessional chores.
2. Provide individual attention and assistance that the classroom teacher is not able to supply to children who are not performing well in a group situation.
3. Tap the human resources of the community for the enrichment of the school program.
4. Develop greater citizen understanding of the problems facing the schools, enlist their support in securing better budgets, and involve them in the total effort to improve public education.[20]

Problems exist, of course, in the utilization of volunteers, some of them identical to those incurred in the employment of paraprofessionals and even professional staff members. The *Education U.S.A.* survey reported in 1973 these problems cited by schools using volunteers: resistance of other staff members, irregular attendance by volunteers, high dropout and turnover rates, improper use of volunteers, inadequate communication, and recruitment problems, particularly in low-income areas. The potential values to a school staff and student body of volunteer and paraprofessional services are so great that continued effort to recruit, select, train, and properly use these additional staff members seems mandatory.

Cross-Age Tutors

Use of students to tutor other students provides still other additions to a faculty. High school students in particular can be and are effective tutors of children in elementary and junior high schools, and even of their high school peers. In the Dallas, Texas, schools the Dallas Tutoring Program started with twenty students at Bryan Adams High School tutoring twenty-four other students. At the close of the 1971–1972 school year 1000 student volunteers had given 100,000 hours of tutorial services to 5000 students in various subjects in twenty-three middle, junior high, and high schools, and the goal was to involve 10,000 high school students during 1972–1973. Results for the program were cited by its originator and director as follows:

> The number of students who were spared scholastic failure because of the extra help given them.

[20] Barbara Carter and Gloria Dapper, *School Volunteers: What They Do—How They Do It* (New York: Citation Press, 1972), p. 15. Much of this book is devoted to instruction of the volunteer, especially in tutoring in reading.

The improvement in self-concept on the part both of those receiving help and those doing the tutoring.

The participants' increased feeling of belonging, even in a large school that sometimes seems to them impersonal.[21]

High school students also benefit by the tutorial services of college students working as school volunteers or as preservice teacher-education participants. Untrained tutors at any age may provide only the spark of motivation to the learner that comes from the attention of an older student, but this advantage can be retained and the services made more valuable by training the tutors. With training and supervision, cross-age tutors may indeed be new staff members of a school.

Learner Exchanges and Networks for High Schools?

The use of cross-age tutors and volunteers in high schools approaches the concept of educational networks proposed by Ivan Illich in his *Deschooling Society*, which describes the general plan of learners seeking out teachers without the coordination of a school. Sometimes tutors and volunteers are sought by students, especially in alternative schools, and the school coordination is loose and informal. A better example of the Illich concept in practice is "The Learning Exchange" in Chicago, described as follows in a 1973 press story:

> It isn't a school with classrooms, grades, entrance requirements or certified teachers—and as often as not there's no tuition. It's a simple design to bring together people who want to teach with those who want to learn. For the price of a phone call or postage stamp, many people are getting access to education they wouldn't otherwise get.
>
> The Exchange's rolls have increased to more than 4,000 participants in less than two years. And the number of people using the Exchange could increase to nearly 20,000 by year-end, its co-founders say. This growth has been stimulated primarily by word-of-mouth and public-service advertising by local media.[22]

In view of the widespread belief today that high school students should have more opportunity to formulate their own learning goals and guide their own learning activities, we raise in all seriousness the question of whether public high schools might create innovative learner exchanges wherein students would advertise their learning needs and specialties. The

[21] Wanda Wassallo, "Learning by Tutoring," *American Education*, 9:28 (April 1973).

[22] Terry P. Brown, "In Chicago, It's Easy to Find Someone to Teach Lion Taming or Anything Else," *Wall Street Journal*, April 10, 1973.

school coordinator (unlike Illich, we would have the exchanges function under school auspices), would tease out unmet needs and available resources including those of other students, and match these. Such an exchange would be only an extension of present use of volunteer and other resources and would utilize the best of Illich's proposal without "deschooling society." In fact, we would see future services of support teams of administrators and counselors giving much attention to identifying learning needs and resources, and bringing these together in far more imaginative and promising ways than classes have usually been formed in high school programs of the past.

EMERGING TEACHER-EDUCATION RESPONSES

Although many innovations described in this book are created by short-comings in teacher education and performance, these innovations create still further demands for new forms and emphases in teacher education. That changing roles for teachers require changes in teacher education has long been argued, but responses in preservice education have been slow to come about and have been less than enthusiastically applauded when tardy and inadequate. Staff development programs in school districts had increasingly carried the burden of preparing teachers for the new roles, until federal aid pressures and various other factors prodded university–school

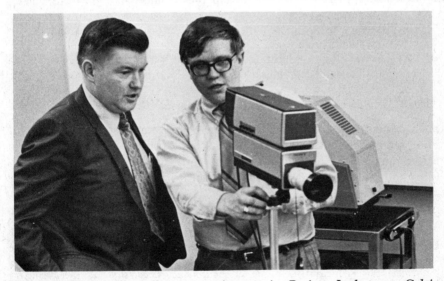

Staff members utilize videotape equipment in Project Lodestone, Calais, Maine.

cooperative endeavors in recent years toward more functional programs of teacher education. As late as 1970 a group of high school teachers from all parts of the United States, convened by the Institute for Development of Educational Activities, Inc. and chaired by J. Lloyd Trump of the National Association of Secondary School Principals, agreed "that the majority of high school teachers now emerging from colleges of education have practically no experience in being able to:

1. relate to the special problems of teen-agers;
2. employ worthwhile teaching innovations; or
3. cope with typical daily classroom situations."[23]

A more comprehensive indictment of current teacher education efforts was made in a 1973 report of the Program for Improving the Undergraduate Preparation of Professional Personnel (supported by funds from the Education Professions Development Act):

1. There is general dissatisfaction with the low quality of current efforts.
2. No one takes responsibility for the education of teachers.
3. Despite its ostensible role as an educational institution, the university devotes little academic attention to the problems of education.
4. Prospective teachers are not being prepared to assume nontraditional roles.
5. The current system is not only inflexible; it is also inefficient.
6. Successful efforts to improve teacher education have often failed to affect other institutions and components of the same institution.
7. The current system fails to tap the resources of individuals outside education.
8. Trends within the teaching profession may diminish the chances for fundamental reform.
9. The failures of education have pressed with particular harshness on the disadvantaged minorities.[24]

School–Univerity Alliances and Teacher Centers

Such criticisms notwithstanding, teacher education institutions have for some years been seeking alliances with school districts that would provide better opportunity for the integration of theory and practice.[25] Internships and full-time student teaching quarters and semesters were better

[23] A *Symposium on the Training of Teachers for Secondary Schools* (Dayton, Ohio: Institute for Development of Educational Activities, Inc., 1970), p. 3.

[24] Study Commission on Undergraduate Education and the Education of Teachers, *Undergraduate Preparation of Educational Personnel Program* (Lincoln, Nebr.: The Commission, Andrews Hall, University of Nebraska, February 1973), pp. 4–7.

[25] See the February 1973 issue of *Educational Leadership* on the theme of "Shifts in University–School Role." Several articles describe cooperative programs of various types.

planned and guided, and frequently preceded by student experiences as observers, participants, and more recently as tutors. Microteaching, with videotaping and playback, was introduced to show better specific teaching activities and skills. Participation of supervising or directing teachers in seminars for the trainees along with assignment of the trainees to teaching teams bridged some gaps between the university and school classrooms. The British teacher center has been recognized in some quarters as a prototype for teacher education reform:

> Perhaps the most significant potential British contribution to American education, however, is only now being identified and discussed: the development of teachers' centers. British experience with these centers, at least in their present form, is a matter of three or four years only. But the idea is so simple, so psychologically sound, as to make one wonder why teachers' centers have not dotted the educational landscape for decades.
>
> Teachers' centers are just what the term implies: local physical facilities and self-improvement programs organized and run by the teachers themselves for purposes of upgrading educational performance. Their primary purpose is to make possible a review of existing curricula and other educational practices by groups of teachers and to encourage teacher attempts to bring about changes.[26]

The Florida legislature in 1973 passed a Teacher Center Act and appropriated planning funds for exploration of the use of cooperatively developed centers in both preservice and inservice teacher education. Whether such centers in the United States should operate only for inservice education or be used for preservice education has been one of many concerns that have undoubtedly accelerated the movement toward performance-based teacher education in the United States, a movement that aims toward great change in both preservice and inservice education. This movement is widely regarded as potentially the most significant innovation in teacher education in its history. It builds on previous efforts toward cooperation in teacher education and must utilize and indeed facilitate the cooperation and involvement of teachers themselves, for instance, in the teacher centers. Illustrative of the cooperative arrangements planned in the various organizations now developing the new programs is this outline of purposes of the West Virginia Kanawha Valley Multi-Institutional Teacher Education Center (MITEC):

1. Strong state department of education leadership and direction.
2. Cooperative arrangements and commitments of public schools and colleges as equal partners in teacher education.

[26] Stephen K. Bailey, "Teachers' Centers: A British First," *Phi Delta Kappan*, 53:146 (November 1971).

3. A reexamination of teacher education programs by colleges and universities in which they identify new roles and responsibilities in the center concept.
4. Linkage with the professions, the community, regional laboratories, Teacher Corps, Triple T (Training the Teachers of Teachers), Job Corps, Career Opportunities Programs, experimental schools, other states and nations.
5. Teachers and total staff retraining and inservicing to improve competencies in teaching and to work in new roles and new staffing patterns.[27]

The 1973 Florida Teacher Center Act stimulated similar cooperation of universities, school districts, and professional associations in planning and operating centers.

Performance-Based Teacher Education

Competency- or performance-based teacher education, as the name implies, attempts to develop required teaching competencies, utilizing more specific criteria, activities, and performance data than conventional teacher education courses and student teacher arrangements. A 1973 report on "The State of the Scene" listed these specific distinguishing characteristics:

Precise objectives stated in behavioral terms

Criteria to be applied in assessing the competencies of students made explicit and public—and negotiable

Students held accountable for meeting these criteria

Decision-making regarding training needs based on successful mastery of objectives

Instructors held accountable for effectiveness of planned program

Achievement held constant and time varied

Emphasis placed upon exit requirements with considerable flexibility in entrance requirements.[28]

This report gave a state-by-state summary of developments toward such teacher education programs, and listed as institutions with "high involvement" ten having their "total" program on a competency base, and eighty others having "alternative" or "parallel" competency-based programs. In

[27] Kathryn Maddox, "Teacher Education Center: Cooperation, Challenge, and Commitment—The West Virginia MITEC Model," in *Innovation Now!* (Washington, D.C.: International Council on Education for Teaching, 1972), pp. 104–105.

[28] Allen A. Schmeider, *Competency-Based Education: The State of the Scene* (Washington, D.C.: American Association of Colleges for Teacher Education and ERIC Clearinghouse on Teacher Education, February 1973), p. 5.

the AACTE's survey of 1200 institutions, only 228 of 783 respondents indicated that they were not involved in performance-based teacher education; 125 had programs that "for the most part" met a generally accepted definition of performance-based teacher education; and 366 indicated that they "are now in the developmental stage and plan to establish a PBTE program."[29]

Modules and Minicourses

A typical feature of the competency-based program is the "module," defined in the report just cited as "a package of integrated materials or an identifiable and related set and sequence of learning activities which provide systematic guidance through a particular learning experience or specific program." Modules vary greatly in length and complexity, but typically include rationale, objectives, pretests, activities, posttests, and other sections as needed for individualized progress and assessment. Centers in several locations maintain collections of statements of competencies and copies of modules; for example, Houston Module Bank, University of Houston, Houston, Texas; National Center for the Development of Training Materials in Teacher Education, University of Indiana, Bloomington, Indiana; Florida Center for (competency-based) Teacher Training Materials, University of Miami, Coral Gables, Florida.

Minicourses represent a related approach to the teacher education program, and have been most fully developed at the Far West Laboratory for Educational Research and Development.[30] A minicourse is defined in the glossary of *The State of the Scene*, as "a specific set of learning experiences, often self-instructional, designed to teach a single skill or a cluster of related teaching skills in a relatively short period of time. Microteaching, self-analysis, and reteaching are typical elements in each unit."

Minicourses and modules in teacher education are comparable to the "learning activity package" of secondary education we described earlier; at both levels the purpose is to focus on specific objectives with means of systematic checking of progress and performance and with considerable provision for self-instruction and variable timing. Modules and minicourses in teacher education also are subject to the same criticisms as learning activity packages in high school: The concentration on performance and assessment tends to neglect less easily measured understandings and atti-

[29] Schmeider, p. 11.

[30] See C. L. Hutchins, Barbara Dunning, Marilyn Madsen, and Sylvia I. Rainey, *Minicourses Work* (Berkeley, Calif.: Far West Laboratory for Educational Research and Development, n.d.), for description of minicourses and their usage in teacher education.

tudes; individualized instruction overlooks the values of group discussion and enterprises; adequate individualization is too time-consuming for instructors. We ourselves believe that the competency approach has much potential to improve the education of teachers and their students. It merits full exploration and utilization with much provision for evaluation and feedback and continued improvement efforts to eliminate the weaknesses and problems that do exist and can be overcome.

ACCOUNTABILITY AND STAFF EVALUATION AND DEVELOPMENT

Mounting public resistance to increased taxes, criticisms of the schools, and evidence of the gap between educational goals and their accomplishment supported the popular movement of the early 1970s toward accountability for school results. Obviously, schools had always been as accountable as other public institutions, but many citizens and their legislatures were dissatisfied with the accounting and called for the schools to systematize better their goals, procedures, and reports. The arguments were indeed commanding, for as Combs commented: "Who in his right mind can really oppose the idea of accountability? That is like being against motherhood."[31]

Accountability and the Staff

Although the notion of accountability finds many diverse expressions, and usually becomes controversial when it is applied to any group of personnel or an individual, certain implications for secondary schools staffs are clear and are being studied and used by knowledgeable school people. We see these principles as especially significant:

1. The goals of the school, and each of its programs, must be clearly defined and understood by all concerned.
2. Responsibility for the accomplishment of the goals must be as clearly assigned as possible, with each party to the educational process accepting the appropriate share of responsibility.
3. When goal accomplishment involves new or increased knowledge and skill on the part of responsible participants, especially staff members, provision must be made for these participants to try to acquire the prerequisite skill or knowledge.
4. The processes of evaluating goal accomplishment and the system of

[31] Arthur W. Combs, *Educational Accountability: Beyond Behavioral Objectives* (Washington, D.C.: Association for Supervision and Curriculum Development, 1972), p. 1.

incentives and penalties must be also defined and understood by all concerned.

A statement prepared by the National Education Association, December, 1972, is pertinent. This statement defined the problem and stated the NEA position, indicated in part in the following excerpts:

> Compulsion about accountability in education has reached crisis proportion in at least thirty states and is spreading fast to all fifty. The compulsion, the obsessive desire to *make* educators and students conform is the crisis, not the need for or desirability of, efforts to be more accountable (responsible). More precisely, there are under way deliberate attempts to legislate or decree performance, testing, and achievement levels —in other words, to remove the prerogatives of professionals and the local school district to devise and carry out programs of education that fit their particular clientele. Most of the proposed legislation and decrees are punitive, ill conceived, and probably inoperative. And they have for the most part been developed without the collaboration and consultation of the organized profession.
>
> Therefore, it is essential that educators, through the organized profession, be appraised of the situation, think through their position, and plan their strategy, if they are to have a part in shaping what happens. The stakes are high. They go beyond the welfare of students and teachers. The very future of public education is in the balance. In many states, the sequence of events is at a stage where the trend of all future developments in accountability is being determined.
>
> We contend that there is a legitimate case to be made for greater accountability in education. People (educators included) want to be more sure that human effort and material expenditure achieve demonstrably the purposes and goals for which they have been allocated. These advocates of greater accountability want first not to short-change the public: they want taxpayers to get the best service and products for the dollars they pay; they want students to get an education that is commensurate with the human and material resources expended—for the benefit of both the learner and the society of which he is a part. . . .
>
> We contend that 1) goals, 2) students, 3) program, 4) staff, 5) resources, and 6) governance of education and the teaching profession are elements of quality education for which responsibility should be fixed and monitored if educators and the public are to assure accountable (responsible) education. We contend further that a review of these elements in terms of the existing operation of education in states and school districts will help professionals and laymen (and legislators and state board members) to identify the measures needed to achieve greater accountability (responsibility) in education. The valuing as to adequacy in each setting is the responsibility of the people involved.[32]

[32] "Accountability," a statement prepared by the NEA, December 1972, pp. 1, 3. Mimeographed.

Chiefly the NEA statement called for involvement of educators in the development of accountability programs; note the concluding paragraph:

> When teachers possess the authority and the decision-making power to perform their professional task, education will improve. When teachers are in that position, and only then, will we be able to address the question of accountability seriously enough to assume that it can make a difference. Until then, the only relevant accountability question is why teachers are not in that position. This is reality.

Undoubtedly a major implication of the accountability movement is that it will increasingly become a matter for negotiation between professional groups and their employers. Consideration of this issue and the processes of negotiation is beyond the scope of this chapter and book, but we do want to note the related and important matters of staff evaluation and development.

Staff Evaluation

Of the various state laws concerning accountability, one advocate, W. James Popham, found California's "precedent-setting," noting that it "transformed educational accountability from fashionable professional chatter to binding statutory reality."[33] He cited as its key stipulations these:

> Each school district must establish its own objective system of evaluation for the annual appraisal of probationary teachers and the biennial appraisal of all other teachers.
> In devising its evaluation system the district school board must seek the advice of the local teachers' organization.
> Each evaluation system must minimally include:
>
> —established standards and techniques for assessing student progress in each area of study.
> —assessment of teacher competence as it relates to the established standards.
> —assessment of duties performed by teachers as an adjunct to their assignments.
> —established procedures for ascertaining that teachers are maintaining proper control and a suitable learning environment.
>
> A written evaluation plus a face-to-face meeting must be used to relay the evaluation to the teacher.[34]

[33] W. James Popham, "California's Precedent-Setting Teacher Evaluation Law," *Educational Researcher*, 7:13 (July 1972).
[34] Popham, p. 13.

In most states and districts, controversy has probably been greatest regarding the establishment of standards for assessing student progress and related teacher competence. In its 1972 report *There's a New School Coming*, a research and development program in Florida, aiming to implement the legislative requirements of assessment, reviewed progress and plans toward the three targets of the program: educational assessment and management, educational personnel training, and alternative educational practices. Indicative of the complexity of state assessment programs, the Florida program aimed to have available only by the end of 1976 techniques for assessment of mastery of basic skills of communication and computation in the elementary grades. Schools in general may not expect acceptable, research-based programs to be available soon on statewide, regional, or national basis.

And so, many districts and schools and organizations are establishing their own approaches to comprehensive planning, including the evaluation of student progress and teacher competence. For example, members of the Rochester, Minnesota, Education Association in cooperation with the National Education Association chose to develop a plan of teacher evaluation for these reasons:

> They were aware that parents, students, elected officials, and state agencies across the country are demanding teacher accountability. They believed that if the profession doesn't deal with the problem, then someone else will. Therefore, they felt that education associations must place a high priority on becoming more fully involved in establishing policies for and carrying out evaluation of education programs and of teaching processes.[35]

The March, 1973, report of this project cited questions that were raised and underlined the complexity of the problem, but also noted some principles we consider to be significant guidelines:

> Opinions differ on all of these questions. Although the Rochester Education Association has spent nearly a year on the project so far, we still don't see the answers falling in place. Teacher evaluation is complex.
> Perhaps it can never be completely objective. But it must be rational. It must be logical. It must be workable. It must be used to improve the teaching process.[36]

[35] Larry E. Wicks, "Teacher Evaluation," *Today's Education*, 62:43 (March 1973).

[36] Wicks, p. 43.

Staff Development

Promising approaches to staff development seem more numerous, or at least reported more frequently, than do complete accountability and evaluation programs. And perhaps it is within the areas of preservice and in-service education that the real progress to better schooling must be made, essential as are the prior or parallel jobs of goal definition and product evaluation.

One of the most promising approaches to staff development has already been described in part: performance-based teacher education, which is fully as applicable to in-service as preservice use and in fact has been much more widely employed in the former, where deficient performance is more glaringly revealed.[37] It is for staff development, too, that another cluster of innovative practices we have described, is especially appropriate: school-university alliances. In fact, these two notions may be almost inextricably related; for example, the modules or packages used in staff development may be produced at the university site and field tested and ultimately used at the school site, with full collaboration in both stages. This possibility is described in an article by an Austin, Texas, coordinator of staff development as the major opportunity for the university's role in staff development:

> The unique role that colleges can play in staff development is very great. Since colleges typically have a variety of research efforts as part of their ongoing program, the research and development of staff development packages as a part of the college program could provide public schools with a wide range of "packaged consultants." . . .
>
> We have the needs for staff development packages for use in public schools, as well as the potential for meeting these needs in colleges. It will be interesting to view the developments over the next several years to see whether these particular needs of the public schools will be met by the colleges, or whether this role will be assumed by private business or perhaps by the public schools themselves.[38]

In addition to collaboration in competency-based in-service staff development of the "package" type, schools and colleges do have many other types of cooperative activity for staff development. Schools also have their own staff development programs, with help and collaboration available from regional educational laboratories, private consulting firms, publishers

---

[37] See Iris M. Elfenbein, *Performance-Based Teacher Education Programs: A Comparative Description* (Washington, D.C., American Association of Colleges for Teacher Education, October 1972) for descriptions of various programs for both preservice and in-service education.

[38] Paul W. Kirby, "In-Service Education: The University's Role," *Educational Leadership,* 30:433 (February 1973).

and educational technologists, and other sources. Over twenty models of staff development presented in two 1972 issues (October and December) of *Theory into Practice* indicate the range of possibilities. Introducing these issues, editor Jack Frymier indicated their possible usefulness as follows:

> A series of fortuitous events . . . have created a situation in which quality staff development programs can become a reality. The economic down-turn across the country, an increase in the number of college graduates prepared to teach, and declining public school enrollments have all interacted to stabilize the teaching profession. For the first time in more than a quarter of a century, in fact, teacher turnover has reduced to the point that we now have an opportunity to learn new professional skills and develop new understandings "on the job." . . .
>
> . . . We recognize the difficulties and dangers in labeling a practice as a "model," but hope that the twenty or so "models" described in these two issues will be sufficiently diverse and provocative to foster a higher level of discourse among educators than has traditionally occurred. We have attempted to present a broad spectrum of practice. . . .[39]

We are commenting on only one of the models, but hope that readers will find many useful. John Goodlad's article on "The League Model" reports his experiences and observations in directing a league of eighteen schools in cooperation with the University of California at Los Angeles and the Institute for Development of Educational Activities (IDEA). The focus of this league was on processes of educational change; a major part of the strategy for continuous school improvement was directed at the in-service growth of faculties, individual members as well as total faculties. The aspect of Goodlad's findings that we find most significant for staff development in general was the attention to the individual school as "the organic unit for educational improvement":

> Focusing on the individual school as the organic unit for educational improvement departs more abruptly from conventional approaches than is at first apparent. The most difficult aspect of this departure is that it calls for us to lift our eyes and efforts temporarily from customary practices which focus only on pupils and individual teachers. It is the school as a social institution that is ailing. Let us concentrate for a time on what is required not only for it to become healthy but also for it to become capable of sustaining itself in a healthy state. Once the condition is established, it will be interesting to see what happens to boys and girls over a period of years in healthful school environments.[40]

[39] Jack Frymier, "This Issue," *Theory into Practice*, 11:206 (October 1972).
[40] John Goodlad, "Staff Development: The League Model," *Theory into Practice*, 11:213–214 (October 1972).

The league notion of collaboration of individual schools in improvement efforts has been influential in earlier secondary school improvement programs such as the Eight-Year Study, the Southern Study, and the various staff utilization studies. It can probably be much more fully put to use by high schools seeking to reach new standards, including those of accountability, and finding strength in collaboration with themselves and other helpful partners.

For the individual school to serve as the unit for improvement and accountability means that efforts toward assessment must be adaptable to its goals and operating conditions. It also means that teachers, counselors, and administrators, along with appropriate representatives of all other personnel involved, must work in concert to define school goals, assign responsibilities for goal accomplishment, undertake staff development as needed by individuals and groups, and fashion, implement, and be guided by adequate evaluation programs. It is the individual school that is accountable in the final analysis for what happens to its students; its staff should have heavy responsibility as well as challenging opportunity to plan, implement, and evaluate its goals and goal accomplishments. The successful innovations of the future, we believe, will be those that are oriented in this conception of the role of the individual school.

additional suggestions for further study

1. Cooper, James M., M. Vere DeVault, and others, *Competency Based Teacher Education*. Berkeley, Calif.: McCutchan, 1973. Symposium on various aspects of the topic, with several articles dealing with a systems approach to teacher education.
2. Dempsey, Richard A., and Rodney P. Smith, Jr., *Differentiated Staffing*. Englewood Cliffs, N.J.: Prentice-Hall, 1972. Description and analysis of differentiated staffing, and means of introducing. Includes numerous models in use.
3. Gorow, Frank F., *The Learning Game: Strategies for Secondary Teachers*. Columbus, Ohio: Merrill, 1972. A specific model of instruction is developed through the cycle of objectives, analysis of content and learning tasks, preassessment, planning and implementation of strategies, and evaluation.
4. Noar, Gertrude, *Individualized Instruction: Every Child a Winner*. New York: Wiley, 1972. Specific and useful descriptions of individualized instructional practices.
5. Poliakoff, Lorraine, "Teacher Centers: An Outline of Current Information," *Journal of Teacher Education*, 23:389–397 (Fall 1972). Useful summary and bibliography of materials on teacher centers, excerpted from an ERIC Clearinghouse on Teacher Education report of May 1972.

6. Scobey, Mary Margaret, and A. John Fiorino (Eds.), *Differentiated Staffing*. Washington, D.C.: Association for Supervision and Curriculum Development, 1973. Critical analysis of differentiated staffing, with illustrative materials on planning, implementation, and evaluation.

7. Travers, Robert M. W., *Handbook of Research on Teaching*, 2d ed. Chicago: Rand-McNally, 1973. A new edition of a comprehensive compilation of research finding on teaching and teachers. An excellent reference for any professional library.

8. Wilhelms, Fred T., *Supervision in a New Key*. Washington, D.C.: Association for Supervision and Curriculum Development, 1973. Describes the use in staff development of new tools available for supervision and staff improvement: new media, interaction analysis, microteaching, clinical supervision, and the teacher center.

9. Wynne, Edward, *The Politics of School Accountability*. Berkeley, Calif.: McCutchan, 1973. Comprehensive treatment of the accountability movement, including its historical development. Chapter 12 presents a checklist of steps to assist accountability.

Media: Getting
Things Together

The mid-sixties excitement about the possibility of electronics for drastic improvements in education has cooled a bit and both educators and managers of the "knowledge industry" have had some second thoughts. Educators have learned that the acquisition of audio-visual materials, electronic equipment, and other media has little impact on teaching and learning unless there is thoughtful concern with the individual needs of students and the processes by which students learn and gain skills and knowledge.

In the mid-sixties, a number of new combines appeared that involved the merging of electronics-hardware industries with book publishing firms. Industry and the education profession made some preliminary efforts to build a working relationship aimed at improving the student's opportunities to learn. Industry brought to the partnership a wide range of resources in communication skills, publishing techniques, systems engineering, and consultative services of many kinds. Educators brought to the partnership a working knowledge of education and of classroom techniques. The business and financial pages of the newspapers of 1964 through 1967 regularly carried news of mergers of publishers and machine manufacturers or other configurations with similar interests in the education market. Major computer companies acquired textbook publishing houses and launched costly programs designed to capture the education market by proving that teaching and learning could be boosted to new levels of achievement by the combination of educational hardware and software. Results have not kept up with expectations, however.

The size of the education market was overestimated, financial problems of the schools continued to increase, and American schools and colleges became preoccupied with pressing problems of student unrest, racial confrontations, problems of the city schools, demands of militant teachers, and taxpayer revolts.

Meanwhile, however, research and development centers, regional laboratories, universities, and other organizations increased their research and development efforts toward finding ways to design instructional media to meet the diverse and individual learning needs of students. Publishing companies with their capacity to apply research findings to the development of instructional materials, combined with the ability to reach the purchasers, shifted their emphasis from devising attractive combinations of hardware and software to designing more effective learning systems. Although advancing slowly, educational technology is predicted to be utilized more and more effectively in future teaching and learning. This prediction is based on the relationship of educational technology to three types of influences currently at work within education: (1) applications of systems theory to education, (2) demands for individualizing instruction so that the needs of individual learners are met, and (3) the influence of future-thinking on education.

Systems Concepts

Basic to modern views of educational technology are applications of systems concepts. Implicit in the utilization of media in systems approaches are the use of clearly stated instructional objectives, selection of resources and methods to achieve those objectives, and feedback mechanisms so that the learning situation for the individual student is constantly being improved.

A decade or two ago, most uses of media were group oriented. Teachers would show a film to an entire class, assign the same print material to the group, and guide all to the same museum exhibits. The introduction of programmed instruction in the early sixties seemed to introduce a new frame of reference for various kinds of media. Planners and developers became more and more creative in finding ways to provide instruction that was individualized, tailored to each student's unique learning abilities and needs and largely self-instructional. A change in

A partial view of exhibits at the annual convention of the American Association of School Administrators indicates the scope and diversity of educational media.

thinking also took place relating to the quality of media utilization by schools. Instead of measuring the effectiveness of a media program by the quantity of equipment and materials available to given numbers of students and teachers, the emphasis shifted to the relationship of the use of media to reaching sound instructional objectives.

Systems approaches provide ways of developing, organizing, and making available appropriate learning resources for focusing on the individual learner. A system approach usually involves the following steps:

1. Assessing needs to determine analytically specific strengths, deficiencies, and problems.
2. Developing instructional objectives and criteria for measuring effectiveness.
3. Planning alternative procedures by selecting media to reach different individual needs and learning styles, locating necessary resources, and planning appropriate instructional strategies.
4. Monitoring the planned procedures to provide constant information on progress and revision of resources as needed for greater effectiveness.
5. Evaluating and utilizing the monitored feedback to alter the program so it meets individual and group needs, changing knowledge inputs, or changing environmental conditions.

The system concept provides a way of thinking about teaching and learning that promises responsiveness on the part of the school to the needs of individual students when guided by perceptive, humane, and competent teachers and administrators.

Individualization

Media, in the context of educational technology, offer almost unlimited possibilities for meeting the unique needs of individual learners. The movement to measure the quality of education by the degree of students' learning and motivation rather than by pupil/teacher ratios, credentials of teachers, and other quantitative measures is supported by new concepts of educational technology.

> Educational technology is a field involved in the facilitation of human learning through the systematic identification, development, organization, and utilization of a full range of learning resources, and through the management of these processes. It includes, but is not limited to, the development of instructional systems, the identification of existing resources, the delivery of resources to learners, and the management of these processes and the people who perform them.[1]

Thus by bringing together the individual learner and his unique needs, a constantly expanding range of resources, and a systematic approach to the efforts of bringing needs and resources together for effective learning, media has a critical role to play in the individualization of learning.

Expanding from the earlier concepts of programmed instruction, whole schools are now involved in individualization of learning programs under such titles as continuous progress, tutorial communities, and many others. Various types of instructional modules or packages (described later in this chapter) are another expression of a systematic approach to the use of media.

In planning individualized instruction, for example, the individual and his needs are considered to be basic factors in the system, and these are constantly evaluated. The services of a computer might be provided to the student and teacher as an information processing, storage, and retrieval tool. The first step in the process would be the statement of behavioral or performance-related educational objectives for the course or unit of learning. Instructional strategies would then be planned, testing devices would be developed for assessing the student's progress in attaining these objectives, and guidance procedures would be planned. Teaching–learning units that include the method–media mix desired for the instructional strategies would be assembled and cataloged. Stored in the computer or in a conventional record file would be detailed information on each student, including special aptitudes, patterns of learning, interests,

---

[1] Donald P. Ely (Ed.), "The Field of Educational Technology: A Statement of Definition," *Audiovisual Instruction*, 17:36 (October 1972).

background, skills, and knowledge acquired prior to the point of entry. The computer or conventional file would also store a systematic index of teaching–learning units with information helpful in matching student and learning activities. Directing the utilization of media toward specific objectives for the individual learner has initiated a trend that has implications for the future.

Future-Thinking

Our lives are so intertwined with the media of a fast-moving technological age that educators cannot afford to be nonparticipants in studies of the future. Achievements in the processing and distribution of information within a short span of twenty years have brought about fundamental changes in governmental and political processes and have altered the psychological and cultural attitudes of millions of people, according to a recent study of the management of change.[2]

In the same study, four major categories of information technology that are of critical importance to human development were identified:

1. *Mass and individual communications:* speech, letters, telephone, telegraph, radio, television, films, books, magazines, newspapers, and the theater.
2. *Computer technology:* storage, retrieval, and processing of information with continuing growth in capacity and memory.
3. *Audio technology:* radio, recordings, the sound component of television, and the cassette tape recorder.
4. *Image technology:* photography in its many dimensions, graphic material of all kinds, and books.[3]

These exist now. But with constantly and rapidly advancing information technology, what are the questions facing educators if technology is to serve the goals of education in a democratic society? What elements must be built into curriculum planning to enable students to draw from a wealth of information so that rational decisions can be made and so that the student is not susceptible to outside manipulations? Is there a danger that schools will overemphasize abstractions because of the information-saturated environment, or will schools also expand the opportunities for students to have reality experiences as a part of their school life? Present trends seem to say that education will be viewed more and more as a lifelong activity, and will take place in a wide variety of settings both inside and outside of the school. Educational programs planned to in-

---

[2] "Information Technology and Its Implications," *The Futurist*, 6:244–245 (December 1972).

[3] "Information Technology," p. 244.

volve students in the affairs of the community and to involve community in the affairs of the school should increasingly provide a reality base. Through television, cassettes, computer resources, and the great range of media presently available and those to come, education can be delivered to unlimited types of locations. Educational service centers, electronic libraries, and resource centers of various types are appearing that indicate the ability of educational institutions to adapt media support systems to constantly changing and expanding future needs and developments.

RESOURCE CENTERS

New terminology reflects new conceptions of the library. Terms such as media center, learning center, instructional media center, resource center, and others are implying that libraries now contain much more than books, that in the newer context the library is at the center of learning, and that it is a place that provides services as well as materials.

In a remote and sparsely populated area of Maine is a media center serving schools in thirty small communities within a 2200-square-mile area. The center, located in Calais, Maine, provides a toll-free WATS (Wide Area Telephone Service) line telephone number to all students and teachers wishing to contact the center and free delivery service to all participating schools. Available on loan are filmstrips, slide sets, tapes, cassettes, records, film loops, learning kits, and a wide variety of printed materials. Services are offered in mounting and laminating pictures, lettering, making transparencies, and producing slide sets. In-service education programs are regularly available for teachers and the center expects to expand its services to students who wish to make their own films.

Alexander Central High School, Taylorsville, North Carolina, carefully planned the media center of its new building to support an innovative and comprehensive school program. The bi-level arrangement of the media center provides large areas in its complex which can accommodate entire classes and are often used for student panels, talks by guest speakers, or dramatic presentations shared with other classes. The center provides a vast array of materials which are readily accessible for students to use in their search for information to fit individual needs. All equipment and materials in the media center may be checked out by students for overnight use. In addition to printed materials, the most frequent overnight usage involves projectors, tape recorders, record players, films, filmstrips, film loops, recordings, and art prints. Many parents have "gone back to school" by sharing with their high school sons and daughters media materials in their own homes.

An unusual resource center is the Educational Facilities Center in

Chicago, which is beamed toward educators and those who select media for school needs. A variety of materials and products are displayed and demonstrations of a variety of teaching approaches are constantly offered to teachers. At the regional level, educational service centers are sponsored by such organizations as the Board of Cooperative Educational Services in New York, Intermediate Educational Districts in Oregon, Regional Educational Centers in Texas, and others.

A survey of teachers' views by the Nassau County New York Regional Center revealed a wide range of desirable resources that should be offered by a large instructional media center. Teachers said the media center should be a place:

—where overhead projectuals, audio and video tapes, activity sheets, units, dioramas and other instructional materials can be designed by teachers, scholars, technicians and students to meet individual and group needs;

—where teachers and administrators can call for information, pamphlets, magazines, books, news articles, research studies, materials and other resources and have their requests filled in 24 hours;

—that demonstrates and helps to adapt innovations and effective techniques in the classroom, e.g., teaching walls, teaching desks, and multiple projection and sound presentations;

—that will evaluate local curricula and work with the staff to develop improved and relevant courses and materials;

—that will use all of the local and regional resources available—libraries, museums, cultural groups, government, industry, colleges and universities, the community—in effective, meaningful ways;

—where scholars and professionals in residence—poets, writers, musicians, scientists, economists—can work with students and teachers;

—that develops materials and techniques for slow learners, the disadvantaged and the handicapped as well as for average and advanced students;

—where teachers can receive training and skills in developing and using all media to improve instruction;

—that will provide continuing consultation and resources to teachers, students and administrators whether in the classrooms, media center or community.[4]

From studies of future trends, Marvin Adelson, of the School of Architecture and Urban Planning at the University of California, Los Angeles, predicts that the learning process will not be so tightly tied to the teaching process and that libraries will be more and more expanded and

[4] Jack Tanzman, "All About Educational Service Centers," *School Management*, 16:16 (May 1972).

modified through new technologies. The libraries, or resource centers, as they become the cores of educational institutions or of educational processes, will step up the pace at which progress in information storage and retrieval technology is being implemented. The increasing use of audio and video cassettes promises to continue to expand and the library will increasingly be a distribution center for recorded presentations. The role of the book as a primary conveyor of stored information may be relatively diminished. Adelson expects nationwide computerized networks of libraries to become a reality in the 1980s.[5]

Through the use of microform technology, printed material may be reduced in size to 35mm or 16mm rolls of film, available in cartridges, that may be used by the student in a "reader" or that may produce printouts for him. Microfiche can provide on a 4 by 6 inch form hundreds of pages of printed matter. It is possible that some libraries may not be "places" but may provide services which direct the learner to resources.

One indication of the type of service that promises to become more and more desirable is the interest and attention given to the innovative volume: *Yellow Pages of Learning Resources*. This is a guide to the city—any city, any town. It consists of seventy alphabetically arranged categories and tells how to learn more about each one. It is a specific guide to people (the pharmacist, the taxicab driver), to places (the airport, the courtroom), and to processes (candymaking, city planning). Other topics include the architect, the bricklayer, the cemetery, insurance company, kindergarten room, quarry, and many others.[6]

LEARNING PACKAGES

There appears to be a clear trend toward providing access through the media center or library to learning packages of various sorts. Presently the education industry and research and development centers are creating, recording, and disseminating various types of educational media packages. For the individual learner, unlimited opportunities can be visualized.

The Learning Activity Packages (LAPs) publicized earlier among the innovations of Nova High School, Fort Lauderdale, Florida, are now widely used by many schools. Although some LAPs may be exportable from one school district to another, probably the most effective results are found when each district writes its own "packages." A Learning Activity Package is designed to individualize instruction and involves at

[5] Quoted in "Information Technology and Its Implications," p. 247.
[6] Richard Saul Wurman (Ed.), *Yellow Pages of Learning Resources* (Philadelphia: Group for Environmental Education, Inc., 1972).

a minimum the four components of pretest, objectives, activities, and posttest. Each LAP specifies the level and conditions of acceptable performance and provides learning activities incorporating multimedia, variations in methodology (i.e., large group instruction, small group instruction, individual work), and differing levels of resource materials both printed and audiovisual with alternative choices for the student. LAPs are based on the concept of individualized instruction. Each student is encouraged to progress at a pace, level, and in a manner that recognize his particular abilities, previous achievement, cultural background, needs, interests, and learning style. Individualized instruction is complex and requires the consideration of a number of factors at the same time. Content, space, staff, equipment, materials, record keeping, and arrangements for varying sizes of working groups must be organized and coordinated to reach each student's special needs. Self-instructional units such as the Learning Activity Packages provide materials from which students can receive many of their directions, thus freeing the teacher to work with individuals and small groups.[7]

Another widely utilized package is the UNIPAC, originally designed through the /I/D/E/A/ Demonstration Schools Project. At the present time a national UNIPAC bank containing more than 5000 UNIPACs which have been prepared by teachers for particular students identified by unique characteristics are available at cost in paper form or in microfiche to participating teachers from the Teachers' UNIPAC Exchange, Salt Lake City, Utah.

The UNIPAC was designed to aid teachers and students in an individualized program, and to stimulate a change in roles. The student's role becomes more responsible and less dependent, the teacher's role becomes more objective and professional or diagnostic-prescriptive, and the school's role becomes less authoritarian and more service-oriented. Teachers are trained to develop UNIPACs that respond to the local curriculum in individualized, product-oriented workshops. Packages are made using the concepts of the local curriculum plan. At a point where all concepts are packaged, the program becomes continuous progress. A teacher may begin with only one package and one dependable student, continuing to teach the others as usual, and expanding the UNIPAC program slowly as the teacher has time to develop it.

Project PLAN (Program for Learning in Accordance with Needs), described in Chapter 5, utilizes packages or modules which consist of a set of directions for the student, the instructional objectives of the module, a list of instructional materials and suggestions for using them, and sample

---

[7] James E. Smith, Jr., "The Learning Activity Package," *Educational Technology*, 12:15–16 (September 1972).

test items to help the student know when he has succeeded in achieving the objectives. Juanita Senior High School of the Lake Washington District, Kirkland, Washington, has designed a student-centered program which utilizes PLAN in four areas of the curriculum and is supported by a unique new facility formed around a Learning Resources Center. An individual program of studies for each student is provided by PLAN in language arts, social studies, mathematics, and science. A computer provides daily printouts for the teacher and student to utilize in assessing progress.

Locally developed learning packages are being created in all subject fields. In Aquinas High School, David City, Nebraska, learning packages have been developed for all chemistry and physics students. Wilcox (Nebraska) Public High School has developed packets for all algebra and geometry courses, grades 9 through 11, and the Omaha Public Schools have produced packages in world history which explore in depth particular concepts, such as nationalism, allocation of resources, international conflict, and political institutions. The State of Washington has funded an instructional materials center at Clover Park, Washington, to develop a depository for teacher-developed individualized learning packages. Thousands of packages have been photographed, placed on separate microfiche, and are ready for dissemination. One of the strengths of the depository is that it contains packages in sequences which provide complete programs rather than just an assorted accumulation of packages.

Numerous organizations are creating multimedia packages on a great variety of subjects. An example within the concept of "money management" is a unit on budgeting provided by the Changing Times Education Service (Washington, D.C.) which ties role playing with three budgeting situations: a student activities file with four independent study projects, a simulation game in which teams may budget family income for a year by making decisions and solving typical family budget problems, a booklet with six budget checklists and worksheets, and reading and resources listings.

Training packages to teach techniques, methodologies, or skills to educators are coming into use. In a project sponsored by the Research and Development Division of Nassau County (New York) Board of Cooperative Educational Services, nineteen teams designed training packages for educators in their local districts. Packages introduced participants to current trends in education including systems approaches, behavioral objectives, newer media, simulation and gaming techniques, and innovation and communication theory. Participants were helped in formulating solutions to specific problems in their districts by using more complex training packages to develop and evaluate other training packages; these, in turn, were field tested.

Regional laboratories sponsored by the United States Office of Education have produced a variety of learning packages. The Far West Laboratory has developed an Analytical Skills Kit that trains teachers in interaction analysis. A dramatic secondary level package from the same laboratory is the human relations training unit "Confrontations," which provides simulation games, films, and discussion leader guides. Training materials are provided for each of four workshop sessions.

DIAL RETRIEVAL SYSTEMS

In applications of electronic aids to the learning process, available knowledge and prototypes of multimedia far exceed the actual installation in schools. Only a few high schools have dial retrieval systems, even though they may have approximately the equivalent amount of hardware throughout the building in a miscellaneous approach. Increasing attention to learning systems, to individualized learning, and to the use of multimedia in education seems to say that a system such as dial retrieval can provide almost unlimited possibilities for teaching and learning, depending upon the ingenuity of the teacher or student who is making use of it.

Dial retrieval systems, sometimes called dial access or media retrieval systems, have capabilities for bringing to individual students working

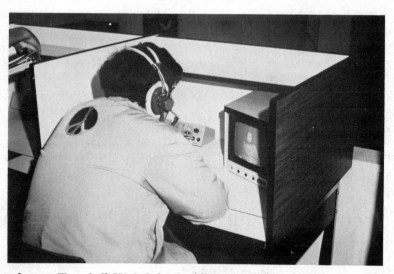

A student at Trumbull High School utilizes the dial retrieval system by watching television in a student carrel in the Resource Center. Pictures courtesy of Trumbull High School, Trumbull, Connecticut.

independently in carrels or to large or small instructional groups, at the push of the right buttons, a wide variety of audio, video, printed, or other illustrative materials.

An example of a dial retrieval installation is that of Trumbull (Connecticut) High School. The system was planned in advance of construction of a new high school facility and it was visualized as a support system for a curriculum designed to encourage students to do as much individual work as possible. The schedule supports the concept of individualization and provides one research and consultation period of the five periods per week devoted to most academic subjects. During the R and C period the student is free to work in areas of his personal interest or on teacher-assigned projects. Although the dial retrieval system is not essential for the R and C period, it is intended to expand the options for learning available to students. The dial retrieval system in the high school connects thirty-six carrels in the school's resource center and science labs as well as seventeen classrooms to the center from which the system is operated. It is possible to obtain live television programs, videotaped programs, 35mm color or black and white slides, 16mm film in color or black and white, and audio reels, cassettes, or records. School announcements and general information are also available through the system. An additional twenty carrels in the resource center are used as a language laboratory and require only audio connections to the equipment center. Portable television sets are available for other spaces where students or teachers wish to receive these services. Students under the supervision of an expert operator provide the necessary maintenance and operational services. As with other innovations, it was found necessary to provide special in-service education for teachers to learn how to take full advantage of the programs and possibilities that the media retrieval system offers. Students were said to be able to adapt to it with no trouble at all.[8]

PROGRAMMED INSTRUCTION

Programmed instruction is essentially an attempt to provide instruction that is more individualized, more tailored to each student's unique learning abilities and needs. However, the term programmed instruction has different meanings for different people. It may include programmed material that resembles something like a workbook with pages divided into frames and accompanied by a sliding strip or device that allows the student to uncover answers as he works along and to check whether his

[8] "What About that Dial Retrieval Business?" *School Management*, 16:25–27 (April 1972).

responses are right or wrong. It may include mechanical devices or teaching machines that inform the student at once whether his response to a problem or a question is correct, thus providing an immediate reward for success. Programmed instruction is based on systems theory in education and may include dial or push-button access systems, electronic language laboratories, automobile simulators for driver education, computer-assisted instruction, learning packages and systems, and various combinations of media.

Some authorities emphasize that the operational specification of behavioral objectives is the beginning step in the development of programmed instruction. The optimum use of programmed instruction implies not only precise specification of behavioral goals but also the use of continuous, progressive evaluation, diagnosis, and prescription. Thus, in this view, if instruction is to be programmed and prescribed on the basis of individual diagnosis, the school must have a workable taxonomy of behavioral specifications and student characteristics. Teachers must have available a large inventory of pretested instructional materials and media from which to make prescriptions. To develop such a system requires major efforts.

A prominent feature of programmed instruction is that it is largely self-instructional. Access to self-instructional materials and media for portions of the students' study time is essential to the success of individualized programs. The student, to become self-directed, needs blocks of time when he can teach himself and learn how to learn, thus necessitating flexibility of school organization. The changing role of the teacher, which demands skillful direction of the student's independent study time, of balance between guiding group discussions, making large group presentations, and conferring with individual students, must incorporate various self-instructional media for greater effectiveness.

The great promise of programmed instruction has not been fully realized, partly because schools have attempted to adopt programmed materials instead of adopting the principle of programmed instruction. Conceptually, programmed instruction was conceived to meet individual differences of students so that more students could find success in learning. However, as observed earlier, the programmed instruction boom of the late fifties and early sixties stimulated new efforts to individualize instruction. A wide variety of materials and devices are being marketed and educational consumers have been warned to check into the availability of research evidence before purchasing.[9]

---

[9] Evaluations of programmed texts and many other types of instructional materials and equipment are available from EPIE: Educational Products Information Exchange, 463 West St., New York City 10014.

Programmed Printed Materials

Programmed booklets or texts typically present the student with introductory information and require him to make a response such as filling in a blank or writing a word or phrase. He is then directed to the correct answer and can check his own response. If it is correct, he proceeds to the next bit of information, and so on through the entire program. In other examples, the student may receive his instructions through audio recordings. A systematic step-by-step self-instructional program can thus provide a means for each student to set his own pace by listening to the recordings and completing worksheets. When he has completed a unit of work, he is tested, the test is corrected immediately, either by himself, or if it is a culminative test, by an adult (aide or teacher). If his score reaches a predetermined level of performance, he moves on to the next step. If not, the teacher offers a series of alternative activities to correct the weakness, including special individual tutoring if needed. There may be almost no lecturing by the teacher to the class as a whole. Instead the teacher is busy observing students' progress, evaluating tests, writing prescriptions, and instructing individuals or small groups of students who need help. Programmed textbooks are frequently used at secondary levels in mathematics courses, statistical applications, and for self-instruction in computer programming. Audio-instructed programs are used to teach reading and mathematics skills at all levels.

Scrambled books are another type of programmed instruction and are designed so that the student may branch to information that fits his individual needs. For example the student begins reading on page one, where he is presented with a considerable amount of information. He is then given a question and chooses his answer from a series of possibilities. If he makes an incorrect choice, he is directed to a review section where he may reinforce the background. As he proceeds through the book he may also discover pages with information that he failed to master previously. He will be directed to sections where he can relearn this information. Programmed materials make it possible for the student to know at once whether he has selected a correct answer.

Teaching Machines

Teaching machines are programmed instruction devices into which programs are placed. These may be simple write-in machines in which the student writes a response after being shown a bit of information that requires completion or a reply. By advancing the material in the machine through a turning mechanism, the student may compare his response with the correct one and know at once whether he has successfully replied to the question. He proceeds bit by bit through the program. Multiple choice machines may provide punchboard or self-scoring models in which the student makes his response by pushing a button or perforating a paper.

Simulators for Driver Education

Another type of teaching machine is widely used in driver education. The student sits in a simulated model of an automobile and views a film in which he seems to be driving in all sorts of traffic conditions. He must make responses by turns of the wheel, pressure on the brakes, and the like. The simulator tallies the student's errors in judgment on a printout paper tape that is used by the teacher at the end of the film for instructional purposes. During the lesson, the instructor can tell by observing lights flashing on his control panel which students are making more errors than others. He also knows which "driving" conditions seem to be most troublesome and is able to tailor his instruction to the particular needs of the individuals in the class.

Electronic Learning Laboratories

Primarily introduced into secondary schools as language laboratories for drill-type exercises in the audiolingual approach to foreign languages, electronic laboratories are being expanded and programmed to serve self-instruction in music, shorthand, and other fields where recording and listening are important. The student may record a section, then listen to a correct version, then rerecord his own revised version, and proceed through a guided system of drill by contrasting his performance with a "model."

Language laboratories usually consist of approximately thirty booths equipped with headsets, microphones, and sufficient recording facilities for every student in the room to record frequently. A control console for the instructor or laboratory assistant provides monitoring facilities. Variations include mobile laboratories that may be wheeled into a room and utilized as needed to make foreign language instruction more effective. Listening and recording equipment is augmented in some instances by projection equipment for coordinating films and filmstrips with the taped listening materials. In rare instances, language laboratory booths are located in learning resource centers or other locations around the building and served by closed circuit television.

AUDIO TUTORIALS

Ingenious secondary teachers are creating multimedia tutorials which allow a student to work alone on a unit of instruction, aided by audiotapes, filmstrips and other specially created visuals, and printed instructions. Guided by the audiotapes, the student may work at his own speed individually in a carrel, in a science laboratory, or in other settings. Under the tutelage of the audiotapes, he reads, writes, performs experiments, handles materials, makes observations, repeats any segment or procedure desired, and takes tests. Secondary schools that have embarked on audio tutorial programs in the sciences include Temple City (California) High School, chemistry and physical sciences; Newport Harbor High School, Newport Beach, California, biology; and Adams Central High School, Monroe, Indiana, biology. Teachers, working in teams, have written the scripts for the audiotapes, prepared lesson material and supplies, and organized the courses into sequences so that each student may proceed at his best rate. Audio tutorials provide opportunities for learning in a variety of ways with each student using the medium which communicates most directly and effectively with him.

MULTI-IDEAS FOR MULTIMEDIA

Possible combinations of media are almost unlimited. Starting from the assumption that today's students learn in a variety of ways and that no single or narrow range of instructional procedure is adequate, modern teachers are employing imaginative combinations of resources. Far more audiovisual resources are available on the market than have found their way into the schools, however. The most popular items found in schools, according to a national survey, are listed in Table IV (p. 196). Audiotape cassettes were reported to be enjoying a boom, and a rise from previous years was noted in the use of all kinds of television equipment. Videotaping in the classroom for evaluative purposes as well as for rebroadcasts of public and educational programs was increasing. The same survey noted a national average expenditure of four dollars per student in 1971–1972.

Popular items as well as accessories, special models, and variations are listed among hundreds of kinds of equipment available in the *Audio-Visual Equipment Directory*, published by the National Audio-Visual Association, Fairfax, Virginia. As schools become able to finance multimedia equipment and as these approaches are demonstrated to improve student's learning, availability of equipment and materials will not be a problem, apparently.

Meanwhile, high schools are quietly going ahead with the creation of new ideas for uses of media. Condon (Oregon) High School, for example, has introduced a multimedia self-instructional system for the techniques of welding. More than 100 students per semester are learning the skills of welding through a system developed by the Northwest Regional

Educational Laboratory of Portland, Oregon. The system includes eight color-sound continuous loop demonstration films enclosed in cartridges, projectors, programmed texts, mounted model welds, and a complete set of professional welding equipment. With the teacher on hand to help with special problems and to evaluate actual work, the student operates the system himself.

An unpackaged approach to the use of multimedia is that of Hagerman (Idaho) High School. Here it is recognized that the wide range of student abilities, interests, and backgrounds requires that teachers must not only know the possibilities of media, and of combinations of media, but must guide the students to meaningful application of the resources. Available to high school students for learning opportunities are textbooks, supplementary books, paperbacks, and pamphlets; programmed materials; overhead transparencies; various types of audio-recordings; filmstrips and 35mm slides; models, objects, charts, graphs, and maps; instructional television programs; 8mm film loops and 16mm films; amplified telephone; educational games; and access to resource personnel.

Students are becoming more and more involved in creating their own multimedia products. An English-Social Studies team of Valley Forge High School, Parma Heights, Ohio, encourages students to combine studies of literature and history through their own film making. A motion picture based on Steinbeck's *Of Mice and Men* led the students into a study of the Great Depression and of mental retardation, as well as an analysis of the book, and development of skills of producing a drama. These students, like students in other schools, experiment with videotape recorders and monitors and with Super-8 motion picture cameras used with audiotape recorders.

table IV

Expenditures of Public Schools (K–12) by Type of Audiovisual System Employed, 1971–1972

ITEM	PERCENT OF TOTAL AUDIOVISUAL EXPENDITURES
16mm (Projectors and Film)	36.0
Filmstrips and Slides	17.9
Records and Tapes	13.6
Transparencies and Masters	7.6
Miscellaneous (Other)	7.2
Videotape Recorders	7.1
Television	5.7
8mm (Projection and Film)	3.3
Microfilm/Microfiche	1.6

Source: "Audiovisual Instruction Survey," School Management, 15:11–15 (November 1971).

Numerous high school students are illustrating English and social studies projects with various individual film making projects, usually accompanied by an audiotape or recording. One high school student of Clayton, Missouri, prepared a report which contrasted traditional high schools with alternative high schools by making a movie in each type of setting, then splicing skillfully so that the view could be flashed back and forth between the two types of schools to compare various types of instruction. The film was accompanied by taped music appropriately chosen to exemplify a background of rising or diminishing enthusiasm about the particular school learning task being shown.

Still photography is also being widely used by students. New pocket-sized one-inch-thick cartridge loading cameras reflect a trend toward giving students their own cameras for school projects. A variety of models are available: drop-in loading and simple settings for beginners and more advanced cameras for advanced students. Cameras can be checked out by students in the same manner as library books.

The theater-arts field has been enhanced by the addition of multi-

Students electing a course in Media Technology make a telecast of a presentation to be given in English classes. Photograph courtesy of Miami Springs Senior High School, Miami Springs, Florida.

media creations. The Theater Lab of Miami Springs (Florida) Senior High has made it possible for students to discover that imagination can be almost boundless when background photography and sound are added to live presentations. With the use of slides, film, and projected images that are faded in and out as the theme changes, and accompanied by music, lights, and appropriate sounds, new dimensions of dramatic presentations can be generated.

SIMULATION AND GAMING

Games are known to have been used in primitive societies for developing understandings and concepts in the young for their survival. Educational games are well known in the modern home and elementary teachers have frequently devised spelling games, arithmetic games, and others to capture children's interests as well as to motivate them. Far more sophisticated and complex are the simulations that have been developed in the field of business management in the past several years as vehicles for training. In urban planning, simulation exercises have been found useful in acquainting public decision makers with the interplay of factors and the time projection consequences inherent in their decisions. Service organizations such as church groups frequently use simulations to study probable consequences of alternate decisions affecting future issues, problems, and available resources: for example, probable consequences of moving a congregation's endeavors and locale from the inner city to the suburbs. Simulations and games for secondary levels of education are frequently being used to simulate reality situations in order to facilitate understandings related to instructional objectives, such as those related to allocation of income and credit financing in consumer education.

Simulation games are presently more widespread in the social sciences than in other disciplines, although there are some well-known mathematical games, such as the Games for Thinkers produced by WFF'N Proof. Games are also being devised in the sciences. The social sciences are seen to be particularly appropriate for simulation as activities can be devised to reflect the motives and interests of real persons in real situations while such abstract concepts as urbanization, inflation, or social conflict are developed.

An illustration is the game of Democracy, in which students take the roles of legislators and participate in caucuses, committee meetings, and parliamentary sessions. Each player must consider competing interests from his electorate, from fellow party members, from committee associations, and from his own personal conscience. As a result of game participation, the student has a better appreciation for the complexities underlying the decision making process that results in a law. Another illustration is the Life Career game, in which students must make life-career decisions related to education, jobs, family interests, personal interests, and recreation. Problems encountered by a bright lower-class boy whose family cannot provide for his education are studied through alternate courses of action.

Social science simulation games have these steps in common:

1. The objectives must be clearly defined, whether to demonstrate something, to teach, to train, to analyze, to explore alternatives, or the like.
2. The scope of the game must be determined; for example, in Empire, the game is concerned with the twenty-year period immediately preceding the American Revolution in relation to the issue of mercantilism.
3. The key actors in the situation are identified, such as individual decision makers, groups of people, nations, consumer groups, political groups, and forces of nature.
4. The actors' objectives must be determined in terms of their political, economic, military, or cultural role as relevant to this particular situation.
5. An interaction sequence is designed, such as what events go on simultaneously in time and what events follow other events in some order.
6. Decision rules are determined, such as "if the player does not get a raise within two years in the specific job, he will change jobs." Constraints are also identified, such as the conscientious objections of Quakers in a military situation.
7. The criteria for winning must be identified, such as whether everybody can win through cooperative activities or whether everyone can lose by unnecessarily conflictive behavior.
8. Design problems are resolved concerning the form of presentation of the problem, whether it is to be a board game, a role-playing game, or a paper and pencil analysis, and so forth. Computer simulations are increasingly coming into use for simulation games.

After noting that academic games should not be used in isolation but as complementary to other learning methods, simulation innovators cite these advantages:

1. Students learn to use facts in cause-and-effect relationships and in long-range planning.
2. While small group teams are learning different things at the same time, they learn from each other by interacting.
3. Simulation games characteristically can include a broad span of background and ability in membership on the teams that provide for heterogeneity within a given class.

4. Games are found to be motivational for students who have previously been unmotivated in usual school situations.

5. Educational games offer opportunities for students to be involved in systems analyses in which the problem can be continually analyzed and restated as new information is fed in.

At Abraham Lincoln High School, San Jose, California, an educational project is underway that engages students in games and simulations for an hour each day. In a unique association of industry and school, Technicon Education Systems is under contract to provide educational games, simulations, and related in-service training to the San Jose Unified School District. Themes of the units, which last from one to three weeks, are worked out by the teaching staff and representatives of Technicon. A typical game is the Freeway Planning Game, designed to simulate the give and take that must accompany the planning of a major highway. The game illustrates the impact of various segments of society upon the governmental offices that are responsible for planning freeway routes and provides an exercise in which conflicts, negotiation, and resolution can be enacted.

The purpose of simulation differs markedly from the purpose of transmitting information through the use of media. Simulation games provide a much different model of learning. In simulation, the student can practice with the components of life itself and apply information to decision making so he can reach a goal. Information becomes more relevant to the student when he sees it applied to a complex and real-life situation where interrelated actions must be considered.

The pitfalls in simulations and games are that they can be used merely as entertainment or because they are a fad. To counteract pitfalls and promote the use of simulations and games as learning tools, it is important to recognize that these are devices which can bridge the gap between the abstract and the practical; however, the bridging function does not automatically take place but is dependent on the follow-up sessions provided by the instructor. Opportunities should be designed for participants to compare individual and group performance to current theories, concepts, and traditional beliefs. Opportunities should be provided for participants to assess their own growth in performance or change in attitude.[10]

[10] The ERIC Clearinghouse on Media and Technology, Stanford University, will provide reports on simulation and games as well as on instructional films, television, programmed instruction, and computers. Reports on games and simulations within its subject scope are available from the ERIC Clearinghouse on Social Studies/Social Science Education, 855 Broadway, Boulder, Colo. 80302.

PRINTED MATERIALS

Current innovations in printed materials seem focused around variations in the "packaging" format and greater attention to inclusion of high quality treatment of minority group information. Also, materials inspired by the curriculum development groups of the sixties are continuing to enter the educational market through commercial publishers.

Paperbacks are continuing to increase in abundance. Minicourses have created a demand for paperbacks on current topics such as pollution, racism, sexism, drugs, war, peace, and selections from literature.

A typical example of the attention given to paperbacks is the special section of the Resource Center devoted to a paperback collection in the Hauppauge (New York) High School. Students are not required to charge the books in or out and records are not kept. Experience has shown that the original collection constantly changes and tends to increase as students add their own paperbacks to it. Special display shelving is used and the area is usually busy.

The conventional hardbound textbook, which required four to five years planning time, finds itself in competition with materials that attempt to keep pace with changing conditions. Textbook companies are currently producing many types of materials in colorful and attractive formats. Purchasers of textbooks frequently have the choice of a single hardbound edition or the same material divided into four to six booklets. Most textbooks may be purchased with supplementary aids such as filmstrips, overhead transparencies, audiotape cassettes, and others.

Materials produced by the national curriculum studies described earlier, and now available through commercial publishers, have the advantage of field testing prior to publication. The recycling process leading to revisions was time-consuming but worthwhile when data certified that revisions resulted in greater learning effectiveness. In contrast, an EPIE analysis of sixty best-selling textbooks revealed that fewer than 10 percent had ever been field tested prior to publication. The problem of the vast multitude of educational materials on the market is a matter of concern to those who must be responsible for selection and purchasing. The Educational Products Information Exchange Institute (EPIE), as mentioned above, provides reports and evaluations of several classes of educational products, both printed and audiovisual.

Another proof of the contemporariness of printed materials in the classroom is the use of the daily newspaper as teaching material. The *St. Louis Post-Dispatch* offers summer workshops for teachers with free scholarships, on how to use the newspaper in teaching, and provides free sets of newspapers daily to high school classes that participate in the program. In Los Angeles, Garfield High School has a course called Contemporary

Reading in which the *Los Angeles Times* newspaper is used as a text. Each student receives a daily copy and the material is used for increasing vocabulary, for recognition of public figures, and for familiarizing students with the spectrum of political thought. Occasionally a prominent citizen is invited to be interviewed by the class when he has appeared in a *Times* article.

Bias in Instructional Materials

Rising concern in recent years for the problem of instructional materials that are inadequate and undesirable on the basis of lack of recognition of minority groups has brought about some changes in printed content and pictured material. Although black people are credited with bringing the problem of bias in teaching materials to the attention of the public, other minorities are demanding and receiving recognition in the educational press.[11]

Detroit is one of several school systems that has developed a firm policy which rejects textbooks found to contain biased information. The Michigan Association for Supervision and Curriculum Development has developed evaluative guidelines for the use of Board of Education members, superintendents, curriculum supervisors, principals, teachers, and others engaged in the task of examining textbooks and other instructional materials for the purpose of review, selection, and purchase.[12]

Educators, awakened to the unresponsiveness of instructional materials to the contributions of black Americans, Indian Americans, Spanish Americans, Orientals, and other groups in a pluralistic society, are pressing for appropriate ethnic emphases in the curriculum. Professional associations, including the National Council of Teachers of English and the Association for Supervision and Curriculum Development, are exerting influence on writers and publishers for unbiased educational materials.

TEACHING BY TELEPHONE

Through the use of an amplified telephone in an audiovisual teaching system called the telelecture, a master teacher may speak to several classes simultaneously at different locations. If a visual monitor is pro-

---

[11] See Michael B. Kane, *Minorities in Textbooks* (Chicago: Quadrangle Books, 1970).

[12] Michigan Association for Supervision and Curriculum Development, *Criteria for Evaluating the Treatment of Minority Groups in Textbooks and Other Curriculum Materials,* available at modest cost from the Association, 1216 Kendale Blvd., East Lansing, Mich. 48823.

vided, the students may also see diagrams that are transmitted over the telephone lines and displayed on a television monitor. The teacher's voice carried by the speaker system is illustrated on the "chalkboard-by-wire" system, and if an audio return system is provided, students may ask questions by pressing an indicator button in the classroom. By depressing a switch on his console, the instructor then can talk to the students. It is also possible for the students in one classroom to speak to students in one of the other classrooms during the telelecture.

High school classes in Topeka were the first to use the telelecture system in the secondary schools of Kansas. Science lectures on topics of bacteriology, physics, chemistry, and botany were provided by professors of Kansas State University of Manhattan in cooperation with the science supervisor of the Topeka schools. Topeka teachers prepared and presented telelecture talks in American literature and history.

A unique "teaching machine" is used by International Correspondence Schools for home study. The student has a specially designed FM radio to receive an instruction program. The radio has four response buttons that let the student answer questions posed during a talk by the broadcast instructor. From time to time the student is asked to respond to a multiple choice question and, by pressing a button, learns immediately whether he has answered correctly.

Teleteaching, a term that implies use on a continuous basis as contrasted to an occasional telelecture, is used in several California school systems for homebound and hospitalized students. An experiment with homebound students was ~ponsored by the New York City Board of Education in which a radio broadcast on socialization was followed by an opportunity for the speaker to engage in a two-way telephone discussion with the patient. Significantly more positive orientation toward social interaction was achieved than with the usual one-way electronic communication of speaker to student. Predictions from this and other experiments are that the telephone has a greater potential as an instructional communications device than has previously been realized.[13]

Long distance amplified telephones are frequently used in seminars or conferences in which questions and comments may be exchanged between students and resource consultants. The same system can be used for the inservice education of teachers. Seven schools in Wyoming recently utilized the services of a lecturer from the east coast for one hour at a modest cost for the use of long distance lines.

Bell Telephone Laboratories have a rental device called a Portable Telephone which weighs less than 20 pounds and plugs into a standard

---

[13] Paladugu V. Rao and Bruce L. Hicks, "Telephone-based Instructional Systems," *Audiovisual Instruction*, 17:18–22 (April 1972).

telephone jack and electrical outlet. The phone has a loudspeaker built in for listening and two microphones for asking questions. With the unit a class can have a phone conference with anyone in the world for less than the cost of a film rental and far less than the cost of a guest speaker. A conference phone can be used to increase the number of "great speakers," to call the author of a book the class is reading, to contact local or national politicians, directors of films, or a high school class in another country.

TELEVISION

Television, described by a distinguished panel several years ago as a "technology of immense power, growing steadily more powerful,"[14] has moved slowly toward integration into the portion of the educational process that takes place in school. That the impact of television on education will increase seems inevitable when the potential capacity of television as a stimulant to learning is considered. Instantaneous worldwide communication available via television outside of the school has already revised a whole generation's outlook. Secondary students come to school with prior understandings that would have been impossible in the pre-electronic age of communications. However, instructional television has thus far been put mainly to incidental or occasional use as ancillary material; so far there is little evidence that television is a powerful medium of communication capable of making its own impress upon education. Although instructional television is not as widespread as might be desirable, the audiovisual survey mentioned earlier showed that the purchase of television equipment is on the increase in public schools. Also, improvements in engineering have produced television equipment that is becoming easier to use. Relatively recent developments that are contributing to increasing uses of television include portable videotape recorders and players, video cassette players, and expanding educational programming through cable TV services. Educational television continues to expand and improve its offerings both in closed- and open-circuit television. Closed-circuit television can make available to all students within a school building or within an entire district live or taped presentations from a centrally located studio. Open-circuit educational television is often conducted on a public-broadcast basis in cities where a channel is available for this purpose and where the expense of the transmitting station can be borne noncommercially. Ultra High Frequency and Very High Frequency channels are available for

---

[14] The Carnegie Commission on Educational Television. Quoted in James R. Killian, Jr. (Chm.), *Public Television: A Program for Action* (New York: Bantam, 1967), p. 13.

instructional television programs produced by public agencies, including schools. To receive this type of broadcast, ordinary sets with UHF and VHF reception are adequate.

Video Systems

Some of the most exciting innovations in the use of television are in closed-circuit installations, particularly portable video systems, in the schools. In Lane County, Oregon, a teacher watches a videotape of her class presentation and says, "Play that back, please. I sensed that I was losing them right there." Teachers in Lane County use videotapes to study and improve their own classroom presentations in a manner somewhat akin to the micro-teaching technique developed at Stanford University's School of Education. Videotapes are employed as an evaluation aid in a teach-critique-immediate-reteach procedure, employing five- to ten-minute lessons with small groups of pupils.

On a football field at Hall High School in West Hartford, Connecticut, a husky tackle misses a block, and within seconds his coach is pointing out that mistake via "instant replay." In the Lafayette, California, school district a lack of qualified Spanish instructors is compensated for by videotaping an entire language program for transmittal in twenty-minute Spanish lessons.

Video cassette units will expand still further the capabilities of video systems when compatibility problems have been solved. Playback units available on loan from the media center can be utilized by classes and individual students as the video equivalent of library reserve books.

Micro-teaching and micro-counseling are other variations of the use of video systems. Pioneering work in this area was done by the Far West Regional Laboratory which produced minicourses now available through the Macmillan Company. In either micro-teaching or micro-counseling a leader-in-training and four or five volunteer group members are videotaped for short segments of time in which single skills such as group leadership (in the case of counseling) or questioning (in the case of teaching) are emphasized. A usual procedure in micro-counseling consists of videotaping of five- to ten-minute segments of group interaction followed by viewing a video model of an expert group leader demonstrating this skill, thus giving the trainees a gauge against which to examine the quality of their own behavior. The trainee then views his own videotape comparing his performance on the skill in question against the "expert." Seeing oneself on tape within a specific context is a powerful learning experience. A trainer-supervisor provides instruction and support for the trainee. A second five- to ten-minute video group session usually follows with a succeeding analysis to ascertain growth in technique.

Educational Television

Educational television programming may be (1) instructional television, directed at students in the classroom in the context of formal education, and (2) public education directed at the general community.

Instructional television is usually closed-circuit television, and covers programs designed for groups of students or for individuals engaged in independent study. Basic characteristics of instructional television include:

The programs have been planned in consultation with professional educators.

The programs contribute to the systematic growth of knowledge.

They form part of a continuous series and are so planned that their effect is progressive.

They are accompanied by integrated texts, guides, workbooks, programmed learning materials, and complementary media materials.

They provide opportunities for active response, whether individually or collectively.

The impact of the programs is supervised and evaluated.[15]

The Dade County (Florida) High Schools have introduced the inquiry approach with instructional television utilizing the Biological Science Curriculum Study course. New programs have been designed that promote inquiry by posing problems to students, leaving them unsolved, and raising questions that alert students to alternate answers. Inquiry sheets are utilized for feedback. Large group televised instruction in BSCS biology is followed by small group discussion and laboratory experiences.

In New Trier Township (Illinois) the two high schools have available hundreds of especially tailored telecasts taped by student crews in a central educational television studio. These are broadcast upon telephone request to any classroom teacher or student at virtually any time of any school day. Telecasts include informal discussion sessions with notable persons including Margaret Mead, Ralph Nader, B. F. Skinner, Ashley Montagu, and Mike Royko, as well as performances and demonstrations by folk singers, visiting theater companies, scientists, and broadcasts of current happenings in the news. The telecasts form a growing videotape retrieval bank, which, with appropriate utilization with students provides an additional instructional resource.

Public educational television programs directed at the general community are usually produced live over local stations or draw from National Educational Television (NET) or other nonprofit depositories of video-

---

[15] Thomas Perry Strauss, "Instructional Television: A Definition," *Audiovisual Instruction*, 17:11 (April 1972).

tapes. Public affairs programs intended to induce people to think critically about important issues confronting our society have included programs such as "Earth Keeping" a six-part series focusing on ecological problems and solutions. Another series examined the plight of the nation's cities and suburbs. "The Naturalists," a four-part series, studied the lives of America's great naturalists: John Muir, Henry David Thoreau, Theodore Roosevelt, and John Burroughs. A wide variety of historical topics are available as are dramatizations from classical and contemporary literature.

Commercial Television

Through commercial television, students are keenly aware of day-to-day events in all parts of the world. Government is viewed in action as the president and other governmental leaders speak on television or as commentators analyze national issues and worldwide problems. The awe and wonder experienced by many millions of viewers who vicariously traveled to the moon with the astronauts brought a dimension to learning that only television could provide.

Advance information about scheduled programs is available to classroom teachers from the Television Information Office of the National Association of Broadcasters, New York City. Teachers' guides to television are provided that give background on commercial television programs most suited to classroom discussion. The American Library Association provides a similar service and publishes lists of related source materials and readings for programs for the coming month or more.

Cable Television

Cable television is a form of closed circuit but it serves entire communities instead of a single school or school district. Known as CATV (Community Antenna Television) it offers great potential for educational programming because of the large number of channels available and because its programming can take advantage of professional television studios. At the same time, CATV can be tailored to suit the needs of particular communities and in addition, offers the possibility of two-way communication.

A 1972 decision by the Federal Communications Commission requires all cable systems to set aside one channel for use by local educational authorities. So the opportunity is there for a closed-circuit network linking schools and homes day and night if educators get involved early enough in the franchise negotiations and demand their rights. However, only a few of the CATV systems in the country are presently originating programs and even fewer of these are of an educational nature. In Meadville, Pennsylvania, a cable television system is originating local news, features, and documentaries of an educational nature which are received by teachers, parents, and students. The Tulsa cable television operation provides programming facilities for local educators and students. In Casper, Wyoming, the cable system is programming instructional courses as well as originating community programming. A survey of classroom teachers brought in suggestions for cable television broadcasts that included public affairs, medical and health information, live and taped coverage from Washington, D.C., and selected specials, documentaries, and other programs of interest to local communities.[16]

Electronic Video Recording

An imminent educational innovation for homes and hotels as well as schools is the Electronic Video Recording (EVR), a new system that transforms an ordinary television set into a movie screen on which films can be selected for viewing at any time. In 1968, in a classroom in Stamford, Connecticut, it was demonstrated for the first time when a film cartridge was dropped into an existing television monitor (specially equipped for the demonstration), an unused channel was dialed, and the classroom viewed an educational film. EVR is expected to be commonplace in the 1980s and capable of transforming the home into a self-contained educational center or of bringing unlimited film possibilities to the classroom.

COMPUTERS

Computers are performing a variety of tasks for secondary schools ranging from data processing through instruction. A national survey sponsored by the Committee on Educational Technology of the National Association of Secondary School Principals in 1971 located 454 schools throughout the nation that were using computers in instruction.[17] Since that time the number has undoubtedly increased because of moderating costs and increasingly smoother operation.

Schools are finding access to computer services in a variety of ways. During slack periods, schools have found low cost or even free computer services available to schools just for the asking. Other schools have joined in a consortium such as the Region IV Education Service Center of Houston, Texas, which serves a network of high schools in the Greater Houston area. Five neighboring school districts in the vicinity of Boston (West-

[16] J. David Truby, "Happily Hand in Hand: CATV and the Classroom Teacher," *Audiovisual Instruction,* 12:53–55 (May 1972).

[17] Warren J. Koch, *The Use of Computers in Instruction in Secondary Schools* (Washington, D.C.: National Association of Secondary Principals, 1972).

wood, Lexington, Natick, Needham, and Wellesley) have also formed a network. Similar examples could be cited. Schools occasionally buy or lease a computer, although this puts responsibilities on the individual school for employing experienced personnel capable of operating, directing, and maintaining the computer services. With the advent of minicomputers costing less than $10,000 to purchase, many more schools have been attracted to purchasing their own computers.

Batch processing is an inexpensive way of conducting a program of computer instruction. In batch processing, students use mark-sense or key punch cards to put their data into the computer. Output may require only a few minutes or several days depending on the location of the computer and the available service. Time sharing is one of the most popular means of using computers in instruction. In time sharing, a teletype machine is located in the school and is connected by telephone line to the computer which may be nearby or at a distance. In some time sharing systems, the teletype, which provides paper printouts, is replaced by a video screen which is accompanied by a typewriter keyboard to provide input.

Some schools feel that all students should be familiar with the functions of computers and provide orientation ranging from one- to ten-period introductions to what computers are and what they can and cannot do. Interested students are encouraged to use programmed materials or to attend noncredit after-school sessions to learn more about programming of computers.

Courses in Computer Skills

Courses are frequently offered covering a wide area and ranging from how a computer functions to learning a computer language and doing actual programming. Dartmouth College provides time sharing instructional computer services to secondary schools in the New England states. BASIC, an easily learned and effective computer programming language for high school students is taught. In Portland, Oregon, Project REACT (Relevant Educational Applications of Computer Technology) has developed twenty-four instructional units or packages organized into three courses, each providing thirty hours of instruction. The purpose is to develop instructional units to help teachers and administrators increase their basic understanding of computers and learn how they can be used in instruction and administration.

Problem Solving

In this approach, the computer is used as a problem solving tool in mathematics or one of the sciences. A project conducted by the University of

Pittsburgh's Department of Computer Science in cooperation with the public school system has as its goal to introduce the student to problem solving through adult-devised programs and move him on to creating his own programs which he must debug and utilize. The novice is introduced to problem solving by means of a series of curriculum units called modules which are being developed in mathematics, physics, chemistry, biology, social science, and computer science. At Burlingame (California) High School in the San Mateo Union High School District students are using a minicomputer in which they must complete a series of predetermined programs and then are free to write their own. The program problem may involve statistics, probability, calculus, analytic geometry, or other mathematical areas.

Modeling and Simulation

Some infrequent uses of the computer are modeling and simulation applications being devised in economics, biology, chemistry, and physics—subjects that readily lend themselves to computer use. An example is the Man-Made World course. After an initial four-year experimental trial, the course had spread to 7000 students taught by 200 teachers in various schools across the country by 1970. Among these were the regional high school at Amherst, Massachusetts and the Roy (Utah) High School.

The course is unique in its approach. It shows students how a computer works and how to program one. The object of the course is to give students who are not scientifically bent enough knowledge of science and technology to enable them to think about technological issues affecting society. Through the use of computer models designed by Bell Telephone Laboratories and through access to computer centers, students learn the values and pitfalls of predictions based on models. Students learn how to observe, how to measure, how to select from a set of facts or ingredients to achieve a desired result, and how to use concepts such as feedback, stability, amplification, and control. The content of the Man-Made World course demonstrates the relevance of technology to biology, economics, sociology, business, communications, psychology, and the arts and humanities. It offers insight into coping with social, economic, and political problems as well as purely technical ones.

Tutorial Uses of the Computer

Computer assisted instruction (CAI) programs, originally introduced on the elementary school level, have also been initiated in secondary schools. Among the CAI programs in use at Albert Einstein High School (Kensington, Maryland) are geometry, general science, chemistry, algebra, consumer mathematics, and physics. Programs are in tutorial, drill and practice, problem solving, and simulation modes. In Philadelphia, computer assisted instruction is operational in four high schools in reading and biology, with CAI material for algebra and general mathematics being developed.

Instructional Diagnosis

Computer managed instruction (CMI) is used frequently in conjunction with programmed methods of instruction. In CMI the computer tests and keeps a record of each student's progress, and in some cases advises the student whether he is ready for the next unit of instruction. It may also indicate where the student might need additional remedial work. An experiment in computer managed instruction, sponsored by the Middle Country Central School District in Centereach, Long Island, New York, uses Britannica's TEMAC series in individualized instruction in mathematics. The computer scores the student's test at the end of each unit, records his score, keeps track of his progress, and assigns him to a mathematics class section based upon his progress.

Curriculum Management

A unique use of the computer is the curriculum management system of Shawnee Mission Northwest High School, Shawnee Mission, Kansas. Designed to assist the teacher, data are stored in four categories: instructional objectives, activities, resources, and test items. Within the first year of usage, over 5000 items had been developed in several areas of mathematics, science, typing, and environmental studies. All items are cross-referenced at the time they are entered into the pool and the computer keeps track of how they are related and how to prepare and select them for production. From this pool, a teacher can design several programs of study for the several interest groups of students within a given class and have the computer prepare for each student individualized study guides, pretests, and posttests. The data are stored on discs and entered and retrieved via an IBM model 2741 communications terminal.

THE POTENTIAL OF MEDIA

Amazing new possibilities can be visualized through the magic of media. Perhaps the wise use of new media can make the school more humane than ever before. Much of the routine and drill can be assigned to technological tools such as the computer, programmed instruction, and audio cassettes leaving more time for teachers and students to be involved in interpersonal relationships, learnings, and counseling. Perhaps the new media may offer the student new success in learning by appealing to him through sight, sound, movement, and involvement. Today's student, through the use of media, has far greater opportunity than ever before to understand and appreciate cultural differences and to learn from the world about him.

But all of these resources are effective only in proportion to the quality of the people who use them. An audio cassette, like the finest textbook, in the hands of a dull, pedantic teacher can turn into an undesirable instrument for the student. Educational technology is only one of the many alternatives available to education and should never be the only alternative presented. The quality of education will not reside in expensive equipment or imaginative tools of communication but in the sensitivities of teachers to the needs and interests of their students.

additional suggestions for further study

1. Eisele, James E., and others. *Computer Assisted Planning of Curriculum and Instruction.* Englewood Cliffs, N.J.: Educational Technology Publications, 1973. The authors describe how computers can be employed to retrieve lists of resources appropriate to any subject matter and to the needs of specific students. While the computer used in this manner does not teach students directly, it does help to individualize instruction by providing access to materials on an individual basis.

2. The ERIC (Educational Resources Information Center) Clearinghouse on Educational Media and Technology, Stanford University, Stanford, California, disseminates research results and resource information related to educational technology and media. Reports are listed in *Research in Education,* an index to ERIC resources.

3. The Ford Foundation, *An Inquiry into the Uses of Instructional Technology.* New York: The Foundation, 1973. This report examines the new technologies of teaching and learning—television and related techniques, videotape, film, audiotape, radio, programmed instruction, computers, and new kinds of books.

4. Kapfer, Philip G., and Glen F. Ovard, *Preparing and Using Individualized Learning Packages for Ungraded, Continuous Progress Education.* Englewood Cliffs, N.J.: Educational Technology Publications, 1972. How to translate traditional curriculum guides and lesson plans into individualized learning packages is the theme of this book.

5. Simon, Myron, *Ethnic Writers in America.* New York: Harcourt Brace Jovanovich, 1972. Contributions of ethnic writing to the educational field are sampled in this book of readings.

6. Snyder, Clifford L. (Ed.), *Viewpoints: Red and Yellow, Black and Brown.* Minneapolis: Winston Press, 1972. In this collection of readings, the predominant theme is a growing sense of pride among minority peoples for their rediscovered heritage. The problem of

The Potential of Media   213

racism in education occupies one section and other portions provide
background information.
7. Teachey, William G., and Joseph B. Carter, *Learning Laboratories—
A Guide to Adoption and Use*. Englewood Cliffs, N.J.: Educational
Technology Publications, 1973. A nonhardware approach to the techniques of the learning lab and how it can improve learning are
described in this book.
8. Zuckerman, David W., and Robert E. Horn, *The Guide to Simula-
tions/Games*, 2d ed. Lexington, Mass.: Information Resources, 1973.
A descriptive survey of available simulations/games at all levels with
information on how to design and introduce them in instruction.

7

Space: New Places for Learning

New shapes and forms of space for learning are, at long last, appearing in nearly every school district of the nation. New views of how learning takes place, new styles of teaching, new knowledge, and pressures of social change have broken the hundred-year reign of the boxlike school and batch processing of students. Following the lead of the Quincy Grammar School, a fully graded public school established in Boston in 1848, schools for more than a century were designed in the form of a large box made up of a series of smaller boxes set side-by-side. Each box or classroom served a class of twenty-five to thirty pupils who were instructed in the same way by a person who did most of the talking while the students listened. Based on the assumptions that sameness for everyone was good and that the school's business was to "tell" or to impart information to students who had no other means of acquiring it than from teachers and books, the nineteenth century model continued to be duplicated over and over again until its widespread use came to be regarded as the standard to be copied whenever a new building was built.

It seemed to be the nature of the box forms to invite the use of drab colors for the walls and woodwork, to use hard echoing materials for floors and ceilings, to accompany sterile physical surroundings with a grimness of tone expressed in the lock-step organization, the use of uninspired materials, and the undemocratic attitude of high schools that they were there to sort out the students who should go on to college and direct the others into trades, or screen out the rejects who were not able to keep up with the uniform requirements.

CHANGING FUNCTIONS

Then, beginning about the middle of the twentieth century, new ideas about education began to take hold. America committed itself to universal education, and secondary schools began to broaden their scope beyond the singular college preparatory function. Increasingly, new knowledge was generated. Access to information through printed materials, films, television, audiotape recordings, and travel became widely available. The school lost its status as the student's chief source of information. Unfamiliar social problems also invaded the schools. No longer could the school stand as an isolated fortress with its sole mission that of transmitting information from teacher to student. Consequently, the expanding scope of secondary education called for changes in the physical forms of the high school to support new goals and procedures.

Places for learning in the newer mode are conceptualized to meet the general goals of American education: to constantly search out knowledge needed for living in an increasingly complex world, to contribute to the good of all, and to find joy in personal development.

School buildings also reflect new realizations about learning: that students learn and teachers teach in diverse and individual ways, that learning is enhanced by discovery and exploration, by interaction with other students and with adults, and that learning comes from many sources rather than a narrow channel or uniform requirement for all. Schools are determined to reach all students and to encompass the rich cultural pluralism of their young people. Those students who were formerly left out are being included in innovative ways that frequently utilize new places for learning and new space arrangements. Schools are being built with space that provides places for an individual to work by himself, for twos or threes to work together, for ten to twenty students to form a group for a specific purpose, or for hundreds to meet together for a more general purpose.

Recognition of the great diversity of human beings calls for space where students may confer with teachers and seek personal advisement on many types of matters. Both teachers and students need places to search, read, write, confer, interact, view, listen, think, experiment, and record. Students need places to transact student affairs or to gather for social purposes. Teachers need office space, conference rooms for team planning, facilities for diagnosis of pupils' needs, and facilities for preparing instructional presentations. New views of the teaching–learning process that move beyond memorizing of knowledge toward involvement of students in applying, analyzing, synthesizing, and evaluating knowledge stress the need for flexibility of space in the secondary schools.

School planners are recognizing that the environment must not only be adaptable for present objectives but amenable to constant renewal and change. A promise of the future is that students now in school will have several changes of career through their life time and thus the school must gear itself to teaching how to learn, how to search for information, and how to draw on technology effectively. Innovative schools are providing opportunities for students to use electronic storage and retrieval devices for efficient utilization of knowledge and major consideration; attention is being given to adequate electrical power capabilities. New teaching and learning styles have called attention to the need for good acoustics; year-round climate control with adequate ventilation, heating, and cooling; proper lighting; and strategic uses of carpeting.

Still another major influence on school buildings is the growing movement to integrate the school with the community. As our society has emerged into new social and economic patterns, the role of the school has become more complex and in the future seems destined to be a major instrument for promoting lifelong learning. Schools will become more and more accessible for learning by adults as well as young people; schooling will take place during hours beyond the regular school day and throughout the year. To meet these new challenges to secondary education, new functions and forms of space are emerging and new places for learning are being created.

OPEN SPACE

Open space schools, more common at the elementary school level, are beginning to appear at the high school level. As an expression of the concept of openness—encouraging an open atmosphere for learning in which a great variety of options are available to nurture student talents that might otherwise be undeveloped—open space schools provide a setting for breaking the lock-step of traditional patterns in favor of programs designed to reach the individual differences of learners. When properly planned and utilized, open space schools provide a more spacious and responsive environment for learning and provide flexibility for unknown futures in educational programs. In the traditional high schools, particularly large ones, students are programmed into patterns in which their contacts with other people are very limited. Schedules control the student's day from room to room, into an assigned bank of lockers, and contain him in a set timetable for a required length of school day, during which time he may not leave the building.

The major difference between open space schools and traditional schools is that in the latter, space is divided into rooms that are assigned on a permanent basis without much flexibility in use. Open space is flexible and, given proper furniture and equipment, the use of the space can change almost instantly. Students and teachers may move from a large group activity to small group or individual study, and learning activities can flow from one place to another.

Secondary schools are likely to have more traditional views of space than elementary schools. Secondary schools are basically more complex in nature and some spaces must be committed to special purposes, for example, music rooms or chemistry laboratories. Thus we find that open space secondary schools usually are semi-open with a combination of open and committed space. Frequently pods or classroom clusters are open within themselves but not to each other or to other areas of the building.

Open spaces or pods appear in a variety of shapes—hexagons, circles, and so forth—and are particularly adaptable for team teaching, differentiated staffing arrangements, and new uses of instructional media. They offer more varied options available to students, more adults to guide and assist, and a richer scene for stimulation and motivation.

Open Campus Possibilities

Open space schools provide possibilities for the student to use many different areas of the school, to interact with a greater variety of people, and sometimes to continue his learning away from the school building under open campus plans which are further expressions of the concept of openness. Under an open campus plan, students are not required to be in the school building except for their scheduled classes. Assigned study halls and passes are not needed and students may go to the library, to the science laboratories, to the electronic learning areas, to other work areas of the school, or may leave school entirely when they do not have a class. More space is thus available for classroom use and teachers have more time for planning and preparation when they are relieved of study hall and cafeteria supervision. Jones High School in Beeville, Texas, has, by combining open campus with an extended school day, increased its capacity by 25 percent. Lawrence High School in Falmouth, Massachu-

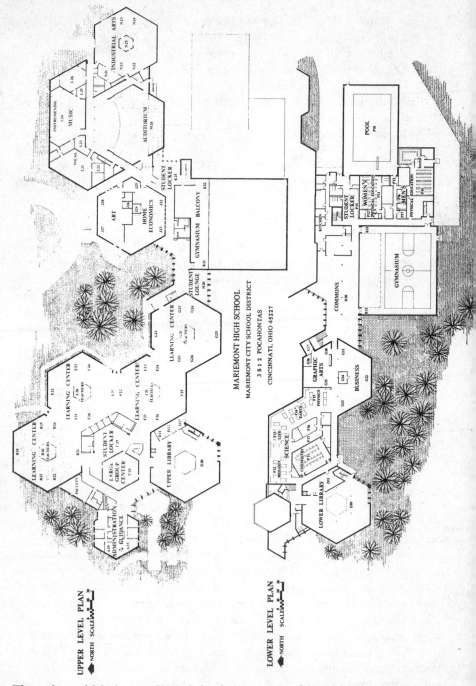

Floor plans of Mariemont High School, Cincinnati, Ohio. Plans reproduced by permission of Baxter, Hodell, Donnelly, and Preston, architects.

Open space in use at Mariemont High School, Cincinnati, Ohio. Photograph courtesy Baxter, Hodell, Donnelly, and Preston, architects.

setts, after initiating an open campus plan, made its cafeteria available as a student lounge and opened its auditorium for panel discussions, folk singing, films, and guest speakers. The building, originally designed for 950 students, was able to house 1200 students comfortably with its new organization.

An Overview

To see how open plan high schools were working, a space planning consultant of the Educational Facilities Laboratories visited schools from New Hampshire to California with enrollments ranging from 800 to 3000 students and operational experience ranging from six months to six years. A few were fully open space high schools but most were flexible or transitional schools in which some departments and some areas were open. School administrators and architects tended to describe transitional buildings as "open plan" even though a traditional program was in operation in a building with movable partitions. It seemed to be easier to run a traditional program in an open plan school than an open program in a transitional school. Success of more advanced and innovative concepts of secondary education seemed more likely to occur in an architecturally open facility. The most successful programs existed where a strong administrator was providing leadership. Best use of open space was found where appropriate furniture and furnishings were in use. Individual student desks were used less and were generally replaced by chairs around a table for up to six students; there were also informal uses of stools, hassocks, and carrels.[1]

Cautions

Although open space high schools offer an environmental tool with unlimited possibilities for creative teaching and learning, performance of students and teachers has not been successful in some instances. Full understanding of the concept of openness is critical to the success of the use of an open facility. Far more teacher–student planning must occur. A sense of order and method must permeate the school. The open setting requires that teachers be engaged in more interaction with the other teachers, with teacher aides and other adults, as well as with students, than they have experienced in more traditional settings. Teachers must be trained to teach students how to develop and use self-directed learning. Students must be taught the skills of decision making and self-responsibility if they have not had opportunities for developing these processes earlier.

If an open space facility is not accompanied by careful planning and programming with agreement on full sharing of responsibility, an unpleasant situation may develop with teachers and students continually engaged in confrontations rather than working cooperatively and constructively together.

Some of the more serious problems of open plan schools in their early stages had to do with architectural arrangements. Often the first open plan schools were simply huge areas of open space without landmarks or reference points. Later models recognized the need for subspaces which express the purpose of the individuals and groups who will be working there. Subspaces are accomplished with movable panels, furniture, carrels, and use of varying floor levels and sunken areas. Examples of high schools using subspace elements effectively are North Kingston Senior High School (Rhode Island) and Little Falls High School (New York). Colorful and movable dividers with surfaces to mount graphic displays are used flexibly to mark off space for varying purposes. Furniture is also movable and may be used for many types of groupings.[2]

[1] "Open Plan Schools Gain in Numbers and Successes," *Schoolhouse* (Newsletter from Educational Facilities Laboratories, September 1971), p. 2. A directory to open space high schools is available from EFL, 477 Madison Avenue, New York, N.Y. 10022.

[2] *Places and Things for Experimental Schools* (New York: Educational Facilities Laboratories, 1972), pp. 38–41.

CONTEMPORARY ARCHITECTURAL DESIGNS

The latest trends in school architecture are annually exhibited at the convention of the American Association of School Administrators.[3] Recent exhibitions emphasize several important trends. New importance is placed on novel and aesthetic exteriors. A model of Timberline High School, Lacey, Washington, illustrates the use of a heavily wooded, steeply sloping 58-acre site cleared for construction in a manner designed to save as much of the wooded area as possible. A central feature is a student commons area highlighted by a decorative pool and fountain. The academic building of Timberline is virtually all open space planned around four houses with an administrative suite, a science area, and resource materials area at the center. Two other common units for all four houses contain physical education and cafeteria, music, arts, and shops.

Other new schools come in many imaginative designs utilizing multiple levels, open courts, sunken floors, circular and hexagonal units, all with aesthetically pleasing landscaping designs. Windowless schools appear to be growing in popularity and are incorporated with variations of open space plans. Advantages of windowless schools include: less damage due to vandalism, economies in costs of heating and air conditioning, and elimination of the need for window-covering devices needed for audiovisual programs.

Technology

Instructional technology continues to be an integral part of new construction with adequate arrangements for its use in all parts of the building. Timberline High has incorporated "wet columns" as a new idea for science laboratories. "Wet column" is an expression designed to convey the concept of a pillar or shaft which contains electrical, gas, and water connections and outlets needed for laboratory work. The terms "wet" and "dry" are also used in relation to study carrels in a learning resource center and distinguish wet carrels—those that have access to electronic media—from dry carrels, that provide only a desk surface in the private study cubicles. In the science area at Timberline, wet columns penetrate the loft space and contain all necessary services for science, so that instead of fixed tables of a certain size, movable tables can be arranged around all four sides of a column to create open spaces or various types of work areas as needed for given tasks.[4]

Other new architectural features are a large student center at Green-

[3] Award-winning designs are reported annually in the January issues of *Nation's Schools*.

[4] American Association of School Administrators, *Open Space Schools* (Arlington, Virginia: The Association, 1971), pp. 94–95.

wich High School (Connecticut) with a circular staircase and massive pillars, which also serves as a dining area, a place for social activities, and a meeting and concert hall. The Greenwich campus has a house plan with four houses arranged on two levels, each with its own student body, housemaster, staff, and space for teachers and guidance counselors. At Ypsilanti Senior High School (Michigan) on a 65-acre site there is a large parking area for students, staff, and for driver education. Also noteworthy is a ramp for physically handicapped students.[5]

The new schools emphasize aesthetics, color, air conditioning, flexibility, and value per dollar. In the new designs there are no long "institutional" corridors, but aesthetically pleasing new uses of space instead.

New Library Forms

Resource centers as the heart of new high schools express the changing concept of the library. Appearing in a variety of physical forms, libraries may also be known as learning resource centers, instructional media centers, and similar terms. It may be located at the center of the building complex or at the periphery. Alternatively, it may be decentralized into resource centers located in subject area units or within each unit of multi-school plans. Or, it may consist of a central core library with subcenters located in specialized areas.

Whatever its name or shape may be, the library is intended to serve an extremely important function: service. The modern library facility is intended to encourage learning, not hinder it; to make information freely and fully available, not dole it out sparingly. It is a place of learning through many types of media and in ways designed to appeal to the unwilling learner as well as the zealous one. The "think" and "quiet" signs are no longer needed and the librarian no longer sees himself as the custodian of books, whose goal is to have every book in its place. His business is serving people and aiding them in their quests. The new library includes far more than printed materials; it is a masterful blend of many kinds of educational media and materials.

Study carrels are innovative additions to conventional library facilities and range from "dry" carrels that provide a private semienclosed study surface and bookshelf to "wet" carrels with elaborate electronic equipment for dial access to a wide range of audio and video resources. Carrels are usually arranged in clusters or rows and are located in areas where traffic is relatively light: possibly in a section of the central resource center, along hallways, or in decentralized resource centers.

Other architectural attractions include various types of media installations, work areas for technical processing by students and faculty, and

[5] "The New Environment: How 16 Award-Winning Schools Compare," *Nation's Schools*, 89:45–51 (January 1972).

Interior of Phoebus High School, Hampton City Schools, Hampton, Virginia, showing student mall bridged by upper level library. (Architects: Rancorn, Wildman & Krause [Hampton] and Perkins & Will [Washington, D.C.])

rooms for small group discussions, projects, and viewing and listening activities.

A unique library design is a part of the new Phoebus High School of Hampton, Virginia. The two-level school is designed around a spacious student mall. Spanning the mall is a wide bridge—the library—easily accessible and visible from both levels. Semi-open academic spaces on the upper level and specialized areas on the lower level face the mall.

A two-level library is a major component of the innovative and aesthetically pleasing open space Mariemont High School in suburban Cincinnati. The school is designed as a grouping of hexagonal pods and follows the contour of a hill on a wooded site of 38 acres. The hexagonal library unit, near the main entrance of the complex, serves a modern program and is readily accessible from both upper and lower levels.

Facilities for Nonstudy Hall Programs

Abolishment of the study hall in numerous high schools has had an effect on facilities. Places for learning are being designed into high schools in heretofore unusual uses of space. Cape Elizabeth High School (Maine) issued this invitation to its students:

"UNASSIGNED PERIOD" POSSIBILITIES [6]

We are most fortunate at our "new" Cape High to have many worthwhile facilities available for student use during unassigned periods. Each Cape student is considered to be a young adult, capable of planning an educational, as well as enjoyable use of this time. Supervised study halls are provided when an individual appears unable to handle this free time. Listed below are the numerous facilities open for student utilization.

WHAT IS YOUR SPECIAL INTEREST? LIKE READING, PEACE & QUIET?
The Library offers:
    50 individual carrels and informal readings areas.
    Typing room for special assignments.
    Conference rooms for quiet meetings.
    Audiovisual room for assigned student aides.

LIKE EATING, CHATTING, ETC.? The Student Center is open all during school hours.

LIKE TO BE BUSY? Volunteer to assist in the: Library, P.E. Offices, General Office, Guidance Office, Laundry, Trainers' Room, Student Store, School Guide Service, Nurse's Office, Audiovisual Facility.

LIKE TO WORK ALONE? The Student Work Rooms offer space for working independently, or in small groups in Math, Social Studies, and English.

INTERESTED IN PHOTOGRAPHY, SCIENCE, MATH? Special work rooms are available in each of these areas: Photography Dark Room, Plant and Animal Room, Science Project Room, Math Laboratory.

ARE YOU ATHLETICALLY INCLINED? Open areas for Physical Education will be announced.

LIKE VARIETY? "Rap" - location of "Sessions" will be announced. "Sun n' Study" - when weather permits - in the outside Amphitheatre. Get involved in Student Publications. Attend announced "Auditorium and "Lecture Room" programs. Be a "Student Tutor Volunteer" - help another High, Middle, or Elementary, student catch up in college requirements, information, etc., in the "Guidance Office."

MUSICALLY OR ARTISTICALLY INCLINED? Music rooms are available for practice of musical instruments or small group rehearsals of folk, rock, instrumental or vocal music, with faculty approval. Get permission for use of Fine Arts facility.

HOW ABOUT INDUSTRIAL ED., BUSINESS ED., OR HOMEMAKING?
Permission to use these facilities may be obtained from the supervising teacher.

---

[6] Multilithed brochure from Cape Elizabeth High School, Cape Elizabeth, Me.

John Marshall High School of Portland, Oregon, makes extensive use of open laboratories and resource centers throughout the school as well as a main instructional materials center. An all-school modular flexible program involves the entire student body of more than 2000 ninth-through twelfth-graders. There is extensive use of teaching teams, large and small group instructional periods, open laboratories, and independent study time for students. The schedule is based on a weekly cycle using a twenty-minute modular system consisting of twenty-one modules per day. Although conventionally designed as a three-level rectangular structure built around a large open central courtyard, the school has rearranged its facilities to support the innovative program.

THE PLANNING PROCESS

In the postwar building boom of the fifties, scores of boxlike high schools were built and these, unless remodeled, continue to control and limit the educational program. In the fifties, the planning process was notable for noninvolvement of the people who were going to use the buildings. Planning followed a simple linear flow chart that started at the point of hiring an architect by the school board and perfunctory meetings of the architect with the superintendent of schools and/or the chairman of the building committee (composed usually of a few school administrators, sometimes with department chairmen and one or two board members). Chief decisions were those regarding the size of classrooms and locations of the gymnasium, principal's office, and other conventional areas. Next followed the drawing of specifications by the architect and letting of construction bids, with the process concluding with installation of standard furniture and equipment.

Today, the planning process is much more complex and the resultant flexible space for learning much more responsive to needs and effective in reaching goals for universal as well as individual education. An early step in the planning process is a procedure for developing understandings about flexible space and open flow with the many different groups to be involved. Persons who are accustomed to traditional buildings may question the advantages of openness. An educational program for community and school persons will require both time and money. Carefully planned educational exposures to learning theories that support modern philosophical considerations underlying the goals of public education may mean visits to observe modern concept schools in operation, new staff development efforts, individual study on the part of educational leaders, use of appropriate printed and visual materials, and interaction with consultants, teachers, administrators, and students who have had first-hand experiences in open space schools or other flexible arrangements.

The selection and training of staff are key factors in the success or failure of an open, flexible school. Adequate time must be provided for the school staff to work as a unit at all stages of the planning process for the new or remodeled facility and, certainly, adequate preparation for instruction in new modes prior to the opening of the building.

The timing of the entire planning process is of critical importance, including: timing the appropriate point at which to move from general understandings to specific considerations, meshing with bond issues, and moving the process along with dispatch so that costs do not change so drastically from the preliminary budget that the building program fails. System techniques (see applications in Chapter 8) are utilized by modern school planners to assure quality in the process.

Although the peak of the building boom has passed and there are fewer new buildings, many others are being renovated. In constructing new buildings as well as in adapting and remodeling old structures, planners are concerned with adaptability and overall quality rather than accommodating large numbers within a given budget—a need that characterized the hastily contrived plans to meet the building needs of the postwar enrollment boom.[7]

Involvement

Today, a great number of people are involved in the decisions accompanying planning procedures for building new schools, altering old ones, or planning unique places for learning. Teachers, students, parents, and other citizens of the community expect to have a part in determining the objectives of education at the local level and the facilities that will assist in carrying out the objectives. With wide involvement of people, new ways are being found to provide information. Architectural models, simulations, visits to schools, and other types of participation in planning require the use of more sophisticated management techniques and ample time for interaction among the persons involved in school planning as well as communication with the whole community.

Planning Teams

In the process of planning an addition, the Dennis-Yarmouth High School (Massachusetts) rented a store front in a shopping mall as a community planning center in which citizens could drop in to discuss the issues of curriculum evaluation, vocational–technical offerings, alternative scheduling forms, adult education, and the use of community resources. A task force composed of six community leaders, six parents, six

[7] *Open Space Schools*, pp. 28–29.

students, and six faculty members held scheduled public meetings in the planning center for a three-month period during the planning process. Students of the Dennis-Yarmouth Regional High School traveled with teachers, administrators, board members, other citizens, and architects to seek ideas for the new facilities. Ten students were involved in visits that took the group from Maryland to Toronto with stops in between.

Students observed that open space did not necessarily make an open school and that in one of the open plan schools, students were scheduled and taught just as they were in traditional box classrooms. Students liked the use of movable, versatile furniture with tables to replace desks. They liked open, carpeted, air conditioned space, but wanted separations available with nooks and crannies for individual study. Overly large schools were rejected and school-within-a-school ideas were recommended so that students could get to know one another better. Other concepts the students wanted to include were the use of teacher-advisors instead of traditional guidance counselors and individualized programs in which students who could handle freedom should be able to use it while those who could not would be held in more traditional programs. Students liked programs where they could obtain instruction in the community as well as in the school. Other attractions with great appeal for the students were the bright colors used on the walls of many schools, open walls available for student art, and the concept of a central media depot replacing the restrictive aura of the traditional library. Students noted with pleasure that several schools had abandoned the large cafeteria and replaced it with snack bars, often scattered throughout the school. The architect who traveled with the group reported that this type of student-adult involvement was invaluable even though there were some differences of opinion between adults and students which had to be resolved as the planning for the new facility progressed.[8]

A planning team whose work spanned more than three years, beginning before the bond election which financed the new Juanita High School of the Lake Washington School District (Kirkland, Washington), is another example of an effective planning process. Citizens of the community and the professional staff, with frequent consultations with students, engaged in intensive planning which began long before the architect made his drawings. The committee was charged with the responsibility of developing an educational philosophy relevant to the needs of individuals in a constantly changing society and with developing educational specifications to implement the philosophy. Much attention was given to the development of goals and objectives for achieving student

---

[8] "Students Report on What They Like in Other Schools," *Schoolhouse*, September 1972, pp. 1–2.

outcomes. General goals included individualization of instruction, humanization of instruction, comprehensiveness of programming, and flexibility of program and facilities. From these general goals more specific objectives were designed with procedures for reaching them. Job descriptions were written in detail for staff utilization in the high school to be built. Specific statements of student rights and responsibilities, teacher responsibilities, and types of programming to be included were developed prior to the planning of the architecture. It was determined that the individualized learning program of Project PLAN (see Chapter 6) would be utilized for some of the subject areas. The nucleus of the new building was seen as a learning resource center with other activities flowing in and out of the specialized learning areas. The result of thorough planning is an imaginative and innovative high school complex in which the use of space is a continuous intermixture of various disciplines in constantly changing patterns. For example, if science gains in popularity and requires more area, its space can be expanded to meet the program with other areas regrouping. Thus the areas can shift in position and change in form as the educational needs shift and change.[9]

Charettes

Initial planning for the new Paul Dunbar Community High School in the heart of Baltimore (Maryland) was accomplished through a two-week charette. A charette is an intensive planning session where a community, with the guidance of consultants, hammers out the problems of planning and designing educational facilities. Follow-up committees, frequently of an ad hoc nature, coordinate the charette's findings and keep interest in the new school alive. In Baltimore, a wide-ranging and free-wheeling discussion among students, faculty, community representatives, city officials, and professional consultants brought out some smouldering community resentments including hostility toward the nearby Johns Hopkins Medical Center. The hospital, eager to cooperate with the school and community, subsequently offered the use of its laboratories and personnel for a new curriculum involving training for health-related occupations. Another result of the charette was the inclusion a neighborhood facilities center with space for several civic agencies including an Office of the Mayor, the Bureau of Consumer Services, the Model Cities Program, the Legal Aid Society, the Department of Parole and Probation, and others. Some facilities of the school are available for community use during nonschool hours. The theater may be used to show movies, and vocational shops are opened to interested citizens. The dining room may be used as needed.

[9] John F. Strauss, Jr., *Juanita High School* (brochure), P. O. Box 619, Kirkland, Washington 98033, September 1971.

Planning committees for curriculum development and for staff and management procedures have continued on a long-range basis.[10]

Simulations and Models

Miniature models made to scale with manipulable components frequently serve as a means of simulation: a way to "play" before final commitment to a set of plans is made. In designing the new Harlem Prep High School in Manhattan, students built a model to assist them in studying alternate patterns for interior design. Using small scale furniture and advice from interior designers, the students and faculty used a trial-and-error method to arrive at an arrangement for their new school in a former supermarket which would satisfy the unique program of the Harlem Prep Street Academy (see Chapter 4).

Chelmsford Park High School (Massachusetts) was also planned in advance by the use of simulation techniques. By employing a physical model, educators and architects were able to work out physical environments for changing instructional programs with optimum use of the new facility. The planners discovered that conventional interior materials would not be suitable for necessary future changes in the educational environment and with the use of simulation avoided errors in judgment that might otherwise have been committed.

Resources and Management

Sophisticated techniques borrowed from industry are available to school planners. Roles of architects, consultants, and other experts are being revamped so that sustained service may be given to their clients over a long period of development of the facility. This represents a departure from the temporary type of service in which architects and other experts delivered a "finished" facility and then disappeared. Innovative school planners have learned that a facility used by a dynamic organization is never finished but constantly needs changes as the educational program changes. New management techniques include the use of data in planning. In Ann Arbor, Michigan, a computerized system constantly studies population densities and educational facilities, with capability of automatically changing district lines as changes in population or facilities occur. The Office of Physical Plant of Baltimore, Maryland, has developed a program called the Management Information System for Facilities Planning, which is plotted on a network including planning and specification guidelines, cost and area analysis techniques, cost control procedures, facility evaluation procedures, and countless other items which may be drawn on for reference.

[10] *Places and Things*, pp. 94–96.

Management teams, assisting in school plannings where many different publics must have a voice, are becoming more and more expert at utilizing a wide variety of resources. Many of these are recently developing areas of environmental expertise and in some instances are not yet organized as consulting services. Although it requires some effort to probe for their input, management teams find a range of resources to be valuable in helping administrators, teachers, students, parents, and other community members examine their values, goals, and financial means in planning a school to provide the program they desire. Useful types of resources to be contacted by the planners and the management team are: acoustical design engineering, audiovisual design engineering, behavioral sciences, building systems design, community and press relations, ecological studies, electronic data processing of hardware specifications, electronic data processing for program development, use-of-facilities training, financial planning, food service planning, graphic design, health care planning, information management, installation supervision, interior design, laboratory planning and engineering, lighting design, management consulting, project planning, safety engineering, site planning, technical equipment specification, and urban planning.[11]

Modern facility planners also make use of some form of analysis that provides a perspective on the value of the proposed new or remodeled school facilities. Propst has identified these essential components and assigned symbols for mathematical computation:[12]

CI	Capital Investment in Plant and Equipment
YCO	Yearly Cost of Operating School
BSE	Basic Shell Efficiency
ISE	Interior Systems Efficiency
DEP	Dynamics of Educational Programs
EE	Exceptional Events
CPA	Cost of Physical Alterations
CD	Contingency Design
ODT	Organizational Downtime, Loss of Program Momentum
LSS	Lost or Underutilized Services and Space
RC	Response Capability
VEF	Value Effectiveness of Facility

Capital Investment usually receives major attention at the outset of a planning process; however, Yearly Costs of Operating are essentially more significant. The original cost of a high school is repeated every three years in its operating budget. Thus, if a school building is used for 60 years, the initial cost is only about 6 percent of the total cost of

[11] Robert Propst, *High School: The Process and the Place* (New York: Educational Facilities Laboratories, 1972), p. 107.
[12] Propst, p. 113.

operations, which is a factor deserving attention early in the planning process.

The efficiency of a building consists of two major considerations: the Basic Shell and Interior Systems. If these are at cross purposes the building will deliver very little efficiency. However, commitment to interior flexibility is meaningless unless there are the continuing pressures of a Dynamic Educational Program. Responsiveness is also essential for Exceptional Events, which will happen in any school and cannot be preprogrammed.

Factors that will test the quality of the plans for the facility include Cost of Physical Alterations, inclusion of a Contingency Design to accommodate problems that may arise, the extent of Lost or Underutilized Services and Space, and the degree to which the school program and personnel lose momentum while the facility is down for change (Organizational Downtime). Thus the Response Capability of the plan is demonstrated in this formula:

$$\frac{BSE + ISE}{CPA + CD + LSS + ODT} = RC$$

In the end, however, the Value Effectiveness of the Facility depends on how well a building can react (Response Capability) to the effect of Dynamic Educational Programs and Exceptional Events.

$$(DEP + EE) \times RC = VEF[13]$$

COMMUNITY/SCHOOL CONCEPTS

A place where education of students and activities of a community may occur at the same time or at different times is an expression of an emerging community/school concept. New community needs for continuing education, for social services, expressive arts, new skills, and recreation and the need for better skills are being met in the design of new multipurpose facilities. Cooperation provides more economical use of funds with better value for the dollar through more efficient use of space. Joint programming of educational and service offerings is an important part of the community/school concept.

Cooperation

Carson City, Nevada, recently involved its citizens in conceptualizing and planning a facility for a community/school. From cooperative efforts, the new Ormsby County High School and space for municipal and county

[13] Propst, pp. 114–115.

agencies have been combined in a flexible structure planned to serve both school and community simultaneously. Areas that can serve many interests are arranged along walkways on ground level and second floor level.

Joint planning in Portsmouth, Virginia, has resulted in the new Manor High School, a facility which includes a public library, a theater, a planetarium, and office space, all designed for community and school use. In addition, gymnasium facilities are open after school hours and at scheduled times of the school day to the community. A central commons allows access for both students and adults of the community to the mutually shared areas.

Bold and reasoned planning and action by Hartford, Connecticut's Board of Education and City Hall have replaced dilapidated school buildings in decaying neighborhoods with new schools combined with a city program of new housing. An educational complex now serves community needs through swimming pool and gym facilities, dining commons for community-oriented meetings, and a large gymnasium. Joint city and school board action have helped finance new urban housing in the surrounding neighborhoods. Buckeley High School and Martin Luther King, Jr., Middle School now form an air conditioned complex located on a sharply sloping 25-acre site directly next to a city park; they face each other across a plaza that also serves as the roof of the library. An auditorium seating 1000 adjoins the plaza at one end. Science, art, and industrial arts laboratories are designed with open space that adapts easily to team teaching. Academic towers of both the high school and middle school are developed around the house plan concept. The middle school, currently serving grades 7 and 8, is designed to expand or contract to meet pressing needs and will be able to house fifth, sixth, and ninth grades as well as seventh and eighth if the high school or elementary school should need more space.

Air Rights

Construction of schools over railroad yards, highways, or water illustrates the use of alternatives to acquisition of costly school sites. New York City's new Northeast Bronx High School straddles the Hutchinson River Parkway. Forty acres of Jamaica Bay were filled in to create the site for the new South Queens High School, and other schools in New York City are planned over railroad yards and subway storage yards. In North Philadelphia an air rights plan for a prekindergarten-through-higher-education-and-continuing-education complex would provide school facilities in a "land poor" section over a railroad station. Schools-within-a-school would spread out on multilevels through adjacent buildings connected by concourses spanning railroad tracks.

In a densely populated section of Miami, where an adequate school site would have cost $2 million and displaced up to 150 families, an unusual solution to finding a site for a desperately needed school has been worked out. The only unoccupied land in the area lies under an expressway built 80 feet above the community. The school district has acquired a forty-year lease on almost 6 acres from the state highway department, without charge, and purchased another two acres adjoining the site. Despite the strange location, there will be normal elementary school facilities including a playground and 900 children will be housed at a considerable saving in cost. Among the safety features to be built in is a cable net between the divided expressway structures to prevent any objects, including automoblies, from falling on to the school. Although this happens to be an elementary school, the problem of locating school sites in densely populated areas is common to secondary schools as well.

Joint Occupancy

In the joint occupancy concept, school facilities are built into high-rise apartment buildings, commercial office buildings, and private or public housing projects. Solutions to several problems are to be found in joint occupancy. Scarcity of available land sites and prohibitively high real estate costs are problems that can be avoided in this manner as commercial enterprises assist in the financing. If the school's enrollment should increase or decrease radically, the school may release part of its facilities to the commercial interest, or, if enrollments require, additional space may be included in the school facilities. The ideal arrangement is to include enough taxpaying commercial space to carry the cost of debt service on the school. The school, in this sense, pays for itself from the expanded tax base.

A number of plans for joint occupancy have been on the architectural drawing boards for several years. In Chicago, the six-story Jones Commercial High School has been designed to support a fifteen-story commercial tower above. In New York, a commercial high school occupies the lower floors of a high-rise office building on the east side of the midtown commercial district. A 1200-student school is part of a Bronx apartment cooperative, and another is to be the base of a thirty-five-story apartment building in Manhattan. The New York City Educational Construction Fund is a state authority with the power to issue its own bonds to develop joint occupancies within New York City. In 1973, $140 million of schools and $300 million of commercial space in various stages of planning and/or construction were underway in New York City.[14]

[14] *Places and Things*, pp. 121–122.

Planned Schools in Planned Cities

An estimated 250 planned communities were in the process of development in 1972.[15] A planned community is defined as a complex that includes all of the life-support systems of a city: government, education, transportation, industry, health, communication, recreation, law enforcement, and so on. New cities offer unique opportunities to introduce and demonstrate educational reforms and innovations. For the most part, planning for innovations can be accomplished before the new citizens move in; thus, new cities do not have to sell the innovative ideas to the citizenry for whom the schools are planned, as the new citizens choose to live there because of the new concepts in education and community living. Planning for new communities is a definite contrast to the usual community-school concept. Instead of planning school facilities that can be made available to the community, community facilities are planned that will meet the needs of students. Thus, instead of asking how the auditoriums or libraries can be used by the community, the new communities plan auditoriums or libraries which can be made available to students. An example of a planned community with a promising educational program and facilities to support it is Columbia, Maryland.

Another illustration of a planned community is the Welfare Island Development, a city planned for completion in 1976 on an island in New York City's East River. The new city will contain 5250 units of mixed-income housing, retail stores, offices, and parks. A community education system running from day care through adult education is being cooperatively planned by the New York City Board of Education and the New York State Urban Development Corporation. School space would be dispersed throughout all of the space on the island, jointly occupying land with housing, stores, offices, parks, and so on, and using all of New York City as a place for learning.

REVISED USES OF SPACE

The Educational Facilities Laboratories use the term "found space" to describe revised uses of space that occur chiefly in two forms: space within outdated school buildings that can be reshaped, renovated, or modernized in some way, and found space that may be utilized for education in unused or partially used industrial, commercial, or public buildings.

[15] Myron Lieberman, "Education in New Cities," *Phi Delta Kappan*, 54:407–411 (March 1972).

University City, Missouri, Senior High School (top) with little-used courtyard, constructed in 1930. Courtyard being converted (center) to modern skylighted library, shown in last picture.

School Modernization

About one-third of the funds spent on elementary and secondary school construction were being spent on modernization and remodeling projects in 1972; this fact was reported in *School Renewal*, published by Educational Facilities Laboratories.[16] The report, prepared by an architectural firm, presents a process including a flow chart for programming educational requirements, making feasibility studies, cost and funding considerations. Money can be saved in a long-range master plan for modernization if schools will abandon piecemeal work left largely to decisions made by the maintenance department. Millions of dollars are regularly squandered in haphazard projects that add little to a modern learning environment, concluded the architects who prepared the report.

The same systematic planning is needed for a modernization program as for a new building program. When professional consultants are brought into the evaluating and planning process at the earliest possible moment, the feasibility of modernizing an existing structure can be predicted. Generally, extensive remodeling is feasible in buildings constructed since 1920 and modernization possibilities are limited in those constructed earlier. Basic questions to be asked include: Can the building be made safe for children? Can it be adapted to meet the educational goals of the district? Is it located in an area where school enrollment is not declining? Is the site large enough to meet current standards and, if not, is it possible to add to it? Negative responses to these questions will suggest that an old building should be abandoned rather than remodeled.

For successful modernization, the district must first define the educational program desired and consult with an architect to determine whether the existing structure and proposed additions or renovations can accommodate a new educational approach with all of its various activities.

Space needed but not often found in old buildings includes professional facilities for the faculty such as team planning areas, office space, clerical space, workrooms, professional development libraries, faculty dining rooms, storage space, and others that may be suggested by the planning groups. Modern student programs need these kinds of space: student conference areas, guidance services, areas for large group instruction, spaces for instructional media, library-resource centers, science facilities, art and music studios, individual study spaces, and physical education facilities.

General types of additions and modernizations include (1) perimeter modernization of an existing building in which one or more additions are built around a major portion of the perimeter of the old facility, (2)

---

[16] *School Renewal* is available from Educational Facilities Laboratory, Inc., 477 Madison Ave., New York, N.Y. 10022.

link types of modernization in which an addition is connected to the existing building by a connecting passageway, (3) plug-in types of modernization in which single or multiple additions are inserted into an existing building where the floor plan has logical points for location of new construction, (4) addition of one or more stories to an existing building, and (5) enclosure of a court in which roofing is built over an open court or space between wings of a building.

High ceilings frequently offer opportunities to add or update plumbing or other mechanical systems, including air conditioning. High ceilings can be an asset and in some types of space provide opportunities for aesthetic dimensions with a change in heights.

The reuse of old materials can sometimes be emphasized as a cost factor and an art form. The value of objects of antiquity, particularly natural materials or artifacts made by hand, has a fresh appeal in school construction. Green plantings within the building and the use of decorative fountains can also add aesthetic dimensions. A prime consideration in modernization programs is to plan additions or remodeled areas so that they are harmonious with the original structure and so that the building and its addition or renovated areas become a single continuous space, not a series of individual, loosely related areas.[17]

An example of long-range planning for modernizing a program with corollary modernization of the plant is a project in Norfolk, Virginia, which resulted in renovation of the Maury High School. The high school, housing 2300 students in grades 9 to 12, is the oldest high school in the city, dating back to the early 1900s. It is an inner city school whose students constitute a cross section of the city's socioeconomic levels. The innovative instructional program includes individualized programs, phase-elective and nongraded arrangement of courses, large and small groups, use of laboratories, resource centers, emphasis on independent study, and assistance for some students from tutors. A flexible modular schedule supports the instructional program. Renovations of the building included expanded library facilities, installation of a dial access video-audio system, a student lounge, lecture demonstration centers, seminar rooms, resource centers, and faculty offices. Lecture demonstration rooms were formed by redesigning the auditorium into three centers with other lecture demonstration areas constructed by removing walls between standard size classrooms. Seminar rooms for interaction were constructed by dividing existing classrooms into minirooms for fifteen students. Space was found for resource centers in several departments of the school.[18]

[17] Ben E. Graves, "Modernization," *Nation's Schools*, 87:58–64 (April 1971).
[18] *The Pacemaker* (newsletter), Maury High School, 322 West 15th Street, Norfolk, Va. 23517, June 1972.

Another old and unwieldy building remodeled into up-to-date quarters is East High School in Madison, Wisconsin. Space existed on four levels and traffic patterns moved up and down in awkward ways. A long-range plan, divided into five phases is underway. In the first phase, space between buildings was roofed to create interior malls and a student commons. Stairwells at appropriate places along the malls now allow students to move freely among the various elevations. Bright colors were used to alleviate the previously depressing atmosphere. Phase two involved remodeling of the gymnasium and industrial arts area to include additional space, a mall and lobby, shower and locker facilities, and a field house. Phase three provided renovation of science classrooms, administrative areas, and general class space. Phases four and five are scheduled to renovate the upper levels by adding specialized classrooms and general instructional areas.[19]

Evergreen Park High School (Illinois), built in 1955, doubled its capacity to house 1400 students by adding a perimeter section to the conventional H pattern of the fifties. The air conditioned addition gave the school a new look as well as more space for a library, team teaching space, science areas, commercial teaching rooms, and speech and language laboratories.[20]

Security

Technology is coming to the aid of security programs in schools with a high incidence of crime and violence. For some years, many large cities—Chicago, Los Angeles, Baltimore, Detroit, Washington, D.C., and New York—have operated school security programs with safety personnel and protective physical arrangements including, in some cases, fences around the grounds and checkpoints at entrances.

An electronic security check system for schools, piloted at John F. Kennedy High School in Sacramento, California, equips each teacher, administrator, and employee with a pencil-sized ultrasonic transmitter, which can light a bulb on a large map of the school in the principal's office and sound a small horn alerting the office for assistance. As a result, help can be dispatched to the trouble scene within 30 seconds. The principal reported that the electronic system has effectively reduced the number of undesirable incidents.[21]

At a recent conference of the International Association of School Security Directors, it was emphasized that electronic aids and other types of trouble-shooting devices and techniques are not the best solutions to

[19] Graves, pp. 65–70.
[20] Graves, pp. 71–72.
[21] Reported in *Education Training Market Report*, September 25, 1972.

school security problems, but that security officers must join with educators in taking humane approaches that stress prevention, not punishment. Cooperative programs that are designed to reach the causes of vandalism, to listen to students, and invite their aid in solving security problems were recommended by school security officers.[22]

"Found Space" in Nonschool Buildings

Some of the most interesting and successful uses of space are schools located in converted factories, warehouses, and other unused buildings.[23] A publicly owned bath house in Boston was recently converted to a high school annex for 450 students at a saving of about two-thirds of the cost of new high school space. One of Chicago's most successful schools is located in a former milking machine factory in the Lawndale section. The school is an industrial education center which provides alternative education for 320 students, aged sixteen to twenty years, who for one reason or another could not find success in Chicago's regular high schools. Students may earn a high school diploma and learn a marketable skill while earning money at the same time. Sixteen staff members are combination teacher-counselors concerned with the individual needs of students. The building is divided roughly into three parts; the upper floor houses a learning center—a carpeted open plan area where students spend about half their time. The learning center includes study areas for science, social science, mathematics, and English, with intensive reading and math centers for students who are below eighth-grade level in these skills. The ground floor contains two shops, sponsored by Western Electric and Motorola. Students are paid for work in these shops and their products are sold on the market.

In the Bronx, New York City, an old hotel has been developed into a school. Students attend minischools organized within the facility around separate interests, including humanities, business, and medical technology. Half of their time is spent in learning situations in the community outside the former hotel. In St. Paul, Minnesota, a warehouse has been leased by a group of parents with partial funding by the school district, and the building has been renovated into an interesting series of spaces which house an alternative K through 12 school.

In Cleveland, a four-story lamp factory with four and one-half acres of usable floor space has been given to the Board of Education by the General Electric Company. Known as the Woodland Job Center, the building houses a youth training program. A vocational school emphasiz-

[22] "School Security: A New Humane Approach," *Education U.S.A.*, August 6, 1973, p. 230.
[23] Examples from *Places and Things*, pp. 10–13.

ing heavy industry occupies areas on all four levels. The Board of Education leases space to General Electric and General Electric then hires the students at minimum wages for on-the-job training and experience in its lamp production line. Additional space may be leased to other industries who want to join the program.

The Olney High School Annex in Philadelphia is located in a former government testing laboratory. A free school in Berkeley, California, found space for rent in a warehouse. The George Westinghouse Vocational High School of Chicago occupies a former candy factory and Portland, Oregon, has established a vocational village in a former Green Stamp display room. The Shoreline School District, outside Seattle, with a decrease in numbers of elementary and junior high school students and over-enrollment at the high school level has revamped two schools that are no longer needed—a junior high school and an elementary school that share a common 22-acre site. Remodeling has provided modern facilities for 1200 high school students.

PLACES FOR LEARNING BEYOND THE SCHOOLHOUSE

Numerous high schools are effectively operating programs that capitalize on the concept of student responsibility by moving students outside of the school for part or all of their educational experience. The schools-without-walls and some forms of alternative schools described in Chapter 4 operate on the "reach out" principle. In some programs a home base school provides half of the student's educational experience in the school building and half in community activities or work-study programs. The Lexington (Massachusetts) High School operates an "Education Without Walls" program in which students divide the day between classes and work, independent projects, or volunteer community service such as teaching at elementary schools.

The 1972 International Design Conference in Aspen, Colorado, emphasized "The Invisible City," and engaged 1500 participants in ways to uncover facets of a city that can be used as part of a school's learning resources. Antique shops and sports areas are among the many types of places for learning in a city.

A different kind of innovation is the mobile unit which brings a place for learning to the learner who remains near his home base. In Great Neck, New York, a self-propelled, 30-foot mobile classroom serves as a study center for secondary and elementary students and adults from 9 A.M. to 10:30 P.M. The unit has its own electrical, heating, and air conditioning system with sink, refrigerator, snack closet, study carrels, carpeting, and materials to meet the special needs of children and adults in selected neighborhoods. In Illinois, the Office of the Superintendent of Public Instruction for the State sponsors a motorized mobile unit to serve as a traveling art resources museum. Its function is to educate children and youths about the heritage of art, to train teachers through in-service workshops, and to expose adults to the world of art.

Disadvantaged youths on the eastern shore of Maryland are provided with a classroom-on-wheels which provides five-week courses at school stops in six counties. Short-term courses in typing, auto tune-up, and merchandising help the drop-out get back in school, give the slow learners a chance for better grades, and offer training in marketable skills to the jobless. The van brings to a student who cannot type 35 words per minute in high school the opportunity to increase speed and possibly land the job he wants in an office in the city.

Four mobile vocational education shops, each one for a different industry, visit high schools in the eastern part of Arkansas regularly. Of the 429 high schools of Arkansas, only 3 have vocational education programs other than agriculture. The mobile units make it possible for 80 students to use the mobile vocational education unit in the course of a school day with adult education scheduled in the evenings. In nine-week courses, students are given an opportunity to explore career possibilities and also learn that some of their regular high school courses are more relevant than they had seemed at one time. These are only some examples of learning centers on wheels. Others include instant libraries, tutorial centers, language laboratories, and certain types of study centers for special learning needs.

SUMMARY

Innovations in space for learning provide tangible evidence of the changing nature of secondary education. Efforts to make the schoolhouse a humane place, to nurture the educative process for diverse individuals, and to be adaptable to a changing future are evidenced by new places for learning. Instead of beginning with courses, texts, and class periods in making decisions about school facilities, today's educators begin with the individual student and the wide variety of options (media, materials, staff, time, space, community resources) that functional facilities can make possible. Furthermore, in planning space for secondary education, educators also consider the economics, politics, geography, social needs, and potential resources of the community. The involvement of the school's many publics is essential. No one standard model for all communities can possibly be designed to meet the complex mix of variables to be considered in the different localities, but fundamental principles do prevail.

The shape and atmosphere of the new schoolhouse must serve a variety of approaches and practices, must be flexible and versatile, and must be capable of constant adaptation to new goals and new functions.

additional suggestions for further study

1. The American Association of School Administrators, 1801 N. Moore St., Arlington, Va. 22209, will provide a listing of publications related to school facilities.
2. *American School and University, The American School Board Journal,* and *Nations Schools* (issues) are journals that regularly provide information on space and places for learning, including: school plant planning, innovations, purchasing guides, practical advice, and specific illustrations from local school districts.
3. Educational Facilities Laboratories, Inc., 477 Madison Ave., New York, N.Y. 10022, a nonprofit corporation, regularly provides publications on trends in school facilities. Examples are: *High School: The Process and the Place,* 1972; *Places and Things for Experimental Schools,* 1972; *Schools: More Space/Less Money,* 1971; *Places for Environmental Education,* 1971; and issues of the newsletter *Schoolhouse.*
4. The ERIC (Educational Resources Information Center) Clearinghouse on Educational Management, University of Oregon, Eugene, Ore., disseminates research results and resource information regarding the planning, renovation, and modernization of school buildings. Reports are listed in *Research in Education,* an index to ERIC resources.
5. Hawkins, Donald and Dennis Vinton, *The Environmental Classroom.* Englewood Cliffs, N.J.: Prentice-Hall, 1972. How to use the environment as a total learning resource is the message of the authors. They describe how to move from a traditional classroom to a "global village" and how to use communications media in a community-centered school.
6. Modernization information is available from the New Life for Old Schools Project, Suite 1734, 20 North Wacker Dr., Chicago, Ill. 60606.
7. "The New Schoolhouse" issue of *The National Elementary Principal,* September 1972, offers advice to school planners on many aspects of school facilities planning, construction, and furnishing.
8. Research information on open plan schools is available from the School Planning Laboratory, Stanford University, Stanford, Calif. 94305.
9. Teacher training programs related to open plan schools are being developed by I/D/E/A/ of the Kettering Foundation. For information, write to Innovative Programs, I/D/E/A/, Inc., 5335 Far Hills Avenue, Suite 300, Dayton, Ohio 45429.

Processes of Innovation
and Change

In this final chapter we focus on the processes of innovation and change—
the ways in which innovation is introduced and utilized to effect change
in secondary education. The all-important role of the teacher is first
emphasized.

ROLE OF THE TEACHER IN INNOVATION

The point of view throughout this book is that the teacher—the
professional school person—is a key figure in innovation. Any significant
change in education must ultimately affect the relationship of the teachers
and the taught. Whether it is change desired in the teacher himself, or
in the plans, materials, processes, organizations he uses—and it may be
impossible to separate change in the thing from change in the person—the
teacher is inextricably involved. If the teacher seeks change and is involved
in making it, its chances of success are high. If the teacher avoids change,
and is involved reluctantly, if at all, in making it, its chances of success
are correspondingly low.

This is not to say that the teacher single-handedly can effect all of the innovation needed in the school. One can hardly overemphasize the role of school administration in creating a school climate conducive to innovation and change. Many of the innovations we have described involve administrative arrangement, budgetary help, and even modification of physical facilities, and most, if not all of them, need the input of students, their parents, and the entire school community. Indeed it is from the expressed dissatisfactions and problems of the latter that innovations arise. But it is the teacher and students who must make the problem solutions— the innovations—work, or at least determine whether they will work.

We have regarded an innovation as a novel practice in an individual school. Although a particular innovation may spread throughout other schools and even be introduced simultaneously in more than one school of a district, its success and the data used to judge its success are unique to an individual school. It is here that change occurs or does not occur; Goodlad calls the single school "the largest organic unit for educational change" and emphasizes the role of its personnel in these words:

> If the school is to become the dynamic, self-renewing unit it should be, the energies of its personnel must be focused on its needs and problems. The in-service education of teachers should arise out of the demand placed upon them by these needs and problems.[1]

Similarly, in introducing this description of various approaches to innovation and change, we are emphasizing the principle of involvement of the personnel of a school in whatever approach is used. Without staff involvement, change is ultimately impossible; with it, ideas can get into action for testing and perhaps adoption.

INNOVATION AND CHANGE: A CONTINUUM

Generally speaking, we have used "innovation" in this book to describe an individual practice that is novel in the situation where it is introduced. In this chapter we are turning attention to the process whereby one or more such innovations get identified, introduced, tested, and adopted or rejected—the process of innovation and change. Change to us represents the goal of an innovation. That is, an innovation is sought and introduced to produce change in the situation, usually regarded as change in the relationships of learners and others involved. The whole process may be represented by the acronym IDEAS, as follows:

[1] John I. Goodlad, "Lag on Making Ideas Work," in *Change and Innovation in Elementary and Secondary Organization.* Maurie Hillson and Ronald T. Hyman (Eds.) (New York: Holt, Rinehart and Winston, 1971), p. 425.

I—Identify a need for change

D—Determine one or more new practices (innovations) that seem likely to meet the need

E—Evaluate the chosen innovation in a tryout situation

A—Activate the findings of the tryout: reject or adopt the innovation, or modify and try it again

S—Stimulate the continuation of this process of innovation and change

Although we recognize that this acronym may be an oversimplification of a very complex process, it is beyond the scope of this book to present a detailed analysis and theory of the process of innovation and change or even to review in detail the several excellent works that do present such analyses and theories.[2] Instead we have presented many innovations and illustrated their utilization as clearly as possible, and in this concluding chapter seek to establish a basic principle and describe and illustrate its implementation: the principle that an innovation as a means to an end (change) must be selected in terms of the end sought, with a definite plan (the process) for using it to attain the end. We, too, have observed the frequent substitution of the means for the end, as commented upon by Sarason in his analysis of educational change, for which he used in part the introduction of new math as a case in point:

> The goals of change, the outcomes sought, surely are not to see if it is possible to substitute one set of books for another, change the racial composition of a class or a school, or have children read or listen to black or Mexican history—those possibilities are relatively easy to realize, and I have seen them realized in precisely the same way as in the case of new math, with precisely the same outcome: the more things change the more they remain the same.
>
> Realizing these types of possibilities simply begs the question of their *intended consequences*, and in these as well as in other instances the intended consequences—the basic goals and outcomes—always intended a change in the relationships among those who are in or related to the school setting. But these intended consequences are rarely stated clearly, if at all, and as a result, a means to a goal becomes the goal itself, or it becomes the misleading criterion for judging change. Thus, we have the new math, but we do not have those changes in how teachers and children

---

[2] See S. Bailey, J. Ross, L. Sumnicht, and A. Teich, *Significant Research and Development* (Syracuse, N.Y.: Syracuse University, 1972); David S. Bushnell and Donald Rapport, *Planned Change in Education* (New York: Harcourt, 1971); Michael Fullan, "Overview of the Innovative Process and the User," *Interchange*, 3:1–46 (Nos. 2–3, 1972); R. Havelock, *A Guide to Innovation in Education* (Ann Arbor, Mich.: University of Michigan, 1970); L. Maguire, *Observations and Analysis of the Literature on Change* (Philadelphia: Research for Better Schools, 1970); Everett Rogers and F. Shoemaker, *Communication of Innovations: A Cross-Cultural Approach*, 2d ed. (New York: Free Press, 1971); and Seymour B. Sarason, *The Culture of the School and the Problem of Change* (Boston: Allyn and Bacon, 1971).

relate to each other that are necessary if both are to enjoy, persist in, and productively utilize the intellectual and interpersonal experience—and if these are not among the intended consequences, then we must conclude that the curriculum reformers have been quite successful in achieving their goal of substituting one set of books for another.[3]

Thus we see the process of innovation and change as a continuum from the prior existing condition to some goal or combination of goals that represent the planners' conception of the ultimate condition desired:

MAXIMUM	OPTIMUM
RESTRICTIONS	ENCOURAGEMENT
ON LEARNING	OF LEARNING

In general terms, the existing condition is one in which an established school program is too limiting or restricting on learners' potentials for learning. Or, more positively, the program can give much more stimulation and learning opportunities for some, perhaps all of, its population. The ultimate condition desired would be optimum encouragement and development of the learning potentials of the entire school population. Under optimum conditions each learner, fully motivated and self-actualizing, would be finding in the environment provided by or available to the school full and complete opportunities for achieving his learning goals. In such an optimum situation, the educative process would be far more "open" than in schools of the present in that learners would be much more responsible for planning and choosing their own learning opportunities, with school personnel being facilitators and resources. Fullan's comment on the role of learners in educational change is relevant and useful:

> A common starting point for educational reform is to take the system as a whole and begin specifying changes (such as in-service teacher training, better information flow) that presumably will help the individual learner. I believe that it is vastly more productive to reverse the emphasis by starting with the individual user and then considering the resources, organizational needs, and eventually the type of social system to support the desired process.[4]

Some educational theorists find present conditions so far removed from this ultimate goal, which most (if not all) of us would accept, that they tend to abandon hope for present schools.[5] We ourselves see

[3] Sarason, p. 48.

[4] Fullan, p. 31.

[5] See Ivan Illich, *DeSchooling Society* (New York: Harper & Row, 1971), and Everett Reimer, *School Is Dead: Alternatives in Education* (Garden City, N.Y.: Doubleday, 1971).

great changes ahead for schools if they are to help meet the real educational needs of our people, but we also believe that the schools represent the best possibility available for developing and managing adequate educational programs. Hence, a well-conceived process of innovation and change is imperative in each school. Each school has its own starting place on the continuum of innovation and process: Some have made very little if any movement toward the ultimate and optimum condition we described; others have gone a long way toward its achievement; and most lie somewhere between these extremes. As we see it, each school's group of planners should size up the status of the school on the continuum—that is, how far the school is from providing an optimum environment for learners—and then deliberately fashion an approach to innovation and change that is the most feasible for moving as rapidly as possible toward the optimum condition. We turn now to brief description of various possible approaches from which planners may select, or perhaps combine or improve upon, in some approach of their own.

ADOPTION OF SINGLE INNOVATIONS

Probably the most common process of innovation and change is that of adopting single innovations, sometimes more than one at a time and sometimes one after the other, but without some predetermined plan of simultaneous or successive adoptions toward a selected goal. The history of secondary education, indeed of education in general, is replete with instances of the adoption of single innovations, for this has been the typical pattern of change: the addition of a new program or practice. Sometimes the innovation is relatively minute (a new course or instructional aid or strategy), and sometimes it is comprehensive (an alternative curriculum plan, a school-within-a-school organization, or a year-round program). Hence it is impossible to make a categorical, valid judgment of the significance of the single innovation approach, although there is in it the inherent weakness of its lack of an orderly plan for relating each step to the total change sought. In all too many instances there is little study of alternative practices and even less provision for evaluating the effectiveness of the innovation in achieving the desired change.

However, single innovations do not have to be without plan and evaluation. Indeed many innovations introduced to meet a particular student need or demand can be a significant entering wedge toward opening the curriculum. Thus a report from the Northwest Ashe High School, Warrensville, North Carolina, related the development of a series of minicourses to the needs of students:

The student body is vocationally oriented, with only 20 percent of the school's 500 enrollment seeking a higher education after high school graduation. With this statistic in mind, the administration has long been searching for a way to turn a traditional, boring, and in many ways, outdated curriculum into something meaningful and interesting to students who could not care less if Hamlet wanted "to be, or not to be" . . . .

We were interested in the versatility which the quarter system offered, so we began an intensive study of the new minicourse idea. This seemed to be the one answer for the many vocational students who were artisans in their trade, but who would rather be punished than attend an English class and read poetry. Both English and social studies were adaptable to the mini idea, since they could so easily be broken down into many units of work, and both were required courses for graduation. To a degree, the mini approach made these courses more elective than required. The strong point was that students could choose particular fields that they especially enjoyed within a subject area, and eliminate those that they disliked from their schedules.[6]

Experience with the minicourses in English and social studies led to further curriculum changes, with still others in process of planning and evaluating: a new program and facility in commercial cooking; a program in service station management developed in conjunction with an oil company; a "micro-mini" course in home economics for students not enrolled otherwise in home economics; "micro" math courses built entirely around the vocational training in which boys were engaged; a pass-fail option in all courses.

Innovation in administrative organization also may relate to the broad goal of changed relationships in a more open school. The concept of an "administrative team" may be more relevant to open and flexible staffing relationships than the traditional line and staff organization of the high school. As used in the Pasco Comprehensive Senior High School in Dade City, Florida, administrative teaming broadens the formal organization while reducing the span of control.[7] Schools seeking to provide more opportunities for responsible learning by their students need to find such alternative ways of increasing the channels for student communication and participation in decision making about their school.

"Crash" programs to alleviate some urgent problem have frequently come into being as single innovations, to be discarded when the need subsides or better alternatives appear. Drug abuse education programs, a recent instance of the crash program phenomenon, may be closer to meet-

---

[6] Statement prepared for the authors by F. L. Barker, Jr., Principal, Northwest Ashe High School, Warrensville, N.C., December 14, 1972.

[7] See Wayne C. Malone, "The Team Concept in School Administration," *Clearing House*, 47:259–262 (January 1973).

Counselors, teachers, paraprofessionals, and students work together as a counseling team at University City (Missouri) Senior High School. This is representative of the changing approach to the entire counseling and advisement process at the school.

ing students' needs and interests than some other programs if the advice of the Committee on Drugs of the American School Health Association and the Pharmaceutical Association is followed. The introduction to their *Teaching about Drugs, A Curriculum Guide, K–12* explains the underlying point of view as follows:

> This guide, then, is designed to assist teachers in presenting correct information about drugs and to help them in directing children to make wise decisions about the use of drugs. It has been developed in response to requests for assistance in teaching about drugs and is intended only to give suggestions to school administrators, teachers, counselors, and others who work with children and youth in the school and in the community. Its potential can be realized best when it is used as a point of departure for local curriculum development. *It is intended for modification according to the needs, interests and abilities of the children and youth in a given community* and for integration into the regular health program.[8]

Unfortunately, many national curriculum projects, even series of textbooks, have similarly suggested local adaptations that were not made in some local situations. Hopefully in such sensitive areas as drug education,

[8] American School Health Association and Pharmaceutical Manufacturers Association, *Teaching About Drugs, A Curriculum Guide, K–12*, 2d ed. (Kent, Ohio: American School Health Association, 1972), p. xiv. Italics supplied.

family life, and sex education, and others that are very critical for youth and the community, innovative practices will not be of a "crash" variety but instead will be painstakingly planned and executed in the school to meet the specific requirements of its population in attaining optimum self-direction.

A national survey of innovations by Cawelti during the great upsurge of single innovations during the 1960s noted their tendency to be "haphazard," a major weakness of this approach:

> The haphazard way changes are introduced in schools leads to highly uneven efforts across the country. Continued and intensified efforts from school administrators will be needed to clarify the change process and to subject new ideas to better scrutiny on a large scale basis. Schools must develop discrete goals, a system for continuous evaluation, and a willingness to acknowledge weakness in planning for change.[9]

The single innovation approach, aiming towards a clearly stated goal and following our IDEAS model, is probably the starting point for most effective programs of educational change. Cawelti's caution, and ours, is that it be a soundly planned and evaluated start on the continuum of change.

SPECIAL FUNDING FOR INNOVATIONS

The wave of innovations beginning in the 1960s was undoubtedly propelled by the availability of new federal funds to support them, especially those funds appropriated for the Elementary and Secondary Education Act of 1965 and its successors. Billions of dollars were expended over the next decade to support innovative programs in the categories set by this legislation and also through programs created by the Vocational Education Act of 1963 and its Amendments, the various Higher Education Acts, and other federal legislation. Title III of ESEA, 1965, was directly beamed at innovation and was designed, according to an early *Manual for Project Applicants,* "to encourage school districts to develop imaginative solutions to educational problems"; it sought to "(1) encourage the development of innovations, (2) demonstrate worthwhile innovations in educational practice through exemplary programs, (3) supplement existing programs and facilities."

For a number of reasons we are choosing not to use our limited space to describe the various procedures, evaluations, and controversies regarding the use of federal funds for innovation. Many such descriptions are

---

[9] Gordon Cawelti, *Special Study: How High Schools Innovate,* reprinted from *Nation's Schools,* April 1967, p. 4.

already in the literature of education.[10] The fact that many of the innovations described elsewhere in this book (as frequently noted there) were initiated and/or supported by federal funds, indicates that this money has been a very important factor in the innovations movement. The purposes and conditions of the federal grants keep changing so that any student interested in particular funding programs should consult the appropriate government source. We are turning attention instead to certain other types of external funding: (1) grants from local community groups and agencies; (2) grants by the school district for innovations; and (3) grants from philanthropic foundations.

First, however, we would note the possibility of combining funds from several agencies as a means of accelerating development of critical programs. For example, a December 1972 account of the Education for Parenthood program noted as federal grant funds being used in a relatively massive approach to this critical need, the following: Vocational Education Act of 1963; Titles, I, III, IV, and VIII of the Elementary and Secondary Education Act; the Talent Search provisions of the Higher Education Act; the Aid to Federally Impacted Areas; Title IVA and B of the Social Security Act; the Department of Housing and Urban Development's Model Cities Program; and the Department of Labor's Neighborhood Youth Corps. Funds for developing curriculum materials and their testing were also being provided by the Office of Child Development and the National Institute for Mental Health, with the Educational Development Center of Cambridge, Massachusetts, responsible for their development, and with the planned participation of 200 school districts in large-scale testing during 1973–1974.[11] If federal legislation and bureaucracy can be tapped and coordinated in the interest of a major educational goal so inextricably related to the optimum educational condition of adequate opportunities for all learners, surely local communities, state departments of education, citizens' groups, businesses and industries, and philanthropy can find ways to join together to support the opening up of a local school to increased learning opportunities and accomplishment for all of its students.

Grants from Local Community Groups and Agencies

The "partnership" high school idea has been instrumental in the provision of grants by industries to support individual programs in urban high schools. Characteristic features of this plan of cooperation between edu-

---

[10] See, for example, Stephen K. Bailey and Edith K. Mosher, ESEA: The Office of Education Administers a Law (Syracuse, N.Y.: Syracuse University Press, 1968), and Joel S. Berke and Michael W. Kirst, Federal Aid to Education: Who Benefits? Who Governs? (Lexington, Mass.: Lexington Books, 1972).

[11] W. Stanley Kruger, "Teaching Parenthood," American Education, 8:25–28 (December 1972).

cation and industry were described in a report from the Institute for Educational Development as follows: "(1) an understanding or exchange of commitments, (2) between representatives of a corporation and an urban school, usually a high school, (3) to the effect that they will try to cooperate over a period of years, (4) in an organized group of projects intended to improve education in the school, (5) for the benefit of the students."[12] Direct grants to individual schools under such arrangements have facilitated many of the innovations described earlier in this book, frequently related to vocational education but also providing other services aimed toward broadening the educational opportunities offered by the school.

Citizen groups can also move toward fund-raising and grants for school improvement programs, as indeed they long have through their PTA's, Dad's Clubs, Boosters' Clubs, and so forth, although past efforts have usually not aimed to introduce innovation. The new-type association is exemplified by the Cleveland, Ohio, PACE Association, a citizen-based education action group that has supported hundreds of small but worthy school projects. A 1973 press description of one such project follows:

> Frequently, minigrant ideas have an impact far beyond the classroom. Two years ago, students at Brush High School in South Euclid, a Cleveland suburb, formed SLOP—Student League Opposed to Pollution—and got a pledge from the city to gather newspapers. Then, armed with a $100 minigrant to pay for publicity, the students made posters and went house to house reminding residents of the drive. Last year South Euclid diverted 908 tons of newsprint from landfill or incineration.[13]

The Association was funded by a private foundation for its first three years, but in 1973 was soliciting funds from the public. Its grants are small, and intended to provide the "extras" for ideas that teachers must either fund out of their pockets or abandon.

Our observation is that local contributions for innovations have the special virtue of involving some local industry, association, or individual who thereby becomes a partner. Innovative schools need many partners!

Grants by the School District for Innovations

One of the spin-offs of the federal ESEA Title III program for support of innovations has been the development by numerous local districts of plans of special support of individual school and individual teacher inno-

[12] Donald E. Barnes, " 'Partnership' High Schools: The Search for New Ways to Cooperate," *Industry and Education Study No. 2, 1969* (New York: The Institute for Educational Development), p. 1.

[13] James C. Hyatt, " 'Minigrant' Program in Cleveland Helps Teachers Provide Some Special Extras," *Wall Street Journal*, March 14, 1973.

vations. Pioneering in this effort was the Dallas, Texas, "Pennies for Innovations" program developed there by Superintendent Nolan Estes, who had left the USOE administration in which he had directed the Title III program to become Dallas Superintendent in 1968. Some such local district programs are originally supported by federal funds, or in part so. Thus the Intermediate School District No. 110, Seattle, Washington, used Title III funds to start 35 innovative programs, many of which were continued after the federal funding ended. This program was part of a statewide minigrant program giving each intermediate school district in Washington a total grant to be distributed on a competitive basis to minigrant applicants; during 1971–1972 Intermediate District No. 110 had $30,017.20 allocated, received applications from 527 teachers and organizations, and funded 35. The amounts ranged from $106.50 to $2,485.00, going to both public and nonpublic schools, teachers, and agencies. The following account of the High School-Elementary Language Project is illustrative of the use of the minigrants in this district:

> Every teacher dreams of teaching on a one-to-one basis. But teachers know that they can't give individual help to every child who needs it. This program, based on the idea of "people helping people," matches Highline High School student volunteers and pupils from next door Sunnydale Elementary in that one-to-one relationship. The high school student tutors his elementary school friend in reading. . . .
>
> Under mini-grant funding of $1040 last year the program had 30 teachers working with children in grades 1–6. This fall, the program has 50 "olders" and 50 "youngers," all matched by interest inventories. The "olders," all volunteers, go through nine days of inservice training. They get one credit for their work with the grade-schoolers.[14]

Another pattern of internal funding of innovations is provided by the use of a curriculum council to review applications and award grants in terms of curriculum improvement priorities in the district. A report of the Curriculum Council of the Great Neck, New York, Schools described this operation as follows:

> The Council continues to consider, for possible recommendation to the Superintendent, innovative programs proposed by Building Faculty Curriculum Groups, individuals or groups of faculty members, students, and members of the community. For the purposes of implementing such recommendations, if they are accepted, it monitors a Research and Development Fund provided for in the school budget. It also receives interim reports and final evaluations of such projects.[15]

[14] Intermediate School District No. 110, *Mini-Grants and Maxi-Programs* (Seattle: The District, 1972), p. 15.

[15] "Curriculum Development Council, Annual Report, 1969–70" (Great Neck, N.Y.: Great Neck Public Schools, September 30, 1970), p. 14.

Community service is one of the changing emphases of programs at University City (Missouri) Senior High School. Here we see a student tutoring an elementary pupil on a regular schedule for which she received high school credit.

Such projects underway at the time in secondary schools included these:

Biology Project Using BSCS Laboratory Blocks

Creative Metal Work

Young Filmmakers Elective

Computer Guidance Information System

Trips of Mechanical Drawing Students to Architectural Sites

There are a number of advantages and possibilities in school district funding of special grants for innovation. In the first place, the competition to receive such grants and the recognition they provide is a wholesome incentive to the innovation process. In the second place, the commitment of the district to the process, as evidenced by such budgetary commitment, encourages school personnel to innovate and to regard innovation as normal and expected, even if more difficult and expensive. In the third place, considering the state of school budgets, it is to be expected that administrators will need to look for results and carefully guard the funds for well-conceived plans appropriate to school goals. Furthermore, it is recommended that school personnel, parents, and students be involved, as in the Great Neck Curriculum Council, in the process of reviewing minigrant applications and determining awards. Such inclusion in decision making is critical, we believe, in developing the relationships sought in the more open school system, which is the goal of innovation and change.

Grants from Philanthropic Foundations

Long before 1965 and the granting of massive federal funds to improve education, philanthropic foundations were subsidizing various educational innovations. The various practices introduced in the Eight-Year Study and the Southern Study of the 1930s and 1940s and many other once innovative programs were originally made possible by foundation grants. Many practices that have moved from innovative status to common practice were at one time helped into being by the support of philanthropy; for example, health education by the Kellogg Foundation and others, and television education by the Ford Foundation.

Foundation grants have been given to school districts both to support some particular innovation and to make possible comprehensive studies and services designed to facilitate educational change. Much can be learned about the relationship of foundation grants to change from the Comprehensive School Improvement Program, 1960–1970, of the Ford Foundation. This was a $30 million, ten-year program supporting twenty-five improvement projects. A "Foreword" to a 1972 evaluation of this program described its intents and nature in part as follows:

> Each project differed from the others in significant ways, but all were related through common strategies, including close working relations with colleges and universities and orchestration of activities in curriculum, use of time, staff, technology, and facilities to create a more comprehensive approach to improving educational programs. In research terms the program broke little fresh ground. It was not intended to invent further innovations; rather the program focused on ways and means to make school systems adaptable, flexible, and open to change so that they could make good use of innovative schemes that had already been developed.[16]

The evaluation of the program was done by an independent assessment team. The implications drawn from the careful analyses and evaluation done by the team are of interest to all persons concerned with the process of innovation and change; excerpts follow of several implications which seem most relevant to our present purposes:

> 1. While obvious, it is perhaps important to restate that innovations took hold best where the number of schools was limited and the objectives and techniques few and sharply defined.
>
> *   *   *
>
> 3. Larger scale change seemed more likely to occur when grantee and grantor agreed before funds were committed on the specific purpose, nature, extent, and limitations of a proposed project. General, broad-

16 Edward J. Meade, Jr., "Foreword," *A Foundation Goes to School* (New York: Ford Foundation, November 1972), p. 3.

purpose grants awarded for "improving educational opportunity" or for testing innovations (unspecified) did not allow for the definition or the commitment by any of the parties to measurable outcomes. Furthermore, beyond certain essential minimums, the size of grant seemed to have little to do with ultimate success of the program.

4. The operating design of a project seemed to determine its influence and ultimate impact. For instance, the school or project funded, organized, and staffed primarily to make it a prominent and conspicuous demonstration center in CSIP did become the "lighthouse." However, the people willing to accept its "lighthouse" function generally were not those for whom it was designed. . . . On the other hand, district-wide influence seemed more likely where projects practiced diffusion of activities and encouraged innovation in schools and classrooms throughout the district.

*   *   *

6. Innovation and change need the broadest possible commitment of intellectual and financial resources. While advice and technical assistance are essential before and during the life of the project, the commitments from multiple funding sources and especially from parent districts are essential ingredients, not simply as they represent broadly based intentions to stay with the program but also as they illustrate for staff and the public a budgetary and philosophical commitment to the concept.

*   *   *

8. Not surprisingly, the less complex the school system's structure, the more easily innovations were introduced and accepted initially. Small schools changed faster than large ones. But the ease and rapidity of innovation in small schools—often attributable to the efforts and convictions of a single dynamic leader—were offset by immediate abandonment after the departure of the charismatic promoter or with reduction of external funding.

9. The most lasting applications seemed to occur in middle-sized suburbs small enough to avoid the divisive debate between powerful interest groups but large enough to require that innovative movements be identified with more than individual or simple localized concerns.[17]

Hence planners of change programs utilizing these findings would use processes of innovation and change that could be specifically defined and were understood by all concerned; that would not assume the dissemination of change in a district from its "lighthouse" school; that had stability of leadership; that had support of more than one funding source and especially of the district itself; and that had an uncomplicated organizational structure. We consider these good guidelines for the process of innovation and change in general, and not just for the use of outside support in the process. Additionally, the Ford program assessment would

[17] *A Foundation Goes to School*, pp. 42–43.

indicate that the grantor has a better chance of a successful program if it does not rely on a university as a force in the improvement program, if the school concerned is small, if the community is a middle-sized suburb, and if crises and confrontations are not involved.

EXPERIMENTAL SCHOOL APPROACHES

Beginning with John Dewey's Laboratory School started at the University of Chicago in 1896,[18] various types of experimental, laboratory, and alternative schools have been widely used as a means of promoting change in schools. Although the somewhat negative findings of the Ford program assessment may bring new questions, there is widespread belief that a particular school or even several schools within a district can be used to experiment, demonstrate, and disseminate. At least three applications of this approach can be discerned.

The Single Experimental School

The original concept of a laboratory school as attached to a university and serving as a testing ground for innovative ideas of the university faculty is changing very rapidly. The single laboratory schools that remain tend to be focused on research and development projects, rather than totally preoccupied with innovation and demonstration.[19] Widespread attention to the need for more careful and systematic approaches to educational change necessitates the utilization of many school centers of various types. Hence an individual school is more likely to be a testing ground for some purpose it shares with other schools that may be scattered throughout the country, than to be a multipurpose laboratory center.

Many schools are utilized as testing grounds for innovations sponsored by state, regional, and national groups, including the manufacturers of educational materials, the federally supported regional educational laboratories and research and development centers and projects, educational foundations, university-school consortia, and other organizations. Least return to the school and district comes when the school is merely providing a testing population with no feedback of value to the school.

[18] For accounts of this school, see Katherine Camp Mayhew and Anna Camp Edwards, *The Dewey School* (New York: Appleton, 1936, 1964); Lawrence Cremin, *The Transformation of the School* (New York: Knopf, 1961); and Harold Rugg, *Foundations for Modern Education* (New York: Harcourt, 1947).

[19] See Felicia West and Thomas Gadsden, Jr., "A Major Role for Laboratory Schools," *Educational Leadership*, 30:412–415, for description of the research and dissemination program of the P. K. Yonge Laboratory School, University of Florida, Gainesville.

Most return probably comes when the research and development program provides the school a genuine possibility of experimentation, with adequate help to promise continuing improvement. Here the school is a partner in the program, utilizing the help of the external agency to test innovations of value to this school as well as others.

An alternative school within the system offers the opportunity for learners to try another type of school, and for the district to evaluate a different program. The alternative school is more than a laboratory for testing out multiple innovations; it is a trial run of a different concept of schooling. Although the establishment of alternative schools proceeded very rapidly in the early 1970s, little evidence was available as to the nature and extent of their deliberate, planned use to expedite change in the system. A 1972 review of some 200 alternative school projects in 60 school districts noted the same limitation of the "lighthouse" effect as the Ford program assessment published later that year:

> A successful alternative school has to do more than teach its own students. It has to show the way to others in and out of its school system, alternative school leaders say. *While some alternative schools have become nationally known, often their pioneering is not noticed by nearby traditional schools.* This is called "the lighthouse effect"—a distant bright beam, but darkness next door. Means of transferring teachers, students and ideas need to be developed. It has to be done softly and without fanfare, if professional jealousies aren't to be stirred up. Likewise, an alternative school should be on the lookout for and receptive to worthwhile practices in other schools.[20]

Multiple Experimental Schools Within the System

We have already described (see Chapter 4) such systems of alternative schools as those operated in Berkeley, California. At school opening in September, 1972, more than 20 alternatives were federally funded, to constitute Berkeley's Experimental School Program, and plans for several additional alternatives were made. Berkeley's description of the program stated that the alternative schools had become "a way of helping to change the system itself—to deal, in particular, with the central weakness of not only this but all school systems—the failure to deliver the basic academic skills on a parity to all kids alike."[21] Several other urban school districts have also moved to multiple alternative schools. A March, 1973, report of

[20] *Education U.S.A.* Staff, *Alternative Schools: Pioneering Districts Create Options for Students* (Washington, D.C.: National School Public Relations Association, 1972), p. 48. Italics supplied.

[21] Berkeley Unified School District, *Alternative Education: Experimental Schools Program* (Berkeley, Calif.: The District, October 1972), p. 7.

the National Association of Secondary School Principals briefly described such operations in Seattle, Philadelphia, St. Paul, Minneapolis, and Denver; this report underlines the need for multiple choices:

> While one can never be quite sure about such things, all signs suggest that we are not dealing here with just another educational fad. Society is moving toward alternatives of all sorts, and a "temporary society" faced with continuing change probably requires small, autonomous units that can respond quickly to pervasive change. Most alternative schools are "open systems" that can survive change and pressure by making minor or major corrections of course without undue strain. Finally, the idea of smaller and quite different schools as options is not new; it's an old practice that is now gaining new strength. So, our best guess is that alternative schools—perhaps under some other name—will be around for some time to come.[22]

We see much similarity in the effort to have many schools serving as "lighthouses." In this case the school system attempts to operate multiple centers of change, each doing a particular job, in some alternative schools serving a particular student population better than prior or other existing schools. Perhaps this is the situation that may be expected to prevail in a school system that moves far toward the concept of openness described early in this chapter. The University City, Missouri, Schools reported this concept of a "lighthouse" program:

> How is University City working toward the lighthouse concept? Programs such as: individualization, self-selected education, continuous progress education, open classrooms, the alternative school, pods and learning centers—all of which can be part of a lighthouse school—are part of the District.
> In the eleven elementary, two junior highs and senior high schools, programs such as math and social studies and the reading project are going on. *However, each school has some special faceted program to help it achieve its educational goals.*[23]

Networks of Experimental Schools

Collaboration in experimentation by schools in different districts, even across state and regional lines, has been employed in many programs for educational improvement. The Eight-Year Study of the Progressive Educa-

[22] NASSP Curriculum Service Center, "More Options: Alternatives to Conventional School," *Curriculum Report,* 2:3 (March 1973).

[23] Board of Education of Univerity City, Missouri, "University City Moves Toward 'Lighthouse' Concept," *University City Schools,* January 1973, p. 5. Italics supplied.

tion Association, with its 30 schools and some 200 cooperating colleges and universities, begun in the 1930s, is an early example. Beginning in the 1940s the Horace Mann-Lincoln Institute of School Experimentation, Teachers College, Columbia University, worked with various school districts and individual schools to study problems of curriculum and instruction. The /I/D/E/A/ project of the Kettering Foundation has recently operated a League of Cooperating schools for research and development purposes,[24] and is also developing its Individually Guided Education program (see Chapter 5) through leagues of cooperating elementary, middle, and junior high schools, and high schools. Many other examples of such collaborative endeavors have existed during the past few decades and are currently popular. A special type of cooperative organization, the "voluntary educational cooperative" (one not mandated by legislation or regulation), tends to be an organization for change:

> Voluntary educational cooperatives generally try to coordinate or harness the strengths and capabilities of the constituents to develop or generate a structure to provide flexibility, power, potential, and direction for change and innovation.[25]

The Ford Foundation's Comprehensive School Improvement Program reviewed earlier in this chapter, is a noteworthy example of the network idea and the conclusions of its assessment we cited suggest guidelines for planners of change processes interested in the collaboration approach. We do call special attention to the power of collaborative effort —both for the local recognition of the school's or district's involvement in a multischool improvement program, and the help that comes to the individual school and district from the exchange of ideas between schools and districts, and other partners in collaboration such as universities, foundations, state departments of education, industries, and professional and civic associations.

CONTINUING IMPROVEMENT PROGRAMS

Each of the approaches we have described thus far—adoption of single innovations, special funding for innovations, and use of experimental schools—may be a relatively temporary effort toward innovation and

[24] See John Goodlad, "Staff Development: The League Model," *Theory into Practice,* 11:207–214 (October 1972).

[25] Larry W. Hughes, C. M. Achilles, James Leonard, and Dolphus Spence, *Educational Cooperatives,* No. 23 in the Series of PREP Reports (Washington, D.C.: U.S. Government Printing Office, 1972), pp. 5–6.

change, or it may be but one aspect of a program of continuing improvement. We turn now to consideration of the highly desirable approaches to maintenance of a systematic, continuing program of innovation and change that is not to be interrupted or diverted by recurrent crises and personnel turnover. Although these approaches are not really discrete, we do discern certain patterns of such efforts: long-standing organizational arrangements; research, development, and evaluation; systems approaches; and comprehensive planning. Each pattern is briefly identified in this section.

Long-Standing Organizational Arrangements

Many schools and school districts had organizational arrangements for continuing school improvement long before the infusion of federal funds for change and innovation in the 1960s, and were generally more able therefore to capitalize upon these funds for accelerating improvement programs. In the districts in which continuing change is recognized as inevitable and desirable, such provisions as these for underwriting and ensuring it have been and remain common:

1. *Coordinating councils,* especially on curriculum and instruction, are used to share problems and ideas between schools, and to develop, review, and implement improvement plans and proposals. Representation of students and community is increasingly common in these councils, which may be organized on the basis of schools, curriculum areas, school levels, educational functions, or some combination of these. Both separate professional and lay councils and joint professional–lay councils are used. Representation of each school in the district helps to secure adequate communication and feedback.

2. *Systematic needs appraisals,* through surveys by external agencies or local opinion polls or other means, are conducted periodically to determine areas of deficiency and priorities for school improvement efforts. School evaluations may be involved, using either internally developed criteria, or those of accrediting agencies, or some combination.

3. *Vertical curriculum planning and evaluation* brings together representatives of all school levels to develop better-articulated school programs. Intervisitation of schools at different levels is encouraged to promote interlevel and interschool cooperation.

4. *Continuous input of innovative ideas* is sought through use of consultants, attendance at professional meetings, professional libraries, and maintenance of channels for consideration and evaluation of suggestions from school personnel and patrons. Such plans as those discussed earlier of funding of innovative ideas within the district seem especially encouraging to individuals with initiative and creativity.

5. *Staff development plans,* such as we described in Chapter 5, are utilized to provide for continuous retraining and training for new roles. These plans involve the participation of the staff in their development and modification. The induction of new personnel and the orientation of experienced staff for new schools are included.

6. *Budgetary provision for special employment* provides for the maintenance of curriculum development on a continuing basis with the involvement of school personnel who will use the curriculum materials they help develop. Curriculum materials writers, developers, and evaluators are employed during summers, and also during the school year by some plan of alternation between school and special assignments.

7. *Task forces for special purposes* are organized as need arises, to develop new curriculum plans, to search out innovative programs, to plan new school facilities, to carry on evaluation projects, and other purposes. These task forces are created on the recommendation of coordinating and other councils, have relatively specific job assignments, are funded through the operating budget, and involve some of the people directly concerned with execution of whatever results accrue from the work of the task force.

8. *Experimental centers, projects, and schools* are developed on the basis of such task force recommendations, with optimum participation of the school personnel whose work may ultimately be affected by the experimentation concerned. The experimental design provides for feedback of a formative nature, including the observations of participants and visitors.

9. *Evaluation* of each innovative program is an integral part of the operation, with some evaluation unit or center within the district responsible for developing evaluation programs and utilizing such outside resources as may be needed to strengthen and objectify the evaluation process.

10. *Leadership training* is a continuous operation, aiming both at the selection and training of new leadership and the retraining and continuous updating of current leadership personnel. Leadership persons, along with teachers and other personnel, are also involved in all staff development programs.

Our observation indicates that school districts with such established organizational arrangements most readily adapt to changing conditions. In the adaptation process, any such district may also adopt a particular approach to change or an emphasis in change such as the ones to which we now turn.

Research, Development, and Evaluation

Some school districts have emphasized a research and development, perhaps called an evaluation (although this is a more comprehensive term), approach to innovation and change. The effort in this approach (or emphasis) is to test thoroughly experimental and innovative practices. It involves these steps, characteristically:

1. The continuing assessment of needs for change with priorities determined and followed.
2. The development, or temporary adoption for tryout of those developed elsewhere, of prototypes or models of innovative programs or practices, which are frequently developed in a school setting.
3. The systematic testing of such prototypes or models in pilot studies, possibly extended as field tests in multiple situations.
4. The continuing modification and retesting of the innovation until its users have confidence in it.
5. The utilization of the refined programs and practices in appropriate situations, with arrangements for continued study to determine further changes.

A school fully using such a research and development approach will have at any one time some practices being piloted, some being tried out on a wider scale, some in process of full adoption, with other needs just being explored. Too many such studies could be disruptive of a single school, and so such an approach in the district utilizes various schools for particular research and development projects and for particular steps within each project. Some large districts have designated entire subsystems as research and development units.

Utilization of such a research and development approach within a plan for total involvement of personnel is described in a report of the Upper St. Clair (Pennsylvania) Schools:

> The decision for total involvement by all associated with curriculum development was made early in the 1965–1966 school year and has been the foundation of the organization. Curriculum development cannot be an authoritarian series of decisions but rather must be a democratic process with issues being freely discussed and ideas firmly exchanged. . . .
>
> Organization and development and implementation has followed a four stage cycle. This evolutionary approach is represented in Figure 3.
>
> During the first year, Emergence, ideas are solicited and analyzed by all members of the staff. As ideas become principles, these principles are developed in depth by faculty-supervisory-administrative committees.

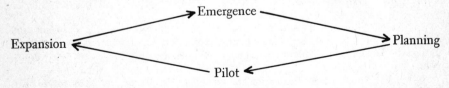

FIGURE 2 Instructional development cycle.

The principles, having been cast into a practical approach, are placed into operation on a limited scale in pilot programs. After evaluation and alteration, expansion of program is carried out.[26]

Whether or not the models for testing—the innovations—are developed on a research and development basis, the need for evaluation is obvious and great. Probably the most frequently cited weakness of the entire innovative movement is the lack of evaluative data about individual innovations. If decisions are to be made wisely about rejecting, modifying, or adopting an innovation, there must be data to guide the decisions. The provision of such data is the purpose of evaluation.

Evidently, there is a particular need for the evaluation of the alternative schools and projects now being so widely developed. Defining the purpose of evaluation as "to improve an enterprise by providing data to its decision-makers which they will use to make more enlightened decisions about it,"[27] Rosen, in an issue of the newsletter of the Educational Alternatives Project, Indiana University, cited special needs for evaluating these schools and proposed a methodology for their evaluation. Without data from the alternatives, any full transference of this phenomenon to the formulation of a complete process of innovation and change is impossible.

Systems Approaches

The accepted concept of a systems approach as composed of interrelated components which interact with each other to reach designated goals, permits one to call most approaches, other than single-innovation ones, "systems approaches." A systems approach involves in its simplest interpretation the statement of goals, the arrangement of components to meet these goals, and the evaluation of progress toward goals; however, most other approaches do involve goal-setting, planning, and evaluation. But the systems approach as developed more fully in education beginning in the late 1950s, and especially after its introduction in the federal government during the 1960s and subsequent reflection in federal educational grants, used such tools of systems analysis as linear programming, PERT (Program Evaluation Review Technique), and simulation, with considerable help from computer technology. A 1972 publication, *How Schools Can Apply Systems Analysis*, noted these efforts that had been made to

[26] Upper St. Clair Township School District, "Instructional Development and Implementation" (Upper St. Clair, Pennsylvania: The District, n.d., provided the authors by Dr. Donald Eichhorn, Assistant Superintendent, in 1973), pp. 1–3. Mimeographed.

[27] David Rosen, "New Evaluation for New Schools," *Changing Schools*, No. 006 (n.d.), pp. 3–4.

apply the systems approach in education: "instructional systems, development, and analysis; teaching and technology; data processing; systems engineering; human engineering; program evaluations; curriculum considered as a social system; program planning; and utopian educational systems."[28]

School districts can and do find useful many systems concepts and techniques in educational planning. The present authors consider the curriculum itself a system; note this concept stated in a current work on this subject in which one of us collaborated:

> Considering a system as a set of components so related and organized as to attain the ends for which the system is established, we can refer to curriculum as a system. We defined curriculum as "a plan for providing sets of learning opportunities to achieve broad educational goals and related specific objectives for an identifiable population served by a single school center." The "set of components" in the system is the "plan for providing sets of learning opportunities" and the "ends" of the system are the "broad educational goals" for the school population served.
>
> Use of the systems concept offers advantages to curriculum planners. Past efforts to plan the curriculum have tended to lose sight of the integral relationship of goals and learning opportunities; in a systems approach the objectives are central in decision-making activities, including those major ones relating to choice of learning opportunities. Past efforts to plan the curriculum have also tended to be piecemeal and fragmentary; in a systems approach the planners are concerned with all relevant factors as they work out the steps to be taken to achieve the goals.[29]

Certainly, school districts which would maintain a continuously current and relevant curriculum must maintain planning systems that relate goals to processes and results with adequate feedback for modification. The term "systems" is also widely utilized in the development of instructional systems (see pages 158–161) especially as produced by instructional designing organizations and specialists to involve management by objectives and somewhat continuous feedback.

Probably the most widespread application of a systems approach in education is the Program-Planning-Budget Systems (PPBS) reported to have been adopted in 1972 by "at least half of the fifty states, a large number of counties and cities, and a host of school systems and educational institutions,"[30] and the adoptions have continued. Such systems

---

[28] Joseph E. Hill, *How Schools Can Apply Systems Analysis* (Bloomington, Ind.: Phi Delta Kappa Educational Foundation, 1972), p. 11.

[29] J. Galen Saylor and William M. Alexander, *Planning Curriculum for Schools* (New York: Holt, Rinehart and Winston, 1974), p. 17.

[30] Hill, p. 12.

are highly relevant to the accountability movement, as noted in this introduction by the Santa Cruz County (California) Schools Superintendent to the documents recording the PPBS system in Santa Cruz County:

> Accountability is rapidly becoming an educational cliché. However, the message included in the accountability theme—stating program targets, allocating resources to gain them, and determining the level of success in meeting program targets—is one which educators must take to heart and apply. At the moment planning, programming, budget system techniques seem to be the most reasonable method for gaining educational accountability.[31]

The development and use of this PPBS illustration are suggested in this further statement:

> This document, PROGRAM DESCRIPTION—Santa Cruz County Office of Education, includes the goals and objectives contained within the county office planning, programming, and budgeting system. No apology is made for the superficial quality of some objectives. Few educators are to the point where they can deliver "finished" statements of intention. However, the thrust is clear—it is to lucidly describe the anticipated outcomes of specific programs.
>
> The companion volume to this program description is the PROGRAM BUDGET—Santa Cruz County Office of Education. That publication gives the financial resource allocations approved by the County Board of Education to gaining stated targets.
>
> During the coming year, the county staff will broaden involvement in developing objectives for programs. The office will review current objectives and revise them appropriately to recognize the changing circumstances in the county. Very obviously a viable planning, programming, budgeting system is one which constantly changes to reflect different circumstances, aspirations, and needs in the community.[32]

The Louisville, Kentucky, program was considered by two reviewers as the first large public school district to begin change on a systems basis; we would agree with their observation therefore that "the Louisville experiment should be closely watched so that other districts can benefit from the promises and avoid the pitfalls."[33] This program involved the identifi-

---

[31] Richard R. Fickel, Superintendent, *Program Description (Goals and Objectives, 1971–72)* (Santa Cruz, Calif.: County Office of Education, July 1971), p. i.

[32] Fickel, p. i.

[33] Daniel U. Levine and Russell C. Doll, *Systems Renewal in the Louisville Public Schools: Lessons on the Frontier of Urban Educational Reform in A Big City School District* (Kansas City, Mo.: Center for the Study of Metropolitan Problems in Education, University of Missouri, n.d.), p. iv. Mimeographed.

cation of fourteen target schools and the implementation of a comprehensive program of change therein, including the social control system, the faculties, the organization, and the instructional system. The nature of the changes introduced and their processes are indicated in the reviewers' appraisal of accomplishment of the Louisville program:

1. Louisville has done more than any other big city we know to provide pertinent training and re-training for teachers and other staff.
2. The importance of obtaining exponential gains in improving administrative leadership has been recognized and acted on in several ways.
3. A serious effort is being made to bring about effective citizen participation in school affairs in general and workable citizen participation in local school decision-making in particular.
4. Concepts for reform in organizing and operating instructional programs as well as in generally improving the utilization of human and material resources in individual schools have been worked out and are undergoing careful testing.
5. A defensible program is being launched to make planning and evaluation activities a central component in many aspects of the district's operation.
6. A variety of significant steps have been taken—particularly the creation and staffing of an Organization Development Office—to enhance problem-solving and organizational improvement capabilities in the system as a whole as well as in individual schools.
7. Most important of all, these discrete components are viewed as related elements in an overall approach to systems change which recognizes that complex organizations like big city schools and school districts desperately need to overcome the dysfunctional conditions typical of a stagnating bureaucracy. It is particularly the acknowledgement and willingness to act on a systems concept of change that has made Louisville important as a case study in urban educational reform.[34]

The Louisville program had its failures and difficulties, too. In an April, 1973, report, under the section title "Louisville Revisited," the original reviewers and a third collaborator wrote: "The presumed strength of the Louisville changes lay in the interlocking strength of the systems approach. Yet the systems approach is not as visible as it was in 1970."[35] However, these evaluators went on to indicate some of the problems and difficulties, posed questions regarding reform in large city districts, and stated their conclusions and "lessons," but in no way found the systems approach itself lacking. In fact, they regarded as of "overall importance"

---

[34] Levine and Doll, pp. 37–38.
[35] Russell C. Doll, Barbara J. Love, and Daniel U. Levine, "Systems Renewal in a Big-City School District: The Lessons of Louisville," *Phi Delta Kappan*, 54:527 (April 1973).

the matters of "concentrating resources and of utilizing a systems approach to innovation and renewal."[36]

Certainly planners of change in school districts will do well to read these sources regarding the Louisville experiment and such other examples of systems approaches as may get into the literature. Despite the difficulties in arranging and managing the variables which make complete systematization so hard to accomplish, the concepts we associate with a systems approach are highly relevant to the process of innovation and change. Two contributions seem of particular significance: (1) the emphasis on the goals-process-results or input-process-output cycle, with its critical relationship to any approach to educational change; and (2) the use of such techniques of systems analysis as feedback, required in any ongoing or formative evaluation of innovation; linear programming for the allocation of resources; PERT for scheduling steps toward mission accomplishment; and simulation for determining possible consequences of particular actions and the relationships of components. As educators become proficient in developing models for use in simulation and as computer technology is employed, time can be compressed and the events of years examined in seconds as guides to action.

Comprehensive Planning

Each of the other approaches we have considered may involve planning of a comprehensive nature, but certain emphases of the early 1970s gave particular connotations to the term "comprehensive planning." Much interest was being expressed in "futures planning,"[37] and long-range planning was being attempted in a growing number of school districts; for example, a report on long-range planning in Chicago was presented "with the sincere hope it will provide a useful guide to solving the complex educational and school building problems facing Chicago during the next half century."[38]

In the state of Florida, comprehensive planning became critical for Florida's county school districts (Florida's districts are all county districts, no independent ones) in 1973 through the impetus given county responsibility by legislative action to provide greater flexibility and at the same time to increase accountability. Specifically, a 1972 legislative act mandated that "each district school board shall maintain an on-going system-

[36] Doll, Love, and Levine, p. 532.

[37] See Harold Shane, "Future-Planning as a Means of Shaping Educational Change," in The Curriculum: Retrospect and Prospect, Robert M. McClure (Ed.), 70th Yearbook, National Society for the Study of Education (Chicago: University of Chicago Press, 1971).

[38] Donald J. Leu and I. Carl Candoli, Planning for the Future: A Long-Range Educational and Facilities Plan for Chicago (Chicago: Board of Education, August 1971), p. vii.

atic evaluation of the education program needs in that district and shall develop a comprehensive annual and long-time plan for meeting the needs," and subsequent state board of education regulations defined the comprehensive plans to be submitted. Especially significant was the provision of flexibility through this clause of the regulations:

> Upon the written request of a district school board the Commissioner is authorized to waive specifically identified State Board Regulations for a specified period of time when, in the opinion of the Commissioner, the evidence presented by the district board is sufficient to show that the regulation is preventing the attainment of a valid objective identified in the district comprehensive plan.[39]

The guidelines for 1973–1974 recommended elements of a systems approach and a five-year planning cycle, but did not prescribe a format for the comprehensive plan, called a "planning and management document." Emphasis was given to comprehensive planning as "a rational base for decision-making by the superintendent, the school board and the professional staff of the district."

As we have reiterated in this book, innovations represent means toward the goals of educational change. Thus the planning of innovations, their implementation, evaluation, and expansion becomes itself a significant part of the comprehensive plan. Shane's analysis of "The 'Drop-Out Problem' in Educational Innovation" deplored the failure of innovations to result in "the kinds of major educational reformation that contemporary revolutionary social change demands" and noted the need "to recast our tactics and our strategies to make educational changes occur more quickly and to give them greater permanence and continuity of influence when they prove beneficial."[40] His article indicated specific problems in past processes of innovations that can be guides to future planning.

An analysis of research, theory, and practice regarding instructional innovation and research prepared by the American Institutes for Research for the United States Agency for International Development, to be used particularly in developing countries, offers suggestions that may be useful for comprehensive planning in American school districts and secondary schools, too. Five components were suggested as critical in any organization capable of producing improvement in education:

1. a management component responsible for setting overall goals, securing funds and other resources, and controlling the operation of the system;

[39] State Department of Education, *Guidelines for District Comprehensive Educational Planning, 1973–74* (Tallahassee, Fla.: The Department, 1973), pp. 1, 3.
[40] Harold G. Shane, "The 'Drop-Out Problem' in Educational Innovation," *Educational Leadership*, 30:507, 509 (March 1973).

2. a development component responsible for planning and innovations, conducting the research, and preparing or locating materials and equipment needed to implement a change;
3. a budgeting component responsible for analyzing costs, projecting expenditures, and allocating funds and personnel;
4. an evaluation component responsible for developing measures to assess the effects of changes, for collecting pertinent data, and for reporting results; and
5. an administrative component responsible for implementing changes within the system through revised scheduling, teacher training, and the procurement of needed materials and equipment.[41]

We would suggest as a sixth or perhaps overall additional component one of massive participation by school and community personnel in planning this organization and in the appropriate activities of the other components, especially the management, development, and evaluation components, since these, respectively, set goals, plan innovations, and secure feedback data.

THE POWER OF INNOVATION

Early in this final chapter of our book, the authors described the process of innovation and change as a continuum. We stated our point of view that innovation and change should move a school toward an optimum development of the learning potentials of the entire school population. Innovation has great power, we believe, to improve learning if it is consciously and deliberately planned to achieve this goal. Each innovation must be carefully selected in terms of a set of criteria such as we presented in Chapter 1 (see section, "What Innovations?"). It is imperative also that the innovators and planners refrain from letting any innovation itself become the goal. Better innovations will likely arise to replace even today's most promising ones. Thus the real power of an innovation lies in its flexibility as well as its utility—it must be presently useful but later replaceable. Innovations are but pegs on the continuum, essential in the renewal process but milestones in the continuing journey forward to ever better conditions for learning. So regarded, each innovation can be carefully considered, fitted into its place, and used as a powerful step forward on the continuum of innovation and change toward an ideal educational environment.

[41] David J. Klaus, *Instructional Innovation and Individualization* (Pittsburgh: American Institutes for Research, 1969), pp. 317–318.

additional suggestions for further study

1. Alexander, William M., *The Changing High School Curriculum: Readings*, 2d ed. New York: Holt, Rinehart and Winston, 1972. Selected readings and interpretations thereof particularly relevant to this chapter are given in Parts III (Trends and Issues in Curriculum Improvement) and IV (The High School Curriculum of the Future).

2. "Curriculum Management: A Panacea?," *Educational Leadership*, 30:299–300 (January 1973). Eight articles explore the concepts of curriculum management and instructional designing.

3. Giacquinta, Joseph B., "The Process of Organizational Change in Schools," Ch. 6 in *Review of Research in Education*, Fred N. Kerlinger (Ed.) (Itasca, Ill.: Peacock, 1973). Careful review of literature and research on organizational change, with particular attention to the characteristics of innovations and their utilization and evaluation in the process of change.

4. Glines, Don, *Creating Humane Schools: Expanded Supplementary Edition*. Mankato, Minn.: Campus Publishers, 1972. Describes a plethora of innovations and the process of their introduction in the Wilson Campus School, Mankato State University.

5. Marien, Michael, and Warren L. Ziegler (Eds.), *The Potential of Educational Futures*. Worthington, Ohio: Charles A. Jones, 1972. Collection of essays by authors who have been actively involved in efforts to use a futures perspective in educational planning. Excellent source for orientation to this approach to educational planning.

6. Martin, John Henry, and Charles H. Harrison, *Free to Learn: Unlocking and Ungrading American Education*. Englewood Cliffs, N.J.: Prentice-Hall, 1972. Restrictive character of today's schools is stressed, and a new design for community education is proposed as an alternative seeking to open learning opportunities.

7. Provos, Malcolm, *Discrepancy Evaluation: For Educational Program Improvement and Assessment*. Berkeley, Calif.: McCutchan, 1973. Presents a model for evaluating school programs on the basis of discrepancy between expectation and performance.

8. Saylor, J. Galen (Ed.), *The School of the Future NOW*. Washington, D.C.: Association for Supervision and Curriculum Development, 1973. See for especially relevant papers, Ch. 1, "A Critical Analysis of Our Schools"; Ch. 5, "The Kinds of Educational Programs We Need for the Later Adolescent Years"; and Ch. 7, "Curriculum Planning As It Should Be."

9. Skeel, Dorothy J., and Owen A. Hagen, *The Process of Curriculum Change*. Pacific Palisades, Calif.: Goodyear, 1971. Interestingly presented description of the process in a hypothetical school district. Uses narrative and dialogue style involving various characters representing teachers, administrators, parents, children, and university personnel.

10. Wilson, L. Craig, *The Open Access Curriculum*. Boston: Allyn and Bacon, 1971. Stimulating statement of a theory of curriculum change through open access to new areas of inquiry and knowledge. See especially Part II on "Power Controls Influencing Open Access"—their nature and means of dealing with them in the process of innovation and change.

Index